the **big book** of

babycakes®

cake pop maker
recipes

Homemade Bite-Sized Fun!

Kathy Moore & Roxanne Wyss

Robert
ROSE

For complete cataloguing information, see page 232.

Disclaimer
The recipes in this book have been carefully tested by our kitchen and our tasters. To the best of our knowledge, they are safe and nutritious for ordinary use and users. For those people with food or other allergies, or who have special food requirements or health issues, please read the suggested contents of each recipe carefully and determine whether or not they may create a problem for you. All recipes are used at the risk of the consumer. Consumers should always consult the Babycakes™ manual for recommended procedures and cooking times.

We cannot be responsible for any hazards, loss or damage that may occur as a result of any recipe use.

For those with special needs, allergies, requirements or health problems, in the event of any doubt, please contact your medical adviser prior to the use of any recipe.

Design and production: PageWave Graphics Inc.
Editor: Sue Sumeraj
Recipe editor: Jennifer MacKenzie
Proofreader: Sheila Wawanash
Indexer: Gillian Watts
Techniques photographer: David Shaughnessy
Techniques stylist: Anne Fisher
Techniques hand model: Shannon Knopke
Recipe photographer: Colin Erricson
Recipe associate photographer: Matt Johannsson
Recipe food stylist: Kathryn Robertson
Recipe prop stylist: Charlene Erricson

Cover image: Crazy Straws (page 189)

We acknowledge the financial support of the Government of Canada through the Book Publishing Industry Development Program (BPIDP) for our publishing activities.

Published by Robert Rose Inc.
120 Eglinton Avenue East, Suite 800, Toronto, Ontario, Canada M4P 1E2
Tel: (416) 322-6552 Fax: (416) 322-6936
www.robertrose.ca

Printed and bound in Canada

1 2 3 4 5 6 7 8 9 MI 20 19 18 17 16 15 14 13 12

Contents

Acknowledgments

WE ARE so grateful for the support we receive. A cookbook like this takes a community of committed, talented, hard-working, patient people, and we are blessed to be surrounded with the best.

We hold our families fast in our hearts, and we so appreciate their love and support. Roxanne's husband, Bob Bateman, and daughter, Grace, have endured countless hours of recipe testing and tasting, and have given up weekend family time so that we could meet our deadlines. Thank you for always being there. Kathy so appreciates her husband, David, and daughters, Laura and Amanda, for their endless love, patience and encouragement, and the immense joy they bring her.

Every time we enter the kitchen, we thank our parents, for they encouraged us, supported us and instilled a deep love of food, cooking and family traditions.

Thank you to publisher Bob Dees and the awesome team at Robert Rose, including our editor, Sue Sumeraj; our recipe editor, Jennifer MacKenzie; publicity manager Martine Quibell; director of sales and marketing Marian Jarkovich; and so many others.

The entire creative team at PageWave Graphics, including Kevin Cockburn, Joseph Gisini and Daniella Zanchetta, is wonderful, and we appreciate their work!

Our thanks also to the team at Colin Erricson Photography for the recipe photographs. As for the step-by-step techniques photos, we loved our days at the photo studio and appreciated working with David Shaughnessy and his talented team: Anne Fisher, Shannon Knopke and Alex Edwards.

A very special thanks to the entire team at Lisa Ekus Group for their fantastic support and guidance, especially our agents, Lisa Ekus and Sally Ekus.

Bill Endres, Eric Endres and Wes Endres have created a wonderful company with Select Brands, and we appreciate their entire team — individuals who are committed to designing, manufacturing, marketing, selling and shipping the best line of appliances.

Cookbooks are collaborative, and we seek out the finest and most creative people to work with in our quest to create and test innovative, great-tasting recipes. Sheri Worrel is the very best, and we cannot imagine creating this book without her imagination, inspiration and friendship. Thank you, Sheri. Thanks to Julie Bondank, our "right hand" in the test kitchen, for tirelessly cooking with us to test recipe after recipe — and doing so with a smile. We are so grateful to Mandy Totoro and Amy Dowell, our awesome test kitchen team, who cooked side by side with us for so many days.

Some friends come into your life and change the way you think, and that is so true of Johnna Perry. Thank you for sharing your skills and knowledge of gluten-free and vegan baking with us. You are awesome.

Heartfelt thanks to our colleagues Karen Adler and Judith Fertig, who continue to share their expertise and guide us on this journey.

Four Babycakes™ books later, we continue to treasure our friendship and awesome business relationship — a priceless bond that began 30 years ago. We are thankful for it each and every day.

Most of all, thanks to our readers. We're so pleased that you, like us, are passionate about creating tasty, innovative Babycakes™ treats and are always craving new recipes.

Introduction

AS FOOD consultants, we have had the pleasure of developing recipes for many publications and iconic food products. We've always been kept busy and treasured what we were doing, but we dreamed of writing cookbooks. Now we are living proof that dreams can come true! This is our second book of recipes for the Babycakes™ Cake Pop Maker (and our fourth in a series of books for the Babycakes™ appliances), and we are having a lot of fun! We so appreciate the many people who enjoy using their Babycakes™ Cake Pop Maker and want to keep baking tasty little treats.

We have been honored to work with Select Brands for many years and have known Bill Endres, the president and owner, for our entire professional career. We were thrilled when Select Brands first asked us to test the Babycakes™ Cupcake Maker prototypes, and we loved what they did. Today, we continue to be delighted by the variety of recipes that can be baked with the Babycakes™ Cake Pop Maker — not just cake pops, but also bite-size doughnuts, muffins, biscuits, scones, ebelskivers, meatballs and appetizers.

At the International Home and Housewares Show, an annual event that showcases all of the newest appliances, gadgets, dishes and everything else for the home, we demonstrated the Babycakes™ Cake Pop Maker, dipping and decorating cake pops by the hundreds. We discovered that cake pops are new to many people. They stopped, intrigued by the cute cake pops on display, and would inevitably ask, "What is that?"

"A cake pop," we'd reply.
"What's inside?"
"Cake."
We had this short conversation at least 10 or 12 times a day. But cake pops are becoming more and more popular, and sometime it seems like they're everywhere: the local coffee shop, neighborhood parties and even weddings and other formal events.

Angie Dudley, aka Bakerella, introduced many of us to cake pops when she featured her creative confections on her blog and on television. Her cake pops, and those patterned after hers, are a candy-like mixture of crumbled cake and frosting. We are forever grateful to her for inspiring us with her beautiful, artistic creations.

Our cake pops are a little bit different. When we say there's cake inside our cake pops, we mean that's all there is. Just cake. Luscious, bite-size spheres of cake, baked in minutes thanks to the Babycakes™ Cake Pop Maker. Neither type of cake pop is wrong, it is just that we (and many others) prefer Babycakes™ cake pops, as they are not as intensely sweet as their predecessors.

Cake pops can be eaten just as they are or topped with a dessert sauce, or you can decorate and even fill them. They are perfect for parties, and, as you'll see in Part 4 of this book, can be the focal point of fun, charming, whimsical, festive and even elegant gifts and centerpieces.

So embrace your creative spirit, let our ideas inspire you and get baking!

Part 1

Getting Started

Baking Sweet and Savory Treats

THE BABYCAKES™ Cake Pop Maker is very easy to use, and we think you will be pleasantly surprised by the variety of bite-size morsels you can bake in this handy appliance. Fun, delicious cake pops are just the beginning. From doughnuts and muffins to biscuits, scones, appetizers and more, the flavors, both sweet and savory, are nearly endless.

- **Doughnuts:** Why go out to a doughnut shop when you can make your own fresh, warm, inviting treats? And these morsels are baked, not fried — a true health benefit.

- **Muffins:** Just the right size for any time of day. Freshly baked muffins call the family to breakfast, are perfect sides at brunch or lunch and make scrumptious snacks.

- **Biscuits and scones:** There's no need to heat up the oven for freshly baked biscuits and scones. These tidbits are the perfect accompaniment for breakfast, lunch, dinner or tea.

- **Appetizers:** Light or hearty, elegant or casual — whatever the event, the Babycakes™ Cake Pop Maker can help you make savory mini masterpieces in minutes.

Cake Pop Maker Options

New models of the Babycakes™ Cake Pop Maker are now available from Select Brands. It is a fast-paced industry, and new features are always being introduced. Make sure to follow the safeguards and directions in the manual packed with your appliance.

As we write this, there are two models of Babycakes™ Cake Pop Makers, both of which bake 12 cake pops at a time.

The Babycakes™ Rotating Cake Pop Maker sits up off the counter and has a rotating mechanism very similar to that of a commercial waffle maker. It heats from both the top and bottom, and you can rotate the appliance so that the treats are turned upside down midway through cooking. This allows the tops of the treats to rest directly down on the heated surface, so the baking may be a little faster and the browning a little more even.

The Babycakes™ Cake Pop Maker also bakes from the top and bottom, but it does not rotate. It is a more compact unit.

While all of the recipes in this book can be baked in either appliance with great results, some treats, including tortilla cups, wonton cups and meatballs, should not be rotated. Each recipe includes baking instructions for both models, so if you're using the rotating cake pop maker, you'll know when you should rotate and when you shouldn't.

How to Use the Cake Pop Maker

It's a piece of cake to make treats, both sweet and savory, in either of the cake pop makers, but here are some tips to help you get started.

Preheating

The appliance preheats quickly. Just plug it in and within moments you are ready to bake. In some cases, as with cooking meatballs, we recommend unplugging the appliance and letting it cool between batches, but in most cases, you can bake batch after batch without pause.

Using Baking Spray

Although the cake pop maker is coated with a nonstick surface, we often find a quick, light spritz with nonstick baking spray is a good idea. Spray before filling the wells the first time, then as needed between batches. Do not use baking spray when brushing the wells with butter or when preparing higher-fat foods, such as meatballs.

Mixing the Batter

Only a small amount of batter — about ¾ cup (175 mL) — is needed to make each batch of 12 cake pops. For recipes that recommend the use of a mixer, we used a handheld electric mixer. A stand mixer is simply not needed for small amounts of batter. Because speed, power and beater design vary from mixer to mixer, the speeds listed in the recipes are guidelines only; you may need to adjust the speed on your mixer to get the best results.

Filling the Wells

The easiest way to fill the wells quickly and neatly is with a pastry bag. We highly recommend using disposable pastry bags, as it is very difficult to wash a reusable bag so it is sanitary. You can also use sealable food storage bags.

There is no need to use a coupler or tip. Simply fold the top edge of the bag down about 2 inches (5 cm) to form a collar. Set the bag in a glass to hold it upright, then fill the bag about half full with batter. Twist the top of the bag, then clip off the point (or, if you're using a sealable food storage bag, clip off one corner).

To fill the wells, press down on the top of the bag very gently so the batter flows out. Stop pressing as you move to each new well. To stop the flow when you're done filling the wells for a batch, twist the tip end, then set the bag upright in the glass.

Fill each well with about 1 tbsp (15 mL) of batter. The rounded well should be just about full. If you don't use enough batter, each cake pop will be a little less rounded. If you overfill the well, the cake pop may have a ridge or ring around the center. After you have used the appliance a few times, you'll find it easy to gauge the perfect amount of batter for each well.

If your cake pop maker came packed with a batter bottle, or if you have purchased one as an accessory, feel free to use it in place of a pastry bag to fill the wells.

Another way to fill the wells is to use a small scoop that holds about 1 tbsp (15 mL) of batter. We often use a scoop when the batter is quite thick and chunky with fruits and nuts. Looks for scoops at shops that specialize in kitchen utensils and baking supplies.

In general, fill all 12 wells of the cake pop maker for each batch. But if the last bit of batter only fills 3 or 4 wells, that is fine.

Yield

The number of cake pops a recipe makes will be affected by how much batter you add to each well. With measurements so small, even the slightest variance can affect the yield. When we were testing the recipes in this book, we often got different yields from one test to the next on the same recipe! The yield listed with each recipe is an estimate based on our tests, but the exact number you get may vary a little.

Baking

Once the wells are filled, close the lid and bake for the time specified in the recipe. Set a timer and check for doneness after the minimum time listed.

- In general, cake pops baked in the Babycakes™ Cake Pop Maker are done in 4 to 6 minutes.
- In the Babycakes™ Rotating Cake Pop Maker, cake pops are usually baked for 1 minute, then rotated and baked for 2 to 3 minutes. Before opening the appliance, rotate it back to its original position.

If you're using the rotating cake pop maker, test for doneness while it is in the upright position, as the appliance will not open when rotated. To test for doneness, insert a tester into the center of a cake pop. If it comes out clean, it is done. (An exception is cake pops that contain chocolate chips; even when the cake pops are done, you will see chocolate on the tester. Bake these cake pops until they are set and light brown. The cake pops should bounce back if gently touched with your finger.) Even slight variations in the volume of batter can affect the baking time, so it is best to check the doneness of several cake pops. If some are done and others aren't, remove those that are done and continue baking the rest for another minute or two, then test again. If using the rotating cake pop maker, continue baking in the upright position, checking every minute, until they are done.

For certain baked items, such as pancakes and some appetizers, we recommend turning the treat over midway through baking to improve the browning. If you're using the rotating model, simply rotate it as directed in the recipe; otherwise, carefully insert the fork tool (see page 16) between the edge of the baked item and the well, gently turn the treat over, then continue baking as directed.

Thermostats and the overall performance of all appliances vary slightly from unit to unit and model to model. This is especially noticeable with short baking times, as with cake pop makers. The baking times in each recipe are based on our tests and typical units, but your appliance may bake a little hotter or a little cooler. If the cake pops are a little darker or lighter than you prefer after the listed baking time, adjust the time slightly up or down. After a use or two, you will be better able to predict the ideal baking time for your unit.

Removing the Treats from the Wells

The fork tool that comes packed with the appliance is perfect for lifting out cake pops and other treats. Hot cake pops are delicate, so it is best to insert the fork tool between the edge of the well and the bottom of the cake pop and lift the treat gently from underneath. Be careful not to tear the cake pop or scratch the appliance. If you have misplaced your fork tool or wish to order another, visit www.thebabycakesshop.com for ordering information.

Place freshly baked cake pops on a wire rack to cool. If you plan to attach sticks and dip the cake pops in candy coating (see page 18), the cake pops must be cooled completely.

Cleaning the Cake Pop Maker

Simply unplug the appliance and let it cool completely. Use a paper towel to absorb any residual oil, then wipe the surfaces with a damp cloth.

What about those extreme instances when a damp cloth can't get the appliance clean? First, be sure to unplug the appliance. Then, while the unit is still warm, wet a kitchen towel or paper towel and place it across the inner surface. Close the appliance and let it steam for about 5 minutes or until the towel is just cool enough to touch. The sugar and any other residuals will then wipe off easily. Always use caution, and never place the towel in the appliance if it is plugged in.

The plates of the appliance do not come out, and there is nothing to take apart. Do not use soap or abrasive cleansers on it. Do not immerse it in water. Always read and follow the safeguards and instructions packed with your appliance.

The Cake Pops Pantry

CAKE POPS don't really require any special ingredients, but we love to share our latest tips and finds. And because we know what it's like to start a recipe, then discover you've run out of a crucial ingredient, we've provided some easy substitutions.

Cake Mix

Some people prefer to use a cake mix; others like to bake from scratch. There are recipes in this book for both methods. When you're choosing a cake mix, keep in mind that different brands bake quite differently. We prefer cake mixes labeled "extra moist" or "pudding in the mix," such as Betty Crocker or Pillsbury, which bake into more rounded cake pops.

Throughout the book, when we call for 1 cup (250 mL) or 2 cups (500 mL) of cake mix, we mean dry cake mix. Spoon it out of the box into a measuring cup and level it off.

Store leftover cake mix in an airtight container and use it by the date stamped on the box.

In general, 2 cups (500 mL) of cake mix — about half the box — makes plenty of cake pops. Because of differences among brands, and even among flavors within brands, there may be a little less than 2 cups (500 mL) left over for the next time you prepare a recipe.

Here is a general cake mix recipe you can use as a guide:

Makes 38 to 40 cake pops

2 cups	cake mix	500 mL
2	large eggs, at room temperature	2
⅔ cup	water	150 mL
¼ cup	vegetable oil	60 mL
	Nonstick baking spray	

1. In a medium bowl, using an electric mixer on low speed, beat cake mix, eggs, water and oil for 30 seconds or until moistened. Beat on medium speed for 2 minutes.

2. Spray cake pop wells with baking spray. Fill each well with about 1 tbsp (15 mL) batter.

3. Bake for 4 to 6 minutes or until a tester inserted in the center comes out clean. Transfer cake pops to a wire rack to cool.

4. Repeat steps 2 and 3 with the remaining batter.

If Baking in the Rotating Cake Pop Maker

In step 3, bake for 1 minute. Rotate and bake for 2 to 3 minutes. Rotate back before testing for doneness. Continue with step 3.

Flour

With quantities as small as these, a slight variation in the amount of flour can have a big impact, so it's important to measure correctly. Spoon the flour into a dry measuring cup and level off the top with a knife or straight edge. Do not pack or shake it down.

All-Purpose Flour

All-purpose flour is our flour of choice for most baking. There are exceptions, which are specifically noted in the recipes.

There is no need to sift all-purpose flour, but we recommend whisking it with the leavening ingredients and salt in a bowl so they are thoroughly blended before adding them to the batter. If you omit this step, your cake pops may have an uneven texture and leavening.

Store all-purpose flour in an airtight container at room temperature for up to 6 months, in the refrigerator for up to 1 year, or in the freezer for up to 2 years. (Whole-grain flours should be kept in the freezer and used within 1 year.)

Cake Flour

Cake flour is softer than all-purpose flour, which for our purposes means it bakes into a fine, tender cake. We use cake flour in a handful of recipes where we wanted a very tender, fine texture. Be sure to use the type of flour specified in the recipe.

In a Pinch

If you don't have cake flour, for each cup (250 mL) of cake flour, measure out 1 cup (250 mL) of all-purpose flour, then return 2 tbsp (30 mL) of the flour to the sack or canister. Add 2 tbsp (30 mL) cornstarch. Sift the two together so they are evenly blended.

Gluten-Free All-Purpose Baking Mix

Gluten-free all-purpose flour or baking mix is a blend of several types of gluten-free flours and starches. The exact blend varies from brand to brand, and you might prefer the baking qualities and flavor of one over another. Popular brands include King Arthur and Bob's Red Mill. Stores and websites that specialize in gluten-free baking ingredients offer a large array of brands and package sizes. For the recipes in this book, do not substitute a gluten-free baking mix that contains fats or leavening agents, such as Gluten-Free Bisquick.

To make your own gluten-free all-purpose baking mix, whisk together three parts white rice flour (not sweet rice flour), three parts brown rice flour, two parts potato starch and one part tapioca starch. Store in an airtight container in the refrigerator for up to 4 months or in the freezer for up to 1 year.

Sugar

Measure sugar in a dry measuring cup and level off the top. Brown sugar should always be packed into the cup.

Store sugar in an airtight container at room temperature; it will keep indefinitely. Choose a plastic container for brown sugar, so it will stay moist. Watch for sales on sugar before the holidays and stock up.

We have not tested these recipes using other types of sweeteners; in general, any substitutions will affect both texture and flavor.

Granulated Sugar

Granulated sugar is a key ingredient in baking, and not just for its irresistible flavor. It also makes baked goods more tender, so reducing the amount of sugar in a recipe could make the treats tough.

Brown Sugar

Light and dark brown sugar both perform well in our recipes. The dark has a little more molasses flavor. Most people choose the brown sugar they are most familiar with. Given a choice, Roxanne opts for dark brown sugar, while Kathy favors light. For old-fashioned recipes, and those reminiscent of Southern cooking, we often specify dark brown sugar.

Confectioners' (Icing) Sugar

Confectioners' (icing) sugar has been pulverized or crushed, and a little cornstarch has been added so it doesn't clump. We used to sift it, but we no longer find that necessary in most cases. If we feel it's critical to sift the confectioners' sugar in a recipe, the ingredient list will tell you to do so. Sift the sugar after measuring it.

In a Pinch

One cup (250 mL) of granulated sugar equals 1 cup (250 mL) of packed brown sugar or 1¾ cups (425 mL) confectioners' (icing) sugar.

Easy, right? Not so fast.

Brown sugar and granulated sugar can generally be substituted for one another; while it may affect the flavor a little, it will work. To add molasses flavor to granulated sugar, combine 1 cup (250 mL) granulated sugar and 1 tbsp (15 mL) light (fancy) molasses, stirring until evenly blended.

When making a frosting or glaze, do not replace the confectioner's sugar with granulated sugar — it doesn't dissolve quickly enough, so you will taste and/or feel the sugar granules.

Eggs

Baking recipes are based on large eggs. If you substitute medium or extra-large eggs, it will affect the results.

Separating eggs is a commonly needed kitchen skill, and we often call for egg yolks or whites in our recipes. The best way to separate eggs is with an egg separator. The American Egg Board no longer recommends passing the yolk from shell to shell, as this method transfers bacteria from the shell to the egg.

Store extra egg whites in an airtight container in the refrigerator for up to 4 days or in the freezer for up to 6 months. Slide leftover egg yolks into a container of cold water, cover and store in the refrigerator for up to 2 days. Drain before using.

Butter

Unsalted butter gives baked goods the best flavor. Although we grew up in the margarine era, those days are gone, and we now prefer the flavor of butter. However, if you prefer to use margarine, it will work in the recipes. Do not use whipped or light spreads, often sold in a tub, or those labeled "diet" or something similar, as these products will create inferior results.

If you use salted butter or margarine, you may wish to decrease the amount of salt in the recipe.

When a recipe calls for softened butter, set it out at room temperature for about 30 minutes before use. If you are short on time and want to soften it quickly, slice the butter into pieces, place them on a microwave-safe glass plate and microwave on Medium-Low (30%) for 10 to 15 seconds for ¼ cup (60 mL) butter, or for 20 to 25 seconds for ½ cup (125 mL) butter, until it just starts to soften. Let the butter stand for about 10 minutes, then proceed with the recipe. Do not melt the butter unless the recipe specifically calls for melted butter.

We buy butter when it is on sale and keep it frozen — it can be stored in the freezer for up to 6 months. You can also purchase good brands of butter, often at a discount, at warehouse and discount stores.

Buttermilk

We have now christened ourselves "the buttermilk queens." Neither of us regularly kept buttermilk on hand until we fell in love with the texture and tangy flavor of cupcakes and cake pops made with it. Now we always have some in our refrigerators, and we encourage you to join our ranks. We appreciate the value of the chemical reaction when the acid in the buttermilk reacts with the baking soda, but most importantly, we love buttermilk because it's tart and thick, and gives baked goods tremendous depth of flavor.

In a Pinch
Do not substitute regular milk for buttermilk in a recipe. If you don't have buttermilk on hand, a common substitution is to stir lemon juice or white vinegar into milk. Use 1 tsp (5 mL) lemon juice or vinegar for every ⅓ cup (75 mL) of buttermilk needed. Pour the lemon juice or vinegar into a measuring cup, then add enough milk to equal the measurement you need. Let it stand for 5 to 10 minutes to thicken.

Another alternative is to use yogurt or sour cream. Substitute 1 cup (250 mL) sour cream or plain yogurt for 1 cup (250 ml) buttermilk, or combine ½ cup (125 mL) plain yogurt and ½ cup (125 mL) milk and use it in place of 1 cup (250 mL) buttermilk.

Dried buttermilk powder, when reconstituted according to package directions, can also be used in place of fresh buttermilk.

Other Dairy Products

The recipes in this book were tested with full-fat dairy products. If you substitute low-fat or fat-free items, the flavor and texture of the treats will be adversely affected.

When purchasing dairy products, be sure to note the "sell by" or "best before" date on the package or carton and buy the freshest product available.

When it comes to whipping cream, it will whip faster if you chill the beaters and the bowl in the freezer for 15 minutes. Also, be sure the cream is very cold.

Vanilla

We choose real vanilla extract for the best flavor. Imitation vanillas just don't deliver for us. One of our favorite brands is Nielsen-Massey. We keep an eye out for sales, then buy a large bottle.

Tools of the Trade

CERTAIN TOOLS make baking and decorating cake pops easy. Here are our favorites.

- **Fork tool:** We use this tool to lift baked cake pops out of the wells. It is also handy when you're dipping cake pops, doughnuts or other baked treats in a glaze. The fork tool is included with the cake pop maker. If you misplace it or want another one, they can be ordered at www.thebabycakesshop.com.

- **Small off-set spatula:** This is the tool to use when a delicate baked treat needs to be supported as it is lifted out of the well. The blade is thinner than that of a typical table knife, so it is easy to insert it carefully between the edge of the treat and the well. Off-set spatulas are readily available where cake decorating supplies are sold. The one you want may be labeled as being 9 inches (23 cm), but much of that is handle; the blade is about $4\frac{1}{2}$ inches (11 cm) long.

- **Cake pop sticks:** Any food-safe sticks can be used for cake pops. Sticks come in a variety of lengths and may be called treat sticks, lollipop sticks, cookie sticks or cake pop sticks. They are available online at www.thebabycakesshop.com or anywhere cake decorating supplies are sold. Or you can get creative and reach for a straw, a plastic fork or a popsicle stick — these also make fun cake pop displays!

- **Pastry bags:** These may take a bit of practice, but once you are familiar with them, you will wonder how you got along without them. We really prefer disposable pastry bags because they are so convenient. Plus, many food professionals caution against reusable bags, as bacteria can lurk if they are not washed and dried thoroughly. Shop around and compare prices. We discovered bakery supply stores that sell disposable bags in rolls of 100 for just a few dollars. In a pinch? We turn to sealable food storage bags and clip a corner off.

- **Squeeze bottles:** Cake and candy decorating stores sell squeeze bottles that are perfect for many decorating techniques. These bottles are food-safe and very flexible, so it is easy to control the flow of the candy coating or glaze. Bottles designed for condiments are made of thicker plastic and are difficult to use for cake decorating.

- **Toothpicks:** A toothpick is the perfect tester when you're checking cake pops for doneness: insert it in the center; if it comes out clean, the cake pop is done. Toothpicks are also great for painting fine details or textures on cake pops, or for placing a tiny drop of candy coating to glue on a decoration.

- **Paintbrushes:** Food-safe paintbrushes of various sizes and widths can be found anywhere cake decorating supplies are sold. Larger brushes are great for painting fur or hair, or for adding texture. Use fine brushes to paint eyes, lips and other small details. You can also paint a fine line or swirl of candy coating or water, then immediately sprinkle it with food-safe glitter or sprinkles.

- **Tweezers:** Fine detail work requires tweezers, so keep a pair in the kitchen. Use them to place an "eye" in just the right spot, hold a "beak" open until it dries or arrange dots in a row.

- **Wire cooling rack:** When removing hot treats from the cake pop maker, transfer them to a wire rack, whether they need to cool briefly or completely. If you place hot baked goods directly on a cutting board or on the counter, the bottoms will get moist; on a cooling rack, they will stay crisp. We also place doughnuts, scones or any treat that is not on a stick on a wire rack before drizzling glaze over them. Be sure to set a piece of parchment paper, waxed paper or foil underneath the rack to catch drips.

- **Containers for melting candy coating:** When selecting a container in which to melt candy coating wafers, choose one that's deep and narrow so the cake pops can be dipped straight down into the coating. Good choices include coffee mugs, glass measuring cups, small microwave-safe glass bowls or small canning jars. Canning jars are a particularly handy choice because, once you've decorated the cake pops, if you have any leftover melted candy coating, you can simply cover the jar with the metal lid and store it in a cool, dry place until you're ready to reheat the candy coating and use it another time.

- **Sharp knives:** A sharp knife is an indispensable tool, so sharpen your knives as needed before getting started. We use a knife to slice off part of each cake pop when making Easter eggs (see page 41) and to create a flat spot for the candy muzzle on a cake pop animal, among other uses. A dull knife will mash the delicate cake pops instead of cleanly slicing through them.

- **Kitchen scissors:** Keep sharp kitchen scissors handy for clipping the tips off disposable pastry bags, trimming ribbons, cutting packages open and cutting candies to the right size.

- **Paper punch:** We often use a 2-inch (5 cm) round paper punch to create paper collars for our cake pops. Of course, if you don't have a paper punch the right size, you can trace a circle with a 2-inch (5 cm) cookie cutter and cut it out. But once you use a paper punch, we think you'll agree that it's a handy tool.

- **Parchment paper:** A sheet of parchment paper, waxed paper or foil placed under a cooling rack makes cleanup quick and easy when you're drizzling glaze over baked goods. We also cover our counters with these disposable sheets when working with intensely colored candy coatings and food colors, to avoid any possibility of staining the counters.

- **Plastic storage containers:** Candies, sprinkles and candy coating wafers need to be stored in an airtight containers, and food-safe plastic storage containers are ideal.

Decorating Your Cake Pops

· ·

WHEN IT comes to decorating cake pops, the possibilities are endless! It can be as easy as attaching the sticks and coating the cake pops with candy coating, or you can take it up a notch and add sprinkles or swirls, or you can go all out, creating fun, fanciful or elegant designs, including characters and animals, that serve as the focal point of gifts or centerpieces. We've provided step-by-step instructions for many simple decorating techniques on pages 29–47, and inspiring recipes for more elaborate designs in Part 4 (pages 168–229).

Attaching the Sticks

Inserting a cake pop or lollipop stick into the baked cake is easy — the trick is keeping the cake on the stick. To make sure the stick is securely attached, dip the tip in melted candy coating wafers and quickly insert it into the center of the cake pop, gently pushing the stick in so the tip rests about halfway or three-quarters of the way into the cake. (See page 27 for more detailed step-by-step instructions.) As you finish attaching each stick, place the cake pops on a baking sheet or tray. When all the sticks are attached, place the baking sheet in the freezer for at least 15 minutes to let the sticks set.

Select the same color of candy coating wafers to secure the sticks and to coat the cake pops, so that any drips are disguised.

Once the sticks are set, you can coat and decorate the cake pops as you like. Or you can transfer them to an airtight container and freeze them for up to 1 month. They are then ready to decorate whenever you wish. We often coat frozen cake pops and find it works well.

Cake Pop Stands

Once the cake pops are coated (see page 19), they'll need to stand upright to dry, without touching each other, so gather some cake pop stands before you dip any cake pops. Select Brands packs one or two stands that hold 12 cake pops with each Babycakes™ Cake Pop Maker. If you're likely to be dipping larger batches than this at one time, you may wish to purchase more cake pop stands from www.thebabycakesshop. com. Alternatively, you can make your own stands. Here are some ideas for do-it-yourself cake pop stands:

- **Styrofoam blocks:** If you are putting the cake pops on crazy straws, ice pop sticks or other creative sticks, you may find that Styrofoam blocks make the best stands, as they can accommodate different sizes of sticks. To keep the Styrofoam particles at bay, we often leave the plastic covering on the block or wrap it in foil. Place the cake pops about 2 inches (5 cm) apart, and space them evenly over the Styrofoam to distribute their weight.

- **Wooden boards:** A wooden board about 2 inches (5 cm) thick makes a sturdy, reusable stand. Drill the board with small holes about 2 inches (5 cm) apart. Be sure to use an appropriate drill bit size so the cake pop sticks will be held securely; you may wish to make a sample hole first, then test it to make sure it holds a cake pop securely without letting it wiggle or lean.

Coating Cake Pops

Candy Coating Wafers

Candy coating wafers (also called confectionery coating wafers, molding wafers, coating wafers and Candy Melts®) are the most popular coating for cake pops. They are little pieces of candy that melt easily and dry to a firm finish. They come in a wide array of colors, and you can easily combine colors to create a nearly endless palette.

Candy coating wafers are available anywhere cake decorating supplies are sold, and companies are continually coming out with new colors and supplies. There are several popular brands, including Wilton, Merckens, Guittard, Peters and Make'n Mold. Experiment to learn which brand you like best: some melt more easily, some flow and coat more easily and each tastes a little different.

Store candy coating wafers in an airtight container in a cool, dry place for up to 18 months. Do not store them in the refrigerator, as moisture can form on the wafers, causing them to become too wet, which affects the texture. In addition, candy coating wafers tend to discolor when chilled.

If you're melting a small amount of candy coating wafers, fill a glass measuring cup, a mug or a small, deep, microwave-safe glass bowl with just the amount you need — perhaps 1/2 or 1 cup (125 or 250 mL). Microwave on High in 30-second intervals, stirring after each, until melted and smooth. Reheat the candy coating as needed to keep the liquid thin and smooth. Keep in mind that if they are overheated, they will harden.

When we're dipping a large number of cake pops, we love to use the Babycakes™ Chocolatier, available at www.thebabycakesshop.com. The 20-oz stoneware insert is microwave-safe, and the appliance holds the chocolate or candy coating at the perfect dipping temperature.

You can also melt large amounts of candy coating wafers in the top of a double boiler over simmering water, or in a heatproof bowl set over a saucepan of simmering water.

To coat a cake pop, hold it by the stick and dip it straight down into the melted coating, covering the cake pop completely. Pull it straight up, allowing the excess to drip off. Gently tap the stick against your fingers, over the melted coating, to encourage all excess coating to drip off.

See page 29 for step-by-step instructions on coating cake pops and page 48 for some helpful hints on candy coating.

Flavoring Candy Coating

Cake and candy decorating shops sell flavorings that work perfectly in the candy coating, adding a whole new dimension of flavor. Do not use typical flavorings or extracts, as they will cause the candy to harden. Read the labels carefully or ask for assistance to make sure you purchase the correct ones.

Every time we look at our store's display, we are amazed to find new flavors available, and each new flavor gives us new ideas. We love to add praline flavoring to the coating for caramel or brown sugar cake pops; champagne flavoring is perfect for cake pops for a wedding shower; bubble gum flavoring adds so much fun to favors for a child's party; and rum flavoring spices up chocolate cake pops for a tailgate party. For a real punch of flavor, you can even add a drop or two of the flavoring to both the cake batter *and* the candy coating.

Add just a small amount of flavoring to the candy coating — the flavorings are concentrated, so a little goes a long way. Begin by adding 2 or 3 drops, then add more drops until the desired flavor is achieved. If you're preparing a larger volume of coating, you might end up needing as much as $\frac{1}{8}$ to $\frac{1}{4}$ tsp (0.5 to 1 mL) flavoring.

Thinning Candy Coating

Thinning the melted candy coating makes painting fine details much easier. You can use shortening, vegetable oil or Paramount Crystals (a product made of palm kernel oil and lecithin that is designed for thinning candy coating or chocolates, and is sold in cake or candy decorating shops). Thin slowly, adding just a small amount of shortening, oil or crystals at a time — you can always add more, but if the liquid gets too thin, it is difficult to thicken it. Also, if you add too much shortening or oil, the candy may taste oily. We melt the candy coating wafers, check the consistency, add a little shortening or some crystals, reheat to melt, check the consistency again and so on.

Almond Bark

Almond bark is an easy and popular candy coating that is readily available at most grocery stores, near the baking supplies. It generally comes in vanilla or chocolate flavors. Follow the package directions for melting almond bark. If it's too thick, thin it with 1 to 2 tbsp (15 to 30 mL) shortening. If you wish to color or flavor almond bark, be sure to use the oil-based colors and flavorings sold specifically for candies. Take note: this candy coating is not to be confused with the chocolate bar–like treat also called almond bark, made of chocolate studded with pieces of almonds.

Glazes

Glazes are similar to frostings, but are thinner. When drizzled over freshly baked cake pops, doughnuts, muffins or scones, a glaze adds the perfect finished look and sweet taste. Because glaze cannot be used to attach a stick securely, it's best to enjoy these treats as miniature morsels that you can simply pop into your mouth.

Arrange the cake pops, without sticks, on a wire rack set over a sheet of foil, parchment paper or waxed paper (to make cleanup easy.) Place the glaze in a small sealable sandwich bag and clip the corner off, then drizzle glaze over the cake pops and let it dry.

You can also dip cake pops in glaze. Place the glaze in a deep bowl and use the fork tool to spear the cake pop, then dip it into the glaze. Dip it completely or dip just the top half — it's your choice. Allow the excess to drip off, then place the cake pop on a wire rack set over a sheet of foil, parchment paper or waxed paper to dry.

Creative Displays

THE OLD saying "You eat with your eyes" is absolutely true for cake pops. These bite-size balls of cake become even more scrumptious when they're decorated, and if you arrange them in an imaginative display, you'll really get the crowd oohing and aahing. While decorating the cake pops and creating the display sound like separate steps, we have found that they need to be planned and implemented together.

First choose a theme. What are the cake pops for? A simple little gift or party favor? A large display for a wedding or formal event? A centerpiece for a child's birthday party or special holiday gathering?

What colors will you be using? Will the cake pops have contrasting swirls of bright colors, or detailed faces drawn on? Remember that it is usually best to match lighter-colored cake pops with lighter colors of candy coating wafers and darker cake pops with darker candy coating wafers.

How many cake pops are you planning to decorate? Displays can be as small as single cake pop in a bud vase, or as large as an elaborate arrangement in a silver punch bowl.

Once you've figured out the theme, colors and size of your display, plan it out and gather all of your supplies *before* you start decorating the cake pops. Your choice of container, for example, may affect the length of sticks you need. Sometimes we use shorter sticks, sometimes longer, sometimes straws, and sometimes no sticks at all.

We've provided plenty of ideas for gifts and centerpieces in Part 4 of this book (pages 168–229). Once you get hooked on making displays with cake pops — as we have — you're sure to come up with many imaginative designs of your own!

Containers

When it comes to containers for your display, think outside the box, vase, basket or bowl. We arrange cake pops in or on coffee mugs, flower pots, decorative tins, canning jars, candle holders, crayon boxes, pencil cans, empty soup cans, story books, soda pop bottles, toys, cakes, cupcakes and so much more. When you begin to dream and scheme, you'll suddenly see potential containers everywhere. Browse at craft stores, flea markets, garage sales, craft sales, kitchen shops, hobby shops and office supply stores.

A piece of Styrofoam cut to fit snugly inside the container is a sure-fire way to hold the cake pops in place. If the container is lightweight and needs added weight to steady it, top the Styrofoam with glass beads, polished pebbles, marbles or candy.

With some containers, you don't need Styrofoam. For example, for a display at a trade show, we used plastic cheese shakers filled with brightly colored candies. The cake pops were held securely in place by the holes in the lid, and the candies gleamed brightly inside the clear jars. It was stunning!

If you use a decorative gift bag (or even a small burlap bag) as your container, simply hide another container, such as a can or box, inside it. Fill the can or box with Styrofoam (and weights, if needed) and insert the cake pops into the Styrofoam.

Whatever containers and weights you choose, make sure they are clean. Avoid containers that once held dangerous chemicals and read the label to be sure the finish is food-safe. If you choose a container that was not designed for food, make sure the food does not come in contact with the container.

Finishing Touches

What else does your display need? We often use ribbons to accent the sticks: sometimes curling ribbon; sometimes tiny, simple bows; sometimes large, flowing swathes of tulle. Sheets of brightly colored tissue paper, cut into squares, can be nestled between the cake pops. Artificial flowers, leaves or holiday picks can be inserted around the cake pops.

To Wrap or Not to Wrap?

Once coated in candy coating, cake pops stay fresh for 3 or 4 days and don't require additional wrapping or covering. You can decorate cake pops a day or two before a party and feel confident that they will taste fresh and moist. Do not store decorated cake pops in the refrigerator or freezer, as condensation may collect and discolor the coating. However, the coating on cake pops does melt easily, so on hot days, keep cake pops in an air-conditioned or other cool room and out of direct sunlight.

If you want to give cake pops as individual treats or favors, wrap each one in cellophane or plastic. Use a treat bag that is about 3 by 4 inches (7.5 by 10 cm) or a 7-inch (18 cm) square of cellophane, and tie it closed with ribbon.

Decoration and Display Tips

- Gather all of your supplies before starting. Make sure you have enough sticks, plenty of candy coating wafers and all of the sprinkles or adornments you might want. It is frustrating to run out of an ingredient just when you need it.

- Stock up when supplies are on sale.

- Keep in mind that certain candies and candy coating wafer colors are seasonal, and buy extras while they're available. Stock up on pastel colors in the spring and black or orange around Halloween. Candy hearts are fun to use all year long, but are most often sold around Valentine's Day.

- Be on the lookout for new colors and techniques. Cake decorating shops, craft shops and hobby shops stock new supplies all the time. Take time to browse and leave with new ideas to try.

- Spread the work out over a couple of days so you don't feel rushed or frazzled. Bake the cake pops and insert the sticks one day, then store the cake pops in the freezer to coat and decorate another day. Bake early in the week for a party on the weekend, then create your display a day or two in advance.

- Remember that the simplest designs can often have the most impact. A single color of cake pops nestled in a clear glass vase makes a very special centerpiece or gift.

Cake Pops 101
Starter Recipes and Decorations

Chocolate Sour Cream Cake Pops

If you usually use a cake mix, this recipe may convert you to baking from scratch — it's that easy! You'll love the moist, decadent chocolate results.

Variation

For a more intense flavor, substitute steaming hot brewed coffee for the boiling water.

2 oz	unsweetened chocolate, chopped	60 g
¼ cup	unsalted butter, softened	60 mL
¼ cup	sour cream	60 mL
¾ tsp	baking soda	3 mL
1 cup	granulated sugar	250 mL
Pinch	salt	Pinch
½ tsp	vanilla extract	2 mL
1	large egg, at room temperature	1
1 cup	all-purpose flour	250 mL
½ cup	boiling water	125 mL
	Nonstick baking spray	

1. In a small saucepan, combine chocolate and butter. Heat over low heat, stirring constantly, until melted and smooth. Transfer to a medium bowl.

2. In a small bowl, whisk together sour cream and baking soda. Set aside.

3. To the chocolate mixture, add sugar, salt and vanilla. Using an electric mixer on medium speed, beat until blended. Beat in egg. Reduce speed to low and beat in sour cream mixture until blended. Add flour and beat on medium speed just until smooth. Using a wooden spoon, stir in boiling water until smooth.

4. Spray cake pop wells with baking spray. Fill each well with about 1 tbsp (15 mL) batter.

5. Bake for 4 to 6 minutes or until a tester inserted in the center comes out clean. Transfer cake pops to a wire rack to cool.

6. Repeat steps 4 and 5 with the remaining batter.

7. If desired, attach sticks to cake pops (see page 27).

If Baking in the Rotating Cake Pop Maker

In step 5, bake for 1 minute. Rotate and bake for 2 to 3 minutes. Rotate back before testing for doneness. Continue with step 5.

See the step-by-step photographs on photo page A. ▶

Tips

Another way to fill the wells is to use a small scoop that holds about 1 tbsp (15 mL) of batter. We often use a scoop when the batter is quite thick and chunky with fruits and nuts. Look for scoops at shops that specialize in kitchen utensils and baking supplies.

In general, fill all 12 wells for each batch. But if the last bit of batter only fills 3 or 4 wells, that is fine.

Filling the Wells

1. Fold the top edge of a pastry bag down about 2 inches (5 cm) to make a collar.

2. Set the bag in a glass to hold it upright, then fill the bag about half full with batter.

3. Alternatively, use a sealable plastic food bag.

4. Twist the top of the bag, then clip off the point (or, if you're using a sealable food storage bag, clip off one corner).

5. Press very lightly on the top of the bag, letting the batter flow into a well. Stop pressing as you move to each new well.

6. Between batches, twist the tip end, then set the bag upright in the glass.

Favorite White Cake Pops

Makes 50
to 52 cake pops

We both love white cake that's moist, rich and packed with flavor. This is the recipe we use when we have lots of cake pops to decorate for a special event.

Variation

Fold ⅓ cup (75 mL) mini semisweet chocolate chips into the batter at the end of step 4.

1¼ cups	all-purpose flour	300 mL
¾ cup	granulated sugar	175 mL
2 tsp	baking powder	10 mL
½ tsp	salt	2 mL
4	large egg whites, at room temperature	4
½ cup	milk	125 mL
1 tsp	almond extract	5 mL
1 tsp	vanilla extract	5 mL
6 tbsp	unsalted butter, softened	90 mL
	Nonstick baking spray	

1. In a medium bowl, whisk together flour, sugar, baking powder and salt. Set aside.

2. In a small bowl, whisk together egg whites, milk, almond extract and vanilla. Set aside.

3. Add butter to the flour mixture. Using an electric mixer on medium speed, beat for 1 minute. Beat in milk mixture for 1 minute.

4. Spray cake pop wells with baking spray. Fill each well with about 1 tbsp (15 mL) batter.

5. Bake for 4 to 6 minutes or until a tester inserted in the center comes out clean. Transfer cake pops to a wire rack to cool.

6. Repeat steps 4 and 5 with the remaining batter.

7. If desired, attach sticks to cake pops (see page 27).

If Baking in the Rotating Cake Pop Maker

In step 5, bake for 1 minute. Rotate and bake for 2 to 3 minutes. Rotate back before testing for doneness. Continue with step 5.

See the step-by-step photographs on photo page B. ▶

Tips

Candy coating wafers are available anywhere cake decorating supplies are sold.

Select the same color of candy coating wafers to secure the sticks and to coat the cake pops, so that any drips are disguised.

Attaching the Sticks

1. To easily remove the cake pops from the wells, use the fork tool, gently inserting the tips between the edge of the well and the cake and lifting gently from beneath the cake pop.

2. Transfer the cake pops to a wire rack to cool.

3. Place $\frac{1}{2}$ cup (125 mL) candy coating wafers in a 2-cup (500 mL) glass measuring cup, canning jar or small, deep, microwave-safe glass bowl. Microwave on High in 30-second intervals, stirring after each, until melted and smooth. Microwave just until melted; do not overheat.

4. Dip the end of a stick into the melted candy coating.

5. Gently push the stick into a cake pop. Be sure to push the stick far enough in—the tip should be about halfway or three-quarters of the way through the cake pop.

6. As you finish attaching each stick, place the cake pops on a baking sheet, a tray or a wire rack. When all the sticks are attached, place the baking sheet in the freezer for at least 15 minutes to let the sticks set. Once the sticks are set, you can coat and decorate the cake pops as you like. Or you can transfer them to an airtight container and freeze them for up to 1 month.

White Spice Cake Pops

<table>
<tr><td>Makes 42
to 44 cake pops</td></tr>
</table>

Roxanne prefers white wedding cake over all other cake flavors. This twist on the traditional has been added to the top of her list.

Tips

No buttermilk on hand? Place 1½ tsp (7 mL) lemon juice or white vinegar in a glass measuring cup, then pour in enough milk to equal ½ cup (125 mL). Let stand for 5 to 10 minutes to thicken. Proceed with the recipe. (See page 15 for other buttermilk substitutions.)

Not in the mood to spice up the white cake? Simply omit the cinnamon and nutmeg.

1⅓ cups	all-purpose flour	325 mL
¾ cup	granulated sugar	175 mL
1½ tsp	baking powder	7 mL
½ tsp	ground cinnamon	2 mL
¼ tsp	ground nutmeg	1 mL
¼ tsp	salt	1 mL
⅓ cup	unsalted butter, softened	75 mL
2	large egg whites, at room temperature	2
1	large egg, at room temperature	1
½ cup	buttermilk	125 mL
1 tsp	vanilla extract	5 mL
	Nonstick baking spray	

1. In a medium bowl, whisk together flour, sugar, baking powder, cinnamon, nutmeg and salt. Using an electric mixer on low speed, beat in butter until well blended. Add egg whites and egg, one at a time, beating well after each addition. Add half the buttermilk and beat for 1 minute. Add the remaining buttermilk and beat for 1 minute. Beat in vanilla.

2. Spray cake pop wells with baking spray. Fill each well with about 1 tbsp (15 mL) batter.

3. Bake for 4 to 6 minutes or until a tester inserted in the center comes out clean. Transfer cake pops to a wire rack to cool.

4. Repeat steps 2 and 3 with the remaining batter.

5. If desired, attach sticks to cake pops (see page 27).

If Baking in the Rotating Cake Pop Maker

In step 3, bake for 1 minute. Rotate and bake for 2 to 3 minutes. Rotate back before testing for doneness. Continue with step 3.

See the step-by-step photographs on photo page C. ▶

Tips

In general, 1 cup (250 mL) of melted candy coating wafers will cover about 24 cake pops. But it depends somewhat on the brand of candy coating wafers, and on how patient you are with letting the excess drip back into the cup.

Candy coating wafers thicken as they cool, so dip the cake pops immediately. Reheat the melts as needed to keep the liquid thin and smooth. If it thickens too much, it will not coat the cake pops evenly.

Coating Cake Pops

1. Add 1 cup (250 mL) of candy coating wafers to those left in the cup, jar or bowl from when you attached the stick. (To disguise drips, be sure to use the same color of wafers as you used to secure the sticks.)

2. Microwave the candy coating wafers on High in 30-second intervals, stirring after each, until melted and smooth.

3. Hold a cake pop by the stick and gently dip it into the melted candy coating, using a straight-up-and-down motion.

4. Hold the coated cake pop over the cup so the excess coating can drip back into the cup.

5. Gently tap the stick against your fingers, over the cup, to encourage all excess coating to drip off.

6. Set the cake pop in a cake pop stand to dry.

Coconut Snowballs

If you're planning a winter celebration, a graduation party or a wedding shower, these moist, coconut-covered white cake pops are the perfect addition to your dessert table.

Tips

Cream of coconut is commonly sold for cocktails and can be found in the mixed drinks section of the grocery store. It should not be confused with coconut milk.

If desired, toast the coconut. Spread flaked coconut in a thin layer on a baking sheet. Bake at 300°F (150°C) for about 20 minutes, stirring every 5 minutes, until coconut is evenly browned.

Decorating Tip

If you want to attach these cake pops to sticks, omit the Cream Cheese Coating and steps 5 and 6. Attach the sticks (see page 27) and coat with melted white candy coating wafers (see page 29). Immediately roll in coconut.

2 cups	white cake mix	500 mL
1	large egg, at room temperature	1
½ cup	water	125 mL
⅓ cup	cream of coconut	75 mL
	Nonstick baking spray	
	Cream Cheese Coating (page 103)	
2 cups	sweetened flaked coconut	500 mL

1. In a medium bowl, using an electric mixer on low speed, beat cake mix, egg, water and cream of coconut for 30 seconds or until moistened. Beat on medium speed for 2 minutes.

2. Spray cake pop wells with baking spray. Fill each well with about 1 tbsp (15 mL) batter.

3. Bake for 4 to 6 minutes or until a tester inserted in the center comes out clean. Transfer cake pops to a wire rack to cool.

4. Repeat steps 2 and 3 with the remaining batter.

5. Place cooled cake pops (without sticks) on a baking sheet and freeze for at least 15 minutes.

6. Dip frozen cake pops in Cream Cheese Coating. Place coconut in a shallow bowl and roll freshly coated cake pops in coconut to cover. Let set on a wire rack for 20 minutes.

If Baking in the Rotating Cake Pop Maker

In step 3, bake for 1 minute. Rotate and bake for 2 to 3 minutes. Rotate back before testing for doneness. Continue with step 3.

See the step-by-step photographs on photo page D. ▶

Tips

Sprinkles come in a variety of colors, sizes and shapes. Select sprinkles that complement the color of the candy melt you used for the coating.

Do you want the sprinkles arranged in a pattern? After coating the cake pop, let it dry. Use melted candy coating wafers to pipe your design onto the cake pop, then immediately sprinkle that design with sprinkles. Or use a small paintbrush dipped in water to paint a design, then immediately sprinkle the moist spots with sprinkles.

Decorating with Sprinkles

1. Select your sprinkles (see tip, at left).

2. Set out a tray or baking sheet to work over. This will make cleanup easier.

3. Following the directions on page 29, coat a cake pop in melted candy coating, but do not let it dry.

4. Hold the freshly coated cake pop over the tray.

5. Sprinkle the cake pop with sprinkles.

6. Set the cake pop in a cake pop stand to dry.

Brown Sugar Spice Cake Pops

Makes 34 to 36 cake pops

Just the right hint of brown sugar and spices imbues these cake pops with old-fashioned flavor. Decorate them as you like for year-round enjoyment.

Tip

For extra spice, add 1/4 tsp (1 mL) ground cloves and 1/4 tsp (1 mL) ground ginger to the flour mixture.

1 1/2 cups	all-purpose flour	375 mL
2 tsp	baking powder	10 mL
1 tsp	ground cinnamon	5 mL
1/2 tsp	ground nutmeg	2 mL
1/4 tsp	salt	1 mL
1/2 cup	granulated sugar	125 mL
1/4 cup	packed brown sugar	60 mL
6 tbsp	unsalted butter, softened	90 mL
1	large egg, at room temperature	1
1	large egg yolk, at room temperature	1
1/2 tsp	vanilla extract	2 mL
1/2 cup	milk	125 mL
	Nonstick baking spray	

1. In a small bowl, whisk together flour, baking powder, cinnamon, nutmeg and salt. Set aside.

2. In a medium bowl, using an electric mixer on medium-high speed, beat granulated sugar, brown sugar and butter for 1 minute or until fluffy. Add egg, then egg yolk, beating well after each addition. Beat in vanilla. Add flour mixture alternately with milk, making three additions of flour and two of milk and beating on low speed until smooth.

3. Spray cake pop wells with baking spray. Fill each well with about 1 tbsp (15 mL) batter.

4. Bake for 4 to 6 minutes or until a tester inserted in the center comes out clean. Transfer cake pops to a wire rack to cool.

5. Repeat steps 3 and 4 with the remaining batter.

6. If desired, attach sticks to cake pops (see page 27).

If Baking in the Rotating Cake Pop Maker

In step 4, bake for 1 minute. Rotate and bake for 2 to 3 minutes. Rotate back before testing for doneness. Continue with step 4.

See the step-by-step photographs on photo page E. ▶

Tips

If you want the contrasting color to be more marbleized or less pronounced, pipe the swirls onto a freshly dipped cake pop.

For sparkly swirls, use candy coating wafers in the same color as the coating. Immediately after piping the swirls, sprinkle them with sparkling sanding sugar or edible glitter.

Adding Spirals, Swirls or Lines

1. After the coating has dried, place 1 cup (250 mL) candy coating wafers in a contrasting or complementary color in a 2-cup (500 mL) glass measuring cup, canning jar or small, deep, microwave-safe glass bowl. Microwave on High in 30-second intervals, stirring after each, until melted and smooth.

2. Fit a pastry bag or squeeze bottle with a fine writing tip.

3. Fill the pastry bag with melted candy coating.

4. Pipe spirals in a decorative fashion over the cake pop.

5. Or pipe swirls in either a tight design or a loose design.

6. Or pipe straight lines in stripes, zigzags or a random decorative pattern.

Pistachio Marble Cake Pops

Makes 40 to 42 cake pops

We remember when pistachio marble cake and Watergate cake were all the rage. This flavor combination got high marks from the entire test kitchen staff, and those of us who are old enough enjoyed the walk down memory lane.

Tip

Toasting nuts intensifies their flavor. Spread chopped nuts in a single layer on a baking sheet. Bake at 350°F (180°C) for 5 to 7 minutes or until lightly browned. Let cool.

2 cups	yellow cake mix	500 mL
3½ tbsp	pistachio instant pudding mix (half of a 3.4 oz/96 g box)	52 mL
2	large eggs, at room temperature	2
½ cup	water	125 mL
¼ cup	vegetable oil	60 mL
¼ tsp	almond extract	1 mL
3 tbsp	chocolate ice cream syrup	45 mL
¼ cup	finely chopped pistachios or pecans, toasted (see tip, at left)	60 mL
	Nonstick baking spray	

1. In a medium bowl, using an electric mixer on low speed, beat cake mix, pudding mix, eggs, water, oil and almond extract for 30 seconds or until moistened. Beat on medium speed for 2 minutes.

2. Transfer one-third of the batter to a small bowl and stir in chocolate syrup until smooth.

3. Fold pistachios into the remaining batter.

4. Drizzle chocolate batter over pistachio batter. Draw a spatula through the batter to swirl. (Be careful not to swirl too much.)

5. Spray cake pop wells with baking spray. Fill each well with about 1 tbsp (15 mL) batter.

6. Bake for 4 to 6 minutes or until a tester inserted in the center comes out clean. Transfer cake pops to a wire rack to cool.

7. Repeat steps 5 and 6 with the remaining batter.

8. If desired, attach sticks to cake pops (see page 27).

If Baking in the Rotating Cake Pop Maker

In step 6, bake for 1 minute. Rotate and bake for 2 to 3 minutes. Rotate back before testing for doneness. Continue with step 6.

See the step-by-step photographs on photo page F. ▶

Tip

Experiment with the melted candy coating to achieve the right consistency for piping initials. Candy coating is quite thin when warm and thickens as it cools. If too thin, the liquid will run as you pipe the initial; if too thick, it will be harder to pipe.

Adding a Monogram and a Ribbon

1. After the coating has dried, place 1 cup (250 mL) candy coating wafers in a contrasting color in a 2-cup (500 mL) glass measuring cup, canning jar or small, deep, microwave-safe glass bowl. Microwave on High in 30-second intervals, stirring after each, until melted and smooth.

2. Fit a pastry bag or squeeze bottle with a fine writing tip.

3. Fill the pastry bag with melted candy coating.

4. Pipe an initial on the cake pop.

5. Set the cake pop in a cake pop stand to dry.

6. Use about 4 inches (10 cm) of narrow ribbon to tie a knot on the stick, or use about 7 inches (18 cm) of narrow ribbon to tie a bow on the stick.

Peanut Butter Cake Pops

Makes 32 to 34 cake pops

Kathy's husband, David, and daughter, Amanda, enjoy all things flavored with peanut butter. Needless to say, these cake pops are among their favorites — especially when coated in chocolate (see decorating tip, below).

Tip

If you prefer, you can use crunchy peanut butter instead of creamy.

Decorating Tip

Coat the cake pops in chocolate candy coating. If desired, immediately sprinkle with finely chopped dry-roasted peanuts.

1 cup	all-purpose flour	250 mL
1 tsp	baking powder	5 mL
¼ tsp	salt	1 mL
⅓ cup	unsalted butter, softened	75 mL
¼ cup	creamy peanut butter	60 mL
1 cup	granulated sugar	250 mL
2	large eggs, at room temperature	2
1 tsp	vanilla extract	5 mL
⅓ cup	milk	75 mL
	Nonstick baking spray	

1. In a small bowl, whisk together flour, baking powder and salt. Set aside.

2. In a medium bowl, using an electric mixer on medium-high speed, beat butter and peanut butter for 1 minute or until creamy. Gradually add sugar and continue beating for 1 minute. Add eggs, one at a time, beating after each addition. Beat in vanilla. Add flour mixture alternately with milk, making three additions of flour and two of milk and beating on low speed until smooth.

3. Spray cake pop wells with baking spray. Fill each well with about 1 tbsp (15 mL) batter.

4. Bake for 4 to 6 minutes or until a tester inserted in the center comes out clean. Transfer cake pops to a wire rack to cool.

5. Repeat steps 3 and 4 with the remaining batter.

6. If desired, attach sticks to cake pops (see page 27).

If Baking in the Rotating Cake Pop Maker

In step 4, bake for 1 minute. Rotate and bake for 2 to 3 minutes. Rotate back before testing for doneness. Continue with step 4.

See the step-by-step photographs on photo page G. ▶

Tips

Paramount Crystals are made of palm kernel oil and lecithin. The product is designed for thinning candy coating or chocolates, and is sold in cake or candy decorating shops.

Thin the candy coating slowly, adding just a small amount of shortening or crystals at a time — you can always add more, but if the liquid gets too thin, it is difficult to thicken it. Also, if you add too much shortening, the candy may taste oily. We melt the candy coating wafers, check the consistency, add a little shortening or some crystals, reheat to melt, check the consistency again and so on.

Making a Simple Face

1. To create a mixture the color of a light skin tone, combine equal parts of yellow, pink and white candy coating wafers. For darker skin tones, combine white candy coating wafers with a small amount of milk chocolate candy coating wafers. Melt 1 cup (250 mL) of the combined wafers as described in step 3 on page 27. Adjust the tone as desired by adding a little more of one color or the other and reheating to melt.

2. Coat the cake pop in the candy coating (see page 29). Set in a cake pop stand to dry.

3. Melt 1 cup (250 mL) yellow, black, orange, white or chocolate candy coating wafers. Fit a pastry bag or squeeze bottle with a fine writing tip. Fill the bag with candy coating. Pipe tight swirls and circles on the top of the cake pop to resemble hair.

4. Before the coating sets, quickly place two red heart sprinkles in the hair, with points touching, to create a bow. Set the cake pop in the stand to dry.

5. a) Melt 2 to 3 tbsp (30 to 45 mL) red candy coating wafers. Use a pastry bag to pipe a dot in the center of the bow. Thin the remaining candy coating with shortening or Paramount Crystals. Use a fine paintbrush to paint a mouth. Set the cake pop in the stand to dry.

   b) Melt 2 to 3 tbsp (30 to 45 mL) dark chocolate, blue or green candy coating wafers. Thin with shortening or Paramount Crystals (see tips, at left). Use a fine paintbrush to paint eyes. Set the cake pop in the stand to dry.

6. Add some white candy coating wafers to the red candy coating and melt together to make a light pink. Use a fine paintbrush to paint cheeks. Set the cake pop in the stand to dry.

Lemon Poppy Seed Cake Pops

These lemon-infused cake pops are like little bites of sunshine. When coated with lemon glaze (see decorating tip, below), they are hard to beat.

Tip

We enjoy poppy seeds in these cake pops, but you can leave them out.

Decorating Tip

Glaze the cake pops with Lemon Glaze (page 104). Remember, if you plan to glaze your cake pops, leave them off the sticks.

2 cups	yellow cake mix	500 mL
1	large egg, at room temperature	1
1	large egg yolk, at room temperature	1
½ cup	water	125 mL
¼ cup	vegetable oil	60 mL
3 tbsp	freshly squeezed lemon juice	45 mL
1 tbsp	poppy seeds	15 mL
	Nonstick baking spray	

1. In a medium bowl, using an electric mixer on low speed, beat cake mix, egg, egg yolk, water, oil and lemon juice for 30 seconds or until moistened. Beat on medium speed for 2 minutes. Stir in poppy seeds.

2. Spray cake pop wells with baking spray. Fill each well with about 1 tbsp (15 mL) batter.

3. Bake for 4 to 6 minutes or until a tester inserted in the center comes out clean. Transfer cake pops to a wire rack to cool.

4. Repeat steps 2 and 3 with the remaining batter.

5. If desired, attach sticks to cake pops (see page 27).

If Baking in the Rotating Cake Pop Maker

In step 3, bake for 1 minute. Rotate and bake for 2 to 3 minutes. Rotate back before testing for doneness. Continue with step 3.

See the step-by-step photographs on photo page H. ▶

Tips

We used a Hershey Cookies and Cream Drop for the muzzle and brown M&Ms for the ears.

Thinning the candy coating wafers makes painting fine details much easier.

Be sure to purchase food-safe brushes from a cake decorating shop.

Making a Simple Bear

1. Slice a small piece of cake off the front of the cake pop to flatten it slightly and create a stable place for the muzzle of the bear.

2. Melt ½ cup (125 mL) dark chocolate candy coating wafers (see page 19) and use to attach a stick to the cake pop (see page 27). Freeze the cake pop for at least 15 minutes to set. Reheat candy coating as necessary and coat the cake pop (see page 29).

3. Before the coating sets, quickly place one white-coated drop candy on the flat spot to make the muzzle. Place two brown candy-coated chocolate candies on top of the cake pop for the ears. Set the cake pop in a cake pop stand to dry.

4. Melt 1 tbsp (15 mL) white candy coating wafers. Thin with shortening or Paramount Crystals (see page 20). Using the end of a thin paintbrush (opposite the bristles), make two dots of candy coating for the eyes. Set the cake pop in the stand to dry.

5. Reheat dark chocolate candy coating as needed. Thin with shortening or Paramount Crystals. Use a fine paintbrush to paint a nose and a mouth on the muzzle and pupils in the eyes. Set the cake pop in the stand to dry.

6. Melt 1 tbsp (15 mL) red candy coating wafers. Thin with shortening or Paramount Crystals. Paint a tongue on the mouth. Set the cake pop in the stand to dry.

Strawberry Cake Pops

Makes 42 to 44 cake pops

A refreshing bite of summer — at least, that's what we think of when we serve these cake pops.

Tip
When fresh strawberries are out of season, you can substitute frozen strawberries (without syrup), thawed and drained.

Decorating Tips
For a treat that will remind you of chocolate-covered strawberries, coat the cake pops in chocolate candy coating. For added finesse, pipe on decorative swirls or lines of white chocolate.

Drizzle the cake pops with Strawberry Glaze (page 105). Remember, if you plan to glaze your cake pops, leave them off the sticks.

Variation
Strawberry Chocolate Chip Cake Pops: Fold 1/3 cup (75 mL) mini semisweet chocolate chips into the batter at the end of step 3.

1/2 cup	halved hulled strawberries	125 mL
2/3 cup	sour cream	150 mL
1 1/4 cups	all-purpose flour	300 mL
2 tsp	baking powder	10 mL
1/2 tsp	baking soda	2 mL
1/4 tsp	salt	1 mL
2/3 cup	granulated sugar	150 mL
1/3 cup	unsalted butter, softened	75 mL
1	large egg, at room temperature	1
1	large egg yolk, at room temperature	1
1 tsp	strawberry extract	5 mL
6 to 8	drops red food coloring	6 to 8
	Nonstick baking spray	

1. In a blender, purée strawberries until smooth. Measure out 1/4 cup (60 mL) purée and stir in sour cream until blended. Set aside.

2. In a small bowl, whisk together flour, baking powder, baking soda and salt. Set aside.

3. In a large bowl, using an electric mixer on medium-high speed, beat sugar and butter for 1 minute or until fluffy. Add egg, then egg yolk, beating well after each addition. Beat in strawberry extract and food coloring. Add flour mixture alternately with sour cream mixture, making three additions of flour and two of sour cream and beating on low speed until blended.

4. Spray cake pop wells with baking spray. Fill each well with about 1 tbsp (15 mL) batter.

5. Bake for 4 to 6 minutes or until a tester inserted in the center comes out clean. Transfer cake pops to a wire rack to cool.

6. Repeat steps 4 and 5 with the remaining batter.

7. If desired, attach sticks to cake pops (see page 27).

If Baking in the Rotating Cake Pop Maker

In step 5, bake for 1 minute. Rotate and bake for 2 to 3 minutes. Rotate back before testing for doneness. Continue with step 5.

See the step-by-step photographs on photo page I. ▶

Tips

To make stripes or swirls on each undecorated cake pop, melt 2 to 3 tbsp (30 to 45 mL) of a contrasting color of candy coating wafers. Fit a pastry bag or squeeze bottle with a fine tip and fill with melted candy coating. Pipe lines or swirls as desired. Set the cake pops in the stand to dry.

To make a sparkly striped egg, after coating the cake pop, quickly dip one end in sanding sugar. Let dry. Pipe a strip of candy coating around the egg and carefully sprinkle it with a contrasting color of sanding sugar. Let dry, then repeat lines until egg is covered.

Use tweezers to grasp and arrange small candies on the cake pops.

Making Easter Eggs

1. Prepare 18 cake pops and slice off about one-third of each. Discard the smaller pieces (or eat them to reward yourself for all your hard work). Insert a cake pop stick into one cake pop piece, pushing it from the rounded side through to the cut side. Repeat with 8 more cake pop pieces.

2. Melt $\frac{1}{4}$ cup (60 mL) white candy coating wafers (see page 19) and use to glue another cake pop piece to one on a stick, matching the cut sides, to make a larger oval cake pop. If there are cracks between the two pieces, use the tip of a knife to evenly dot candy coating in the cracks. Repeat to make 9 egg-shaped cake pops. Freeze cake pops for at least 15 minutes to set. Use a zester, if necessary, to smooth the surface of each cake pop into an even egg shape.

3. Melt a variety of colors of candy coating wafers, using $\frac{1}{2}$ cup (125 mL) each, and coat the cake pops as desired (see page 29).

4. Before the coating sets, quickly decorate the cake pops with sprinkles or tiny candies. Set the cake pops in a cake pop stand to dry.

5. Gently twist the stick out of each egg. If desired, reheat candy coating in the same colors and dab a small amount over the hole left by each stick. Set aside to dry.

6. Arrange the eggs in a decorative container.

Pineapple Cake Pops

Makes 22 to 24 cake pops

With one bite of these cake pops, you can easily imagine yourself sitting on a tropical beach, listening to the sound of the surf.

Tip

If you don't usually keep pineapple juice on hand, you might purchase a six-pack of 6-oz (175 mL) cans. You can open just one can and use what you need for this recipe. Mix the remainder with orange juice for a refreshing drink. Or, for a fun twist, freeze the juice in 1-tbsp (15 mL) portions in an ice cube tray, then serve the fruited ice in a punch or juice drink.

Decorating Tip

For a tropical treat, coat the cake pops in vanilla candy coating, then sprinkle with toasted chopped almonds and toasted coconut.

Variation

Substitute rum extract for the vanilla extract.

1 cup	yellow cake mix	250 mL
1	large egg, at room temperature	1
1/4 cup	unsweetened pineapple juice	60 mL
2 tbsp	butter, melted	30 mL
1/2 tsp	vanilla extract	2 mL
	Nonstick baking spray	

1. In a medium bowl, using an electric mixer on low speed, beat cake mix, egg, pineapple juice, butter and vanilla for 30 seconds or until moistened. Beat on medium speed for 2 minutes.

2. Spray cake pop wells with baking spray. Fill each well with about 1 tbsp (15 mL) batter.

3. Bake for 4 to 6 minutes or until a tester inserted in the center comes out clean. Transfer cake pops to a wire rack to cool.

4. Repeat steps 2 and 3 with the remaining batter.

5. If desired, attach sticks to cake pops (see page 27).

If Baking in the Rotating Cake Pop Maker

In step 3, bake for 1 minute. Rotate and bake for 2 to 3 minutes. Rotate back before testing for doneness. Continue with step 3.

See the step-by-step photographs on photo page J. ▶

Tips

Make a hole flag by cutting a triangle out of colorful card stock and stamping a number on it. Secure the flag to the top of a bamboo skewer with double-sided tape. Insert the flag into the cupcake.

This is a perfect gift for your favorite golfer. Or make several to decorate the clubhouse for the golf tournament.

Making a Cake Pop Golf Ball

1. Melt $\frac{1}{4}$ cup (60 mL) white candy coating wafers (see page 19) and use to attach a stick to the cake pop (see page 27). Freeze the cake pop for at least 15 minutes to set.

2. Using another cake pop stick or the end of a fine paintbrush (opposite the bristles), gently poke holes at least $\frac{1}{4}$ inch (0.5 cm) deep evenly all over the frozen cake pop. (The holes will provide the texture typical of golf balls.)

3. Melt $\frac{1}{2}$ cup (125 mL) white candy coating wafers and coat the cake pop (see page 29), letting the coating drip into the holes, leaving indentations. Set the cake pop in a cake pop stand to dry.

4. For a display, frost a small cupcake with buttercream frosting tinted green.

5. Reheat white coating and dip the top of a brand-new golf tee in candy coating. Insert the tee into the frosted cupcake.

6. Gently twist the stick out of the cake pop. Set the cake pop, hole side down, on the golf tee. Set aside to dry.

Almond Cake Pops

Almond is a classic flavor that is popular worldwide. These treats will whisk you away to a French bakery, an Italian coffee shop, a Scandinavian sweet shop or Grandma's back porch.

Decorating Tip

Coat the cake pops in vanilla or chocolate candy coating. If desired, add almond flavoring to the coating (see page 19). After coating, immediately sprinkle with toasted finely chopped almonds.

Variation

Substitute butter extract for the almond extract for a different flavor profile.

1½ cups	all-purpose flour	375 mL
2 tsp	baking powder	10 mL
¼ tsp	salt	1 mL
¾ cup	granulated sugar	175 mL
6 tbsp	unsalted butter, softened	90 mL
1	large egg, at room temperature	1
1	large egg yolk, at room temperature	1
½ tsp	almond extract	2 mL
½ cup	milk	125 mL
	Nonstick baking spray	

1. In a small bowl, whisk together flour, baking powder and salt. Set aside.

2. In a medium bowl, using an electric mixer on medium-high speed, beat sugar and butter for 1 minute or until fluffy. Add egg, then egg yolk, beating well after each addition. Beat in almond extract. Add flour mixture alternately with milk, making three additions of flour and two of milk and beating on low speed until smooth.

3. Spray cake pop wells with baking spray. Fill each well with about 1 tbsp (15 mL) batter.

4. Bake for 4 to 6 minutes or until a tester inserted in the center comes out clean. Transfer cake pops to a wire rack to cool.

5. Repeat steps 3 and 4 with the remaining batter.

6. If desired, attach sticks to cake pops (see page 27).

If Baking in the Rotating Cake Pop Maker

In step 4, bake for 1 minute. Rotate and bake for 2 to 3 minutes. Rotate back before testing for doneness. Continue with step 4.

See the step-by-step photographs on photo page K. ▶

Tips

Many new brands of prepared fondant are much better-tasting and easier to work with than some brands sold in the past.

Keep any extra fondant covered with plastic wrap so it doesn't dry out.

Making Fondant Flowers

1. Select a fondant color that complements the candy coating you used. Knead the fondant until it is soft and pliable.

2. Lightly dust a cutting board with confectioners' (icing) sugar or cornstarch. Place the fondant on the board and use a rolling pin to roll it out to $1/8$- to $1/4$-inch (3 to 5 mm) thickness.

3. Using a $1/4$- to $1/2$-inch (0.5 to 1 cm) flower-shaped cookie cutter, cut out fondant flowers, rerolling scraps.

4. Using a toothpick or the end of a thin food-safe paintbrush, place a drop of melted candy coating on a coated cake pop as glue for a flower. Place a flower on the drop and hold for a moment, until secure.

5. Arrange several fondant flowers on each cake pop.

6. Use a drop of candy coating to glue a nonpareil (or up to 3 nonpareils, depending on the size of the flower and the desired look) in the center of the flower.

Gluten-Free, Vegan Oatmeal Raisin Cake Pops

Makes 30 to 32 cake pops

These cake pops are so moist and so flavorful, no one will believe they're both gluten-free and vegan! They're sure to become a family favorite.

Tips

Make sure to buy certified gluten-free rolled oats and cook according to package directions. Let the cooked oatmeal cool to room temperature, then measure.

Candy coating wafers are not vegan, and unfortunately there is no suitable substitute at this time, although new products are continually being released. Since vegan cake pops cannot be put on sticks and decorated like other cake pops, enjoy them as is or drizzled with glaze instead.

Decorating Tip

Drizzle with Vegan Cream Cheese Glaze (variation, page 106).

2 tbsp	ground flax seeds (flaxseed meal)	30 mL
1/3 cup	hot water	75 mL
1 cup	gluten-free all-purpose baking mix (see page 13)	250 mL
1/3 cup	granulated sugar	75 mL
1/2 tsp	baking soda	2 mL
1/2 tsp	ground cinnamon	2 mL
1/4 tsp	ground nutmeg	1 mL
1/2 cup	unsweetened plain almond milk	125 mL
1/4 cup	canola oil	60 mL
1/2 tsp	vanilla extract	2 mL
1/2 cup	cooled cooked gluten-free oatmeal (see tip, at left)	125 mL
1/4 cup	raisins	60 mL
	Nonstick baking spray	

1. In a medium bowl, combine flax seeds and hot water. Let stand for 10 minutes.

2. In a large bowl, whisk together baking mix, sugar, baking soda, cinnamon and nutmeg. Set aside.

3. Whisk almond milk, oil and vanilla into flaxseed mixture. Stir in oatmeal until completely incorporated.

4. Add oatmeal mixture to flour mixture, stirring until moistened. Stir in raisins.

5. Spray cake pop wells with baking spray. Fill each well with about 1 tbsp (15 mL) batter.

6. Bake for 6 to 8 minutes or until a tester inserted in the center comes out clean. Transfer cake pops to a wire rack to cool.

7. Repeat steps 5 and 6 with the remaining batter.

If Baking in the Rotating Cake Pop Maker

In step 6, bake for 2 minutes. Rotate and bake for 3 to 4 minutes. Rotate back before testing for doneness. Continue with step 6.

See the step-by-step photographs on photo page L. ▶

Tip
Glazes look beautiful and add a sweet coating, but will not secure a stick in place.

Glazing Cake Pops

1. Arrange cake pops (without sticks) on a wire rack set over a sheet of foil, parchment paper or waxed paper (to make cleanup easy).

2. Spoon the glaze into a small sealable sandwich bag and clip off the corner (or use a disposable pastry bag and clip off the tip).

3. Drizzle the glaze over the cake pops. Let the cake pops dry on the rack.

4. Alternatively, pour the glaze into a deep bowl.

5. Use the fork tool to spear the cake pop and dip it into the glaze.

6. Allow the excess glaze to drip back into the bowl. Place the cake pop on the rack to dry.

Helpful Hints on Candy Coating

- Choose a narrow, deep container, such as a microwave-safe glass bowl, a glass measuring cup or a mug, in which to melt the candy coating wafers. Cake pops coat best if dipped straight down into the coating. If you choose a shallow container, you will be tempted to roll the cake pop in the coating, and it will not be as smooth.

- When you're working with several different colors, melt the candy coating wafers in canning jars. (Thanks to our good friend Sheri Worrel, cake pop baker extraordinaire, for this tip.) Shop around for wide-mouth jelly or pint jars. They are microwave-safe as long as they are not covered. When you are ready to store the coating, cover the jar with the ring and metal lid.

- Candy coating will harden, or "freeze," if overheated or if even a drop or two of water is mixed in. Be sure the containers and utensils you use are completely dry, and melt the candy coating wafers gradually, in 30-second intervals, stirring after each.

- If you're painting fine details on only a few cake pops, you may need to melt a small amount of candy coating wafers — perhaps just 1 to 2 tbsp (15 to 30 mL). Be careful not to overheat them; if necessary, heat in 10- or 15-second intervals rather than 30-second intervals.

- Candy coating is thinnest when freshly melted and hot, and thickens as it cools. If it's too thick, heat it some more; if it's too thin, let it cool slightly. Reheat as needed to keep it flowing smoothly.

- To color candy coating, use only oil-based colorings made to be added to chocolate or candy. Read labels carefully or ask for assistance at the cake and candy decorating store.

- An easy way to achieve different colors is to blend candy coating wafers. For example, you can mix in some white candy coating wafers to lighten a color.

- Candy coating wafers of different brands may not be exactly the same color. Some whites are more cream-colored, and not all reds are exactly the same. If you're dipping a large number of cake pops, be sure to purchase plenty of candy coating wafers in the same brand.

- Candy coating can be melted again and again, so keep any leftovers.

Filling the Wells

(see page 25 for detailed step-by-step instructions)

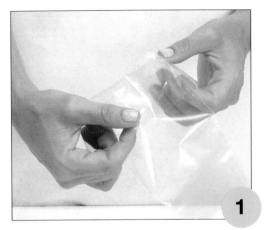

Make a collar on a pastry bag.

Fill the bag half full with batter.

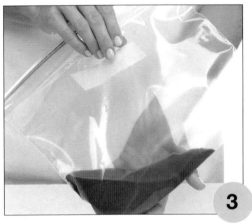

Or use a sealable plastic bag.

Clip the point off the bag.

Fill the wells with batter.

Set the bag upright in a glass between batches.

A.

Attaching the Sticks

(see page 27 for detailed step-by-step instructions)

Lift the cake pops out of the wells.

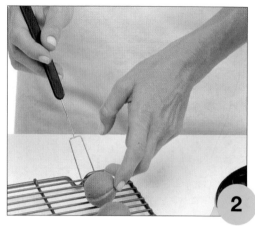

Transfer cake pops to a wire rack.

Melt candy coating wafers in the microwave.

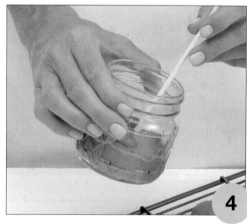

Dip the stick into the coating.

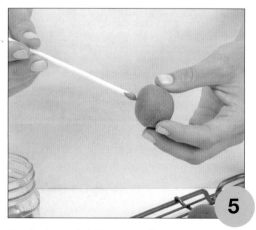

Push the stick into a cake pop.

Freeze the cake pops to let the sticks set.

B.

Coating Cake Pops

(see page 29 for detailed step-by-step instructions)

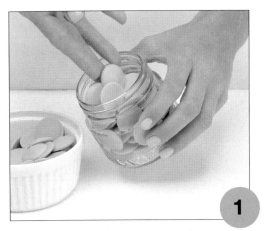

1

Add more candy coating wafers to the cup.

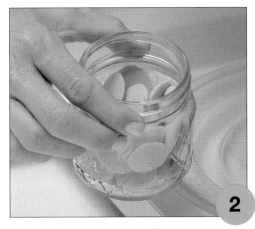

2

Melt candy coating wafers in the microwave.

3

Dip the cake pop into the coating.

4

Hold the cake pop over the cup.

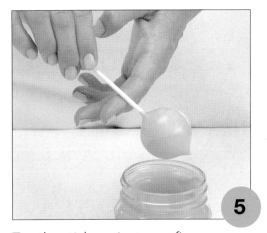

5

Tap the stick against your fingers.

6

Set the cake pop in a stand to dry.

C.

Decorating with Sprinkles

(see page 31 for detailed step-by-step instructions)

Select your sprinkles.

Set out a tray to work over.

Coat a cake pop in melted candy coating.

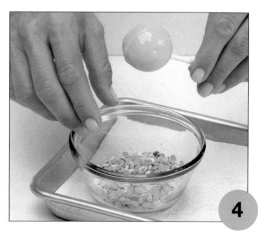

Hold the cake pop over the tray.

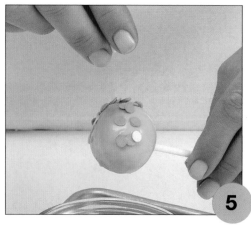

Sprinkle the cake pop with sprinkles.

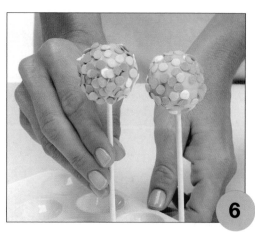

Set the cake pop in a stand to dry.

D.

Adding Spirals, Swirls or Lines

(see page 33 for detailed step-by-step instructions)

Melt candy coating wafers in the microwave.

1

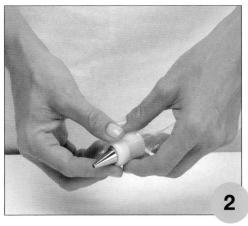

Fit a pastry bag with a fine writing tip.

2

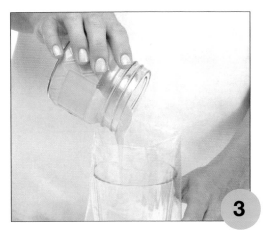

Fill the pastry bag with candy coating.

3

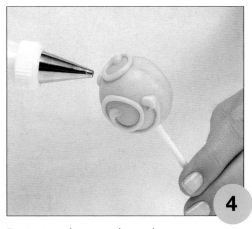

Pipe spirals over the cake pop.

4

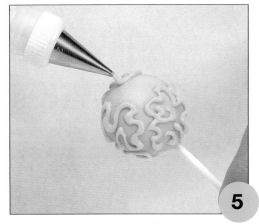

Or pipe swirls in a loose or tight design.

5

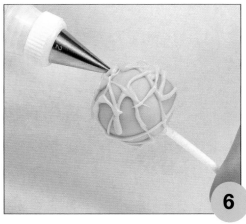

Or pipe stripes, zigzags or a random decorative pattern.

6

E.

Adding a Monogram and a Ribbon

(see page 35 for detailed step-by-step instructions)

Melt candy coating wafers in the microwave.

1

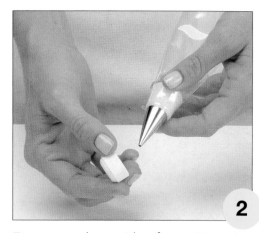

Fit a pastry bag with a fine writing tip.

2

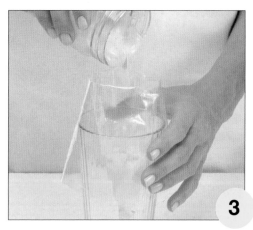

Fill the pastry bag with candy coating.

3

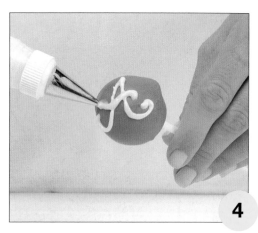

Pipe an initial on the cake pop.

4

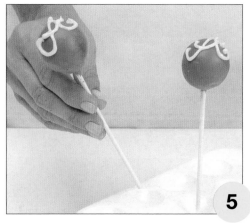

Set the cake pop in a stand to dry.

5

Tie a decorative knot or bow on the stick.

6

F.

Making a Simple Face

(see page 37 for detailed step-by-step instructions)

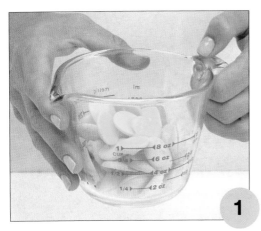

Combine and melt candy coating wafers to make a flesh color.

1

Coat the cake pop in candy coating.

2

Pipe swirls to resemble hair.

3

Make a bow with heart sprinkles.

4

Pipe a knot on the bow and paint a mouth. Paint the eyes.

5

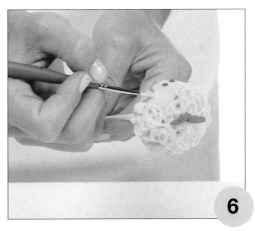

Paint the cheeks pink.

6

G.

Making a Simple Bear

(see page 39 for detailed step-by-step instructions)

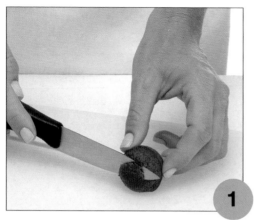

Slice a small piece of cake off the front of the cake pop.

Coat the cake pop in dark chocolate candy coating.

Quickly add a white candy muzzle and brown candy ears.

Make white dots for the eyes.

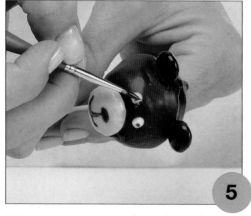

Paint a nose, a mouth and pupils in the eyes.

H.

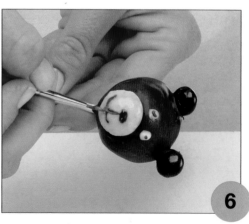

Paint a red tongue on the mouth.

Making Easter Eggs

(see page 41 for detailed step-by-step instructions)

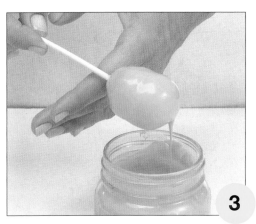

1

Cut off one-third of each cake pop. Insert a stick into one larger piece.

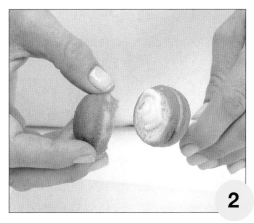

2

Use candy coating to glue another large piece to the one on the stick.

3

Coat cake pop Easter eggs in a variety of colors.

4

Decorate the eggs with sprinkles or candies.

5

Gently remove the stick from each egg.

6

Arrange the eggs in a decorative container.

Making a Cake Pop Golf Ball

(see page 43 for detailed step-by-step instructions)

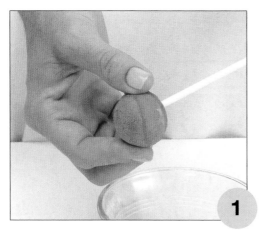

Attach a stick and freeze the cake pop.

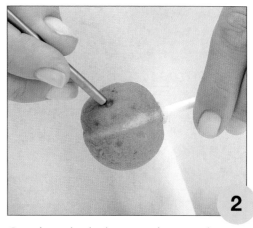

Gently poke holes evenly over the cake pop.

Coat with white candy coating.

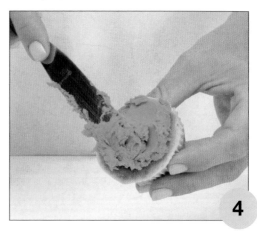

Frost a small cupcake with green frosting.

Dip the top of a tee in candy coating and insert the tee into the cupcake.

Remove the stick and place the cake pop on the tee.

J.

Making Fondant Flowers

(see page 45 for detailed step-by-step instructions)

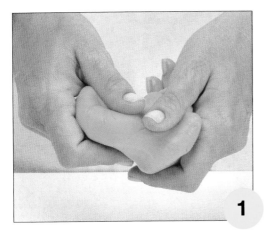

Knead the fondant until soft and pliable.

1

Roll out the fondant until very thin.

2

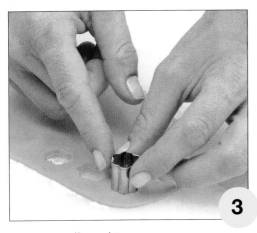

Use a small cookie cutter to cut out flowers.

3

Use candy coating to glue a flower on a cake pop.

4

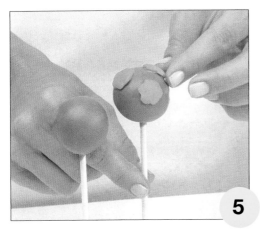

Arrange several flowers on each cake pop.

5

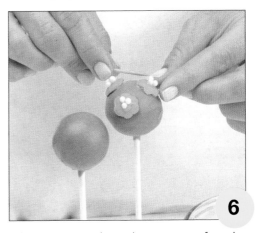

Glue nonpareils in the center of each flower.

6

K.

Glazing Cake Pops

(see page 47 for detailed step-by-step instructions)

1

Arrange cake pops on a rack set over foil or parchment paper.

2

Fill a sandwich bag with glaze and clip off the corner.

3

Drizzle the glaze over the cake pops.

4

Alternatively, pour the glaze into a deep bowl.

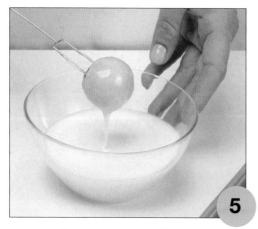

5

Use the fork tool to dip the cake pop into the glaze.

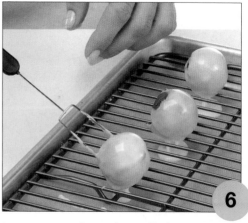

6

Let excess glaze drip off, then place the cake pop on the rack to dry.

L.

Part 2

Sweets and Treats

Chocolate Cake Pops

German Chocolate Cake Pops

Makes 24 to 26 cake pops

German chocolate cake is Roxanne's top pick for favorite birthday cake treats. Now she enjoys the flavor burst all year long with these "just a bite" cake pops.

Tips

A half-recipe of Chocolate Glaze should be enough for these cake pops.

Toasting pecans intensifies their flavor. Spread chopped pecans in a single layer on a baking sheet. Bake at 350°F (180°C) for 5 to 7 minutes or until lightly browned. Let cool.

If Baking in the Rotating Cake Pop Maker

In step 5, bake for 1 minute. Rotate and bake for 2 to 3 minutes. Rotate back before testing for doneness. Continue with step 5.

1 oz	sweet chocolate (such as Baker's German's or Baker's), chopped	30 g
1/2 cup	all-purpose flour	125 mL
2 tsp	unsweetened cocoa powder	10 mL
1/2 tsp	baking soda	2 mL
1/4 tsp	baking powder	1 mL
1/4 tsp	salt	1 mL
1/2 cup	granulated sugar	125 mL
1/4 cup	unsalted butter, softened	60 mL
1	large egg, at room temperature	1
1/4 cup	sour cream	60 mL
1/2 tsp	vanilla extract	2 mL
2 tbsp	buttermilk	30 mL
	Nonstick baking spray	
	Chocolate Glaze (page 104)	
1/2 cup	sweetened flaked coconut	125 mL
1/2 cup	chopped pecans, toasted	125 mL

1. Place chocolate in a small microwave-safe glass bowl. Microwave on High in 30-second intervals, stirring after each, until melted. Let cool to room temperature.

2. In a small bowl, whisk together flour, cocoa powder, baking soda, baking powder and salt. Set aside.

3. In a medium bowl, using an electric mixer on medium-high speed, beat sugar and butter for 1 minute or until fluffy. Beat in egg. Beat in sour cream and vanilla. Add flour mixture alternately with buttermilk, making three additions of flour and two of buttermilk and beating on low speed until smooth. Beat in melted chocolate.

4. Spray cake pop wells with baking spray. Fill each well with about 1 tbsp (15 mL) batter.

5. Bake for 4 to 6 minutes or until a tester inserted in the center comes out clean. Transfer cake pops to a wire rack set over a sheet of foil or waxed paper to cool.

6. Repeat steps 4 and 5 with the remaining batter.

7. Using the fork tool, dip each cake pop in Chocolate Glaze, allowing excess glaze to drip back into the bowl.

8. In a small bowl, combine coconut and pecans. Using the fork tool, dip cake pops into coconut pecan mixture. Return to the rack to set for 30 minutes.

Hot Chocolate Cake Pops

Kathy was a Girl Scouts leader for many years and took lots of overnight camping trips with the girls. They loved sipping hot chocolate on cool mornings while sitting by the campfire. What a fun memory! These cake pops capture the flavor of hot chocolate, and you're sure to create your own happy memories when you serve them.

Tip

If you don't have chocolate milk on hand, you can make your own. Pour 1 tbsp (15 mL) chocolate syrup into a glass measuring cup and add enough milk to equal 1/3 cup (75 mL). Stir until combined.

Decorating Tip

Do you like marshmallows in your hot chocolate? Cut miniature marshmallows in half. Coat the cake pops in milk chocolate candy coating and immediately decorate with marshmallow halves, cut side down.

1 1/3 cups	milk chocolate cake mix	325 mL
1 tbsp	unsweetened cocoa powder	15 mL
1	large egg, at room temperature	1
1/3 cup	chocolate milk	75 mL
2 tbsp	vegetable oil	30 mL
1/2 tsp	vanilla extract	2 mL
	Nonstick baking spray	

1. In a medium bowl, using an electric mixer on low speed, beat cake mix, cocoa powder, egg, chocolate milk, oil and vanilla for 30 seconds or until moistened. Beat on medium speed for 2 minutes.

2. Spray cake pop wells with baking spray. Fill each well with about 1 tbsp (15 mL) batter.

3. Bake for 4 to 6 minutes or until a tester inserted in the center comes out clean. Transfer cake pops to a wire rack to cool.

4. Repeat steps 2 and 3 with the remaining batter.

5. If desired, attach sticks to cake pops (see page 27).

If Baking in the Rotating Cake Pop Maker

In step 3, bake for 1 minute. Rotate and bake for 2 to 3 minutes. Rotate back before testing for doneness. Continue with step 3.

Chocolate Intensity Cake Pops

Makes 44 to 46 cake pops

If you like dark chocolate, these cake pops are for you. Coat with dark chocolate candy coating to maintain the intensity.

Tip

If desired, you can substitute semisweet chocolate for the bittersweet. The chocolate flavor will be milder, but the cake pops will still be good.

If Baking in the Rotating Cake Pop Maker

In step 5, bake for 1 minute. Rotate and bake for 2 to 3 minutes. Rotate back before testing for doneness. Continue with step 5.

3 oz	bittersweet chocolate, chopped	90 g
1 cup	all-purpose flour	250 mL
¼ cup	unsweetened cocoa powder	60 mL
1 tsp	instant espresso powder	5 mL
1 tsp	baking powder	5 mL
¼ tsp	baking soda	1 mL
¼ tsp	salt	1 mL
½ cup	unsalted butter, softened	125 mL
½ cup	granulated sugar	125 mL
¼ cup	packed brown sugar	60 mL
2	large eggs, at room temperature	2
½ tsp	vanilla extract	2 mL
½ cup	buttermilk	125 mL
	Nonstick baking spray	

1. Place chocolate in a small microwave-safe glass bowl. Microwave on High in 30-second intervals, stirring after each, until melted. Let cool to room temperature.

2. In a small bowl, whisk together flour, cocoa powder, espresso powder, baking powder, baking soda and salt. Set aside.

3. In a medium bowl, using an electric mixer on medium-high speed, beat butter, granulated sugar and brown sugar for 1 minute or until fluffy. Beat in eggs, one at a time, beating well after each addition. Beat in melted chocolate and vanilla. Add flour mixture alternately with buttermilk, making three additions of flour and two of buttermilk and beating on low speed until smooth.

4. Spray cake pop wells with baking spray. Fill each well with about 1 tbsp (15 mL) batter.

5. Bake for 4 to 6 minutes or until a tester inserted in the center comes out clean. Transfer cake pops to a wire rack to cool.

6. Repeat steps 4 and 5 with the remaining batter.

7. If desired, attach sticks to cake pops (see page 27).

Triple Chocolate Cake Pops

Makes 58 to 60 cake pops

Roxanne's daughter, Grace, gives these two thumbs up and looks for any excuse to bake them.

Tip

Because of the chocolate chips in this recipe, a tester inserted into the cake pops will not come out clean.

Variation

Substitute vanilla baking chips or white chocolate chips for the semisweet chocolate chips.

2 cups	devil's food cake mix	500 mL
3½ tbsp	chocolate instant pudding mix (half of a 3.4 oz/96 g box)	52 mL
2	large eggs, at room temperature	2
⅔ cup	water	150 mL
¼ cup	vegetable oil	60 mL
1 cup	semisweet chocolate chips	250 mL
	Nonstick baking spray	

1. In a medium bowl, using an electric mixer on low speed, beat cake mix, pudding mix, eggs, water and oil for 30 seconds or until moistened. Beat on medium speed for 2 minutes. Fold in chocolate chips.

2. Spray cake pop wells with baking spray. Fill each well with about 1 tbsp (15 mL) batter.

3. Bake for 4 to 6 minutes or until cake pops bounce back when gently touched with your finger. Transfer cake pops to a wire rack to cool.

4. Repeat steps 2 and 3 with the remaining batter.

5. If desired, attach sticks to cake pops (see page 27).

If Baking in the Rotating Cake Pop Maker

In step 3, bake for 1 minute. Rotate and bake for 2 to 3 minutes. Rotate back before testing for doneness. Continue with step 3.

Chocolate Walnut Cake Pops

**Makes 34
to 36 cake pops**

Walnuts and chocolate are a great combination. For added chocolate flavor, dip these rich cake pops in chocolate candy coating, then decorate as desired.

Tips

The two major kinds of walnuts are English walnuts and black walnuts. English walnuts are more popular, and their taste is milder. You may use either type of walnut in this recipe. Store walnuts in an airtight container in the freezer for up to 1 year.

Toasting walnuts intensifies their flavor. Spread chopped walnuts in a single layer on a baking sheet. Bake at 350°F (180°C) for 5 to 7 minutes or until lightly browned. Let cool.

No buttermilk on hand? Place 1½ tsp (7 mL) lemon juice or white vinegar in a glass measuring cup, then pour in enough milk to equal ½ cup (125 mL). Let stand for 5 to 10 minutes to thicken. Proceed with the recipe. (See page 15 for other buttermilk substitutions.)

- Food processor

¼ cup	chopped walnuts, toasted (see tips, at left)	60 mL
¾ cup	all-purpose flour	175 mL
¼ cup	unsweetened cocoa powder	60 mL
½ tsp	baking powder	2 mL
½ tsp	baking soda	2 mL
¼ tsp	salt	1 mL
¾ cup	granulated sugar	175 mL
¼ cup	unsalted butter, softened	60 mL
1	large egg, at room temperature	1
1 tsp	vanilla extract	5 mL
½ cup	buttermilk	125 mL
	Nonstick baking spray	

1. In food processor, process walnuts until very finely chopped.

2. In a small bowl, whisk together walnuts, flour, cocoa powder, baking powder, baking soda and salt. Set aside.

3. In a medium bowl, using an electric mixer on medium speed, beat sugar and butter for 1 minute or until fluffy. Beat in egg and vanilla. Add flour mixture alternately with buttermilk, making three additions of flour and two of buttermilk and beating on low speed until smooth.

4. Spray cake pop wells with baking spray. Fill each well with about 1 tbsp (15 mL) batter.

5. Bake for 4 to 6 minutes or until a tester inserted in the center comes out clean. Transfer cake pops to a wire rack to cool.

6. Repeat steps 4 and 5 with the remaining batter.

7. If desired, attach sticks to cake pops (see page 27).

If Baking in the Rotating Cake Pop Maker

In step 5, bake for 1 minute. Rotate and bake for 2 to 3 minutes. Rotate back before testing for doneness. Continue with step 5.

Kahlúa Fudge Cake Pops with White Chocolate Dip

Makes 32 to 34 cake pops

Roxanne's niece, Jenna Wyss, has had such fun making brownie cake pops. It's hard for Roxanne to believe that Jenna is now old enough to enjoy this version targeted for adult tastes. Where have all the years gone?

Variation
Fold 3 tbsp (45 mL) mini semisweet chocolate chips into the batter at the end of step 1. Bake until the cake pops bounce back when gently touched with your finger (the tester will no longer come out clean).

2 oz	unsweetened chocolate, chopped	60 g
½ cup	unsalted butter	125 mL
½ cup	all-purpose flour	125 mL
1 cup	granulated sugar	250 mL
2	large eggs, at room temperature	2
2 tbsp	Kahlúa or other coffee liqueur	30 mL
	Nonstick baking spray	
	White Chocolate Dip (page 108)	

1. In a medium saucepan, combine chocolate and butter. Heat over medium heat, stirring often, until chocolate is melted. Remove from heat and whisk in flour, sugar, eggs and Kahlúa.

2. Spray cake pop wells with baking spray. Fill each well with about 1 tbsp (15 mL) batter.

3. Bake for 4 to 6 minutes or until a tester inserted in the center comes out clean. Transfer cake pops to a wire rack to cool.

4. Repeat steps 2 and 3 with the remaining batter.

5. Serve cake pops with White Chocolate Dip.

If Baking in the Rotating Cake Pop Maker

In step 3, bake for 1 minute. Rotate and bake for 2 to 3 minutes. Rotate back before testing for doneness. Continue with step 3.

Favorite Brownie Cake Pops

Simple, straightforward flavors are often timeless classics — take these brownies, for example. Packed with old-fashioned flavor, they will quickly become a favorite for young and old alike.

Tip

If these cake pops are baked until a tester comes out clean, the brownies may be too firm or crisp once they cool. Stop baking when the tester comes out with just a few moist crumbs attached.

Variation

Fold 1/4 cup (60 mL) toasted chopped pecans or walnuts into the batter at the end of step 3.

---

2 oz	unsweetened chocolate, chopped	60 g
1/2 cup	all-purpose flour	125 mL
1/2 cup	granulated sugar	125 mL
1/2 tsp	baking powder	2 mL
1/4 tsp	salt	1 mL
2	large eggs, at room temperature	2
1/3 cup	vegetable oil	75 mL
1/2 tsp	vanilla extract	2 mL
	Nonstick baking spray	

1. Place chocolate in a small microwave-safe glass bowl. Microwave on High in 30-second intervals, stirring after each, until melted. Let cool to room temperature.

2. In a medium bowl, whisk together flour, sugar, baking powder and salt. Set aside.

3. Whisk eggs, oil and vanilla into the melted chocolate. Stir into flour mixture until moistened.

4. Spray cake pop wells with baking spray. Fill each well with about 1 tbsp (15 mL) batter.

5. Bake for 5 to 7 minutes or until a tester inserted in the center comes out with just a few moist crumbs attached. Transfer cake pops to a wire rack to cool.

6. Repeat steps 4 and 5 with the remaining batter.

7. If desired, attach sticks to cake pops (see page 27).

If Baking in the Rotating Cake Pop Maker

In step 5, bake for 2 minutes. Rotate and bake for 3 to 4 minutes. Rotate back before testing for doneness. Continue with step 5.

Cheesecake-Swirled Brownie Cake Pops

Makes 48 to 50 cake pops

Roxanne's husband, Bob Bateman, rates brownies as his number one choice for a sweet treat. His family always serves brownies at their reunions, and this recipe is sure to be added to their list of favorites.

Variation

Fold 3 tbsp (45 mL) mini semisweet chocolate chips into the batter at the end of step 2. Bake until the cake pops bounce back when gently touched with your finger (the tester will no longer come out clean).

2 oz	unsweetened chocolate, chopped	60 g
1/2 cup	unsalted butter	125 mL
1 1/4 cups	granulated sugar, divided	300 mL
3	large eggs, at room temperature, divided	3
3/4 cup	all-purpose flour	175 mL
Pinch	salt	Pinch
1/2 tsp	vanilla extract	2 mL
4 oz	cream cheese, softened	125 g
	Nonstick baking spray	

1. Place chocolate and butter in a small microwave-safe glass bowl. Microwave on High in 30-second intervals, stirring after each, until melted and smooth.

2. In a medium bowl, using an electric mixer on medium-high speed, beat 1 cup (250 mL) of the sugar and 2 of the eggs for 1 to 2 minutes or until fluffy. Beat in flour and salt on low speed. Using a wooden spoon, stir in melted chocolate until smooth. Clean the beaters.

3. In a small bowl, using the electric mixer on medium speed, beat cream cheese and the remaining sugar until smooth. Beat in the remaining egg. Gently swirl into chocolate batter (do not over-swirl).

4. Spray cake pop wells with baking spray. Fill each well with about 1 tbsp (15 mL) batter.

5. Bake for 4 to 6 minutes or until a tester inserted in the center comes out clean. Transfer cake pops to a wire rack to cool.

6. Repeat steps 4 and 5 with the remaining batter.

7. If desired, attach sticks to cake pops (see page 27).

If Baking in the Rotating Cake Pop Maker

In step 5, bake for 1 minute. Rotate and bake for 2 to 3 minutes. Rotate back before testing for doneness. Continue with step 5.

Minted Brownie Cake Pops

Laura Secord, a Canadian chocolate store, sells wonderful chocolate mint candies. These cake pops are a tribute to that favorite combo.

Decorating Tip

To accent the peppermint flavor, coat the cake pops in chocolate mint candy coating. Pipe on a swirl of green candy coating.

1 cup	fudge brownie mix	250 mL
1	large egg, at room temperature, lightly beaten	1
2 tbsp	unsalted butter, melted	30 mL
1 tbsp	water	15 mL
1 tsp	peppermint extract	5 mL
	Nonstick baking spray	

1. In a medium bowl, stir together brownie mix, egg, butter, water and peppermint extract until blended.

2. Spray cake pop wells with baking spray. Fill each well with about 1 tbsp (15 mL) batter.

3. Bake for 4 to 6 minutes or until a tester inserted in the center comes out clean. Transfer cake pops to a wire rack to cool.

4. Repeat steps 2 and 3 with the remaining batter.

5. If desired, attach sticks to cake pops (see page 27).

If Baking in the Rotating Cake Pop Maker

In step 3, bake for 1 minute. Rotate and bake for 2 to 3 minutes. Rotate back before testing for doneness. Continue with step 3.

Gluten-Free, Dairy-Free Chocolate Mint Cake Pops

Makes 28 to 30 cake pops

Crushed candy canes are the perfect choice for sprinkling over these delightful chocolate mint cake pops, but when they're not readily available, use crushed hard peppermint candies.

If Baking in the Rotating Cake Pop Maker

In step 5, bake for 2 minutes. Rotate and bake for 3 to 4 minutes. Rotate back before testing for doneness. Continue with step 5.

1/3 cup	unsweetened plain almond milk	75 mL
2 tbsp	vegan hard margarine	30 mL
3/4 cup	packed brown sugar	175 mL
1/4 cup	dairy-free unsweetened cocoa powder	60 mL
3/4 cup	almond flour	175 mL
1/2 cup	gluten-free all-purpose baking mix (see page 13)	125 mL
1 tsp	baking soda	5 mL
1	large egg, at room temperature	1
1/4 cup	dairy-free sour cream alternative	60 mL
1/2 tsp	peppermint extract	2 mL
	Nonstick baking spray	
	Vegan Chocolate Glaze (variation, page 104)	
2	candy canes (each about 1/2 oz/15 g), crushed	2

1. In a small saucepan, combine almond milk and margarine. Heat over medium heat, stirring frequently, until margarine is melted. Remove from heat and whisk in brown sugar and cocoa powder. Let cool.

2. In a small bowl, whisk together almond flour, baking mix and baking soda. Set aside.

3. In a large bowl, using an electric mixer on medium-high speed, beat egg and sour cream alternative for 1 minute or until fluffy. Beat in peppermint extract. Add flour mixture and beat on low speed until smooth. Beat in almond milk mixture until blended.

4. Spray cake pop wells with baking spray. Fill each well with about 1 tbsp (15 mL) batter.

5. Bake for 5 to 7 minutes or until a tester inserted in the center comes out clean. Transfer cake pops to a wire rack set over a sheet of foil or waxed paper to cool.

6. Repeat steps 4 and 5 with the remaining batter.

7. Using the fork tool, dip each cake pop in Vegan Chocolate Glaze, allowing excess glaze to drip back into the bowl. Sprinkle with crushed candy canes. Return to the rack to set.

Cappuccino Bites

**Makes 22
to 24 cake pops**

All the flavor of cappuccino packed into bite-size treats! It is especially fun to display these cake pops in a large cappuccino cup filled with chocolate-covered coffee beans.

Decorating Tips

Coat the cake pops in chocolate or vanilla candy coating.

Glaze the cake pops with Chocolate Glaze (page 104) and dust with unsweetened cocoa powder or ground sweetened chocolate. Remember, if you plan to glaze your cake pops, leave them off the sticks.

1 cup	milk chocolate cake mix	250 mL
1 tbsp	unsweetened cocoa powder	15 mL
2 tsp	instant espresso powder	10 mL
1	large egg, at room temperature	1
1	large egg yolk, at room temperature	1
3 tbsp	vegetable oil	45 mL
3 tbsp	milk	45 mL
	Nonstick baking spray	

1. In a large bowl, using an electric mixer on low speed, beat cake mix, cocoa, espresso powder, egg, egg yolk, oil and milk for 30 seconds or until blended. Beat on medium speed for 2 minutes.

2. Spray cake pop wells with baking spray. Fill each well with about 1 tbsp (15 mL) batter.

3. Bake for 4 to 6 minutes or until a tester inserted in the center comes out clean. Transfer cake pops to a wire rack to cool.

4. Repeat steps 2 and 3 with the remaining batter.

5. If desired, attach sticks to cake pops (see page 27).

If Baking in the Rotating Cake Pop Maker

In step 3, bake for 1 minute. Rotate and bake for 2 to 3 minutes. Rotate back before testing for doneness. Continue with step 3.

Fruity, Nutty and Spirited Cake Pops

Tie-Dyed Berry Cake Pops

Makes 26 to 28 cake pops

Swirls of bright colors are now trendy again — and are especially fun when captured in berry-flavored cake pops.

Tips

We add non-dairy whipped topping mix to some recipes that begin with cake mix to ensure that the cake pops bake into rounds. We find that some cake mix brands benefit from this addition, while it is not as necessary for other brands.

Substitute other gelatin flavors to create the tie-dyed look you want. For the most distinct look, choose those with sharp contrasts in color. Be sure the two flavors of gelatin complement each other. Also, remember that the color of the cake mix is a light yellow, so if you add blue powder, for example, the batter may take on a green cast unless you also add blue food coloring.

Decorating Tip

Continue the tie-dyed look with the candy coating. Swirl two colors of melted candy coating wafers together, or pipe swirls in contrasting colors.

1 cup	yellow cake mix	250 mL
2 tbsp	powdered non-dairy whipped topping mix	30 mL
1	large egg, at room temperature	1
2 tbsp	vegetable oil	30 mL
2 tbsp	water	30 mL
1½ tsp	blueberry-flavored gelatin powder	7 mL
2 to 4	drops blue food coloring	2 to 4
1½ tsp	raspberry-flavored gelatin powder	7 mL
2 to 4	drops red food coloring	2 to 4
	Nonstick baking spray	

1. In a medium bowl, using an electric mixer on low speed, beat cake mix, whipped topping mix, egg, oil and water for 30 seconds or until moistened. Beat on medium speed for 2 minutes.

2. Spoon ½ cup (125 mL) batter into a small bowl. Stir in blueberry gelatin and blue food coloring until well blended.

3. Stir raspberry gelatin and red food coloring into the remaining batter until well blended.

4. Pour the blue batter into the red batter and, using the tip of a knife, swirl very lightly (do not over-swirl).

5. Spray cake pop wells with baking spray. Fill each well with about 1 tbsp (15 mL) batter.

6. Bake for 4 to 6 minutes or until a tester inserted in the center comes out clean. Transfer cake pops to a wire rack to cool.

7. Repeat steps 5 and 6 with the remaining batter.

8. If desired, attach sticks to cake pops (see page 27).

If Baking in the Rotating Cake Pop Maker

In step 6, bake for 1 minute. Rotate and bake for 2 to 3 minutes. Rotate back before testing for doneness. Continue with step 6.

Apple Spice Cake Pops

Makes 20 to 22 cake pops

We were both raised in the Midwest, where restaurants, bakeries and orchards make wonderful, moist apple spice cakes, cookies, doughnuts and more. We love them and wanted to share a similar recipe with you.

Tip
Fold 3 tbsp (45 mL) toffee chips into the batter at the end of step 1.

1 cup	spice cake mix	250 mL
1	large egg, at room temperature	1
1/4 cup	unsweetened apple cider or apple juice	60 mL
3 tbsp	unsalted butter, melted	45 mL
1/2 tsp	vanilla extract	2 mL
	Nonstick baking spray	

1. In a medium bowl, using an electric mixer on low speed, beat cake mix, egg, apple cider, butter and vanilla for 30 seconds or until moistened. Beat on medium speed for 2 minutes.

2. Spray cake pop wells with baking spray. Fill each well with about 1 tbsp (15 mL) batter.

3. Bake for 4 to 6 minutes or until a tester inserted in the center comes out clean. Transfer cake pops to a wire rack to cool.

4. Repeat steps 2 and 3 with the remaining batter.

5. If desired, attach sticks to cake pops (see page 27).

If Baking in the Rotating Cake Pop Maker

In step 3, bake for 1 minute. Rotate and bake for 2 to 3 minutes. Rotate back before testing for doneness. Continue with step 3.

Blueberry Cake Pops

. . . .

Makes 46 to 48 cake pops

These blueberry cake pops are great dipped in vanilla candy coating. Or, for a light change of pace, leave them off the sticks and drizzle with Lemon Glaze (page 104).

. . . .

Tips

When blueberries are out of season, you can substitute frozen blueberries, thawed and well drained.

To intensify the lemon flavor, beat in 1 tsp (5 mL) grated lemon zest after the eggs.

This batter is thick and chunky, so you may wish to use a small scoop to fill the wells.

1½ cups	all-purpose flour	375 mL
2 tsp	baking powder	10 mL
½ tsp	baking soda	2 mL
¼ tsp	salt	1 mL
3 tbsp	milk	45 mL
2 tbsp	freshly squeezed lemon juice	30 mL
1 cup	granulated sugar	250 mL
⅔ cup	unsalted butter, softened	150 mL
2	large eggs, at room temperature	2
½ cup	small blueberries	125 mL
	Nonstick baking spray	

1. In a small bowl, whisk together flour, baking powder, baking soda and salt. Set aside.

2. In another small bowl, combine milk and lemon juice. Set aside.

3. In a large bowl, using an electric mixer on medium-high speed, beat sugar and butter for 1 minute or until fluffy. Add eggs, one at a time, beating well after each addition. Add flour mixture alternately with milk mixture, making three additions of flour and two of milk and beating on low speed until smooth. Fold in blueberries.

4. Spray cake pop wells with baking spray. Fill each well with about 1 tbsp (15 mL) batter.

5. Bake for 4 to 6 minutes or until a tester inserted in the center comes out clean. Transfer cake pops to a wire rack to cool.

6. Repeat steps 4 and 5 with the remaining batter.

7. If desired, attach sticks to cake pops (see page 27).

If Baking in the Rotating Cake Pop Maker

. . . .

In step 5, bake for 1 minute. Rotate and bake for 2 to 3 minutes. Rotate back before testing for doneness. Continue with step 5.

White Chocolate Blueberry Cake Pops

Jewel-toned blueberries shine in these rich, sweet white chocolate cake pops.

Tips

Select small blueberries for cake pops. If you have larger blueberries, cut them in half.

No buttermilk on hand? Place 1 tsp (5 mL) lemon juice or white vinegar in a glass measuring cup, then pour in enough milk to equal ⅓ cup (75 mL). Let stand for 5 to 10 minutes to thicken. Proceed with the recipe. (See page 15 for other buttermilk substitutions.)

If Baking in the Rotating Cake Pop Maker

In step 6, bake for 1 minute. Rotate and bake for 2 to 3 minutes. Rotate back before testing for doneness. Continue with step 6.

2 oz	white chocolate, chopped	60 g
1 cup	all-purpose flour	250 mL
1 tsp	baking powder	5 mL
½ tsp	baking soda	2 mL
¼ tsp	salt	1 mL
⅔ cup	small blueberries	150 mL
⅓ cup	granulated sugar	75 mL
2 tbsp	unsalted butter, softened	30 mL
1	large egg, at room temperature	1
⅓ cup	buttermilk	75 mL
1 tsp	vanilla extract	5 mL
	Nonstick baking spray	

1. Place white chocolate in a small microwave-safe glass bowl. Microwave on High in 30-second intervals, stirring after each, until melted. Let cool to room temperature.

2. In a small bowl, whisk together flour, baking powder, baking soda and salt. Measure out 2 tbsp (30 mL) flour mixture. Set the remaining flour mixture aside.

3. In another small bowl, toss together blueberries and 2 tbsp (30 mL) flour mixture. Set aside.

4. In a medium bowl, using an electric mixer on medium-high speed, beat sugar and butter for 1 minute or until fluffy. Beat in egg. Beat in melted chocolate. Add flour mixture alternately with buttermilk, making three additions of flour and two of buttermilk and beating on low speed until smooth. Fold in blueberries.

5. Spray cake pop wells with baking spray. Fill each well with about 1 tbsp (15 mL) batter.

6. Bake for 4 to 6 minutes or until a tester inserted in the center comes out clean. Transfer cake pops to a wire rack to cool.

7. Repeat steps 5 and 6 with the remaining batter.

8. If desired, attach sticks to cake pops (see page 27).

Cranberry Nut Spice Cake Pops

Makes 22 to 24 cake pops

Spice cake studded with cranberries and pecans makes for irresistible cake pops. Of course, they are ideal for parties held in the fall, but these days cranberries are popping up on menus all year long.

Tips

This batter is thick and chunky, so you may wish to use a small scoop to fill the wells.

Toasting pecans intensifies their flavor. Spread chopped pecans in a single layer on a baking sheet. Bake at 350°F (180°C) for 5 to 7 minutes or until lightly browned. Let cool.

1 cup	spice cake mix	250 mL
1	large egg, at room temperature	1
¼ cup	milk	60 mL
3 tbsp	unsalted butter, melted	45 mL
½ tsp	vanilla extract	2 mL
¼ cup	finely chopped sweetened dried cranberries	60 mL
¼ cup	chopped pecans, toasted (see tip, at left)	60 mL
	Nonstick baking spray	

1. In a medium bowl, using an electric mixer on low speed, beat cake mix, egg, milk, butter and vanilla for 30 seconds or until moistened. Beat on medium speed for 2 minutes. Fold in cranberries and pecans.

2. Spray cake pop wells with baking spray. Fill each well with about 1 tbsp (15 mL) batter.

3. Bake for 4 to 6 minutes or until a tester inserted in the center comes out clean. Transfer cake pops to a wire rack to cool.

4. Repeat steps 2 and 3 with the remaining batter.

5. If desired, attach sticks to cake pops (see page 27).

If Baking in the Rotating Cake Pop Maker

In step 3, bake for 1 minute. Rotate and bake for 2 to 3 minutes. Rotate back before testing for doneness. Continue with step 3.

Lemon Coconut Cake Pops

Kathy loves the fresh-tasting combination of lemon and coconut. Imagine yourself lounging under a palm tree as you indulge in these scrumptious treats.

Tip

Because coconut milk is often used in Asian foods, it is commonly stocked with other Asian ingredients at the grocery store. Do not confuse it with cream of coconut, which is most often used for cocktails.

Decorating Tips

Glaze the cake pops with Lemon Glaze (page 104). Remember, if you plan to glaze your cake pops, leave them off the sticks.

Coat the cake pops in white or yellow candy coating.

• Food processor

⅓ cup	sweetened flaked coconut	75 mL
1 cup	lemon cake mix	250 mL
1	large egg, at room temperature	1
¼ cup	coconut milk	60 mL
2 tbsp	unsalted butter, melted	30 mL
½ tsp	vanilla extract	2 mL
	Nonstick baking spray	

1. In food processor, process coconut until finely chopped.

2. In a large bowl, using an electric mixer on low speed, beat coconut, cake mix, egg, coconut milk, butter and vanilla for 30 seconds or until moistened. Beat on medium speed for 2 minutes.

3. Spray cake pop wells with baking spray. Fill each well with about 1 tbsp (15 mL) batter.

4. Bake for 4 to 6 minutes or until a tester inserted in the center comes out clean. Transfer cake pops to a wire rack to cool.

5. Repeat steps 3 and 4 with the remaining batter.

6. If desired, attach sticks to cake pops (see page 27).

If Baking in the Rotating Cake Pop Maker

In step 4, bake for 1 minute. Rotate and bake for 2 to 3 minutes. Rotate back before testing for doneness. Continue with step 4.

Orange, Cranberry and Vanilla Cake Pops

Makes 34 to 36 cake pops

The sweetness of vanilla baking chips contrasts with tart cranberries in these delightful cake pops.

Tips

Grated orange zest adds great fresh flavor. Wash and dry the fruit, then grate it with a fine rasp grater, such as a Microplane. Use a light motion and, for the best flavor, grate only the colored portion of the peel, avoiding the bitter white pith underneath.

Because of the baking chips in this recipe, a tester inserted into the cake pops will not come out clean.

1½ cups	all-purpose flour	375 mL
2 tsp	baking powder	10 mL
¼ tsp	salt	1 mL
¾ cup	granulated sugar	175 mL
6 tbsp	unsalted butter, softened	90 mL
2	large eggs, at room temperature	2
1 tbsp	grated orange zest	15 mL
⅓ cup	orange juice	75 mL
⅓ cup	chopped dried cranberries	75 mL
⅓ cup	vanilla baking chips	75 mL
	Nonstick baking spray	

1. In a medium bowl, whisk together flour, baking powder and salt. Set aside.

2. In a large bowl, using an electric mixer on medium-high speed, beat sugar and butter for 1 minute or until fluffy. Beat in eggs, one at a time, beating well after each addition. Beat in orange zest. Add flour mixture alternately with orange juice, making three additions of flour and two of juice and beating on low speed until smooth. Fold in cranberries and vanilla chips.

3. Spray cake pop wells with baking spray. Fill each well with about 1 tbsp (15 mL) batter.

4. Bake for 4 to 6 minutes or until cake pops bounce back when gently touched with your finger. Transfer cake pops to a wire rack to cool.

5. Repeat steps 3 and 4 with the remaining batter.

6. If desired, attach sticks to cake pops (see page 27).

If Baking in the Rotating Cake Pop Maker

In step 4, bake for 1 minute. Rotate and bake for 2 to 3 minutes. Rotate back before testing for doneness. Continue with step 4.

Orange Carrot Cake Pops

Makes 22
to 24 cake pops

The popular flavor of carrot cake is even better when brightened with a touch of orange.

Tips

To increase the orange flavor, beat in 2 tsp (10 mL) finely grated orange zest after the egg.

To quickly shred the carrot, use the fine grating attachment of a food processor. Packaged preshredded carrots are available; if they are coarsely shredded, finely chop them before adding them to the batter.

¾ cup	all-purpose flour	175 mL
1 tsp	baking powder	5 mL
¼ tsp	baking soda	1 mL
¼ tsp	salt	1 mL
⅓ cup	granulated sugar	75 mL
3 tbsp	unsalted butter, softened	45 mL
1	large egg, at room temperature	1
¼ cup	orange juice	60 mL
¼ cup	finely shredded carrot	60 mL
	Nonstick baking spray	

1. In a small bowl, whisk together flour, baking powder, baking soda and salt. Set aside.

2. In a medium bowl, using an electric mixer on medium-high speed, beat sugar and butter for 1 minute or until fluffy. Beat in egg. Add flour mixture alternately with orange juice, making three additions of flour and two of orange juice and beating on low speed until smooth. Fold in carrot.

3. Spray cake pop wells with baking spray. Fill each well with about 1 tbsp (15 mL) batter.

4. Bake for 4 to 6 minutes or until a tester inserted in the center comes out clean. Transfer cake pops to a wire rack to cool.

5. Repeat steps 3 and 4 with the remaining batter.

6. If desired, attach sticks to cake pops (see page 27).

If Baking in the Rotating Cake Pop Maker

In step 4, bake for 1 minute. Rotate and bake for 2 to 3 minutes. Rotate back before testing for doneness. Continue with step 4.

Vegan Carrot Cake Pops

· ·

**Makes 28
to 30 cake pops**

These moist, rich
carrot cake pops are
beautifully studded with
carrots and raisins.

· ·

Tips

To quickly shred the
carrots, use the fine
grating attachment of a
food processor. Packaged
preshredded carrots
are available; if they are
coarsely shredded, finely
chop them before adding
them to the batter.

Read the labels on the
cake mix to be sure it is
vegan. Some popular
national brands are vegan,
so you don't have to buy a
specialty product.

Decorating Tip

Drizzle with Vegan Cream
Cheese Glaze (variation,
page 106).

2 tbsp	ground flax seeds (flaxseed meal)	30 mL
1/3 cup	hot water	75 mL
1 1/2 cups	vegan yellow cake mix	375 mL
1 tsp	ground cinnamon	5 mL
1/3 cup	unsweetened pineapple juice	75 mL
3 tbsp	soy-based dairy-free sour cream alternative	45 mL
1 tsp	vanilla extract	5 mL
1 cup	finely shredded carrots (about 2 large)	250 mL
1/3 cup	raisins	75 mL
1/4 cup	chopped pecans, toasted (see tip, page 72)	60 mL
	Nonstick baking spray	

1. In a large bowl, combine flax seeds and hot water. Let stand for 10 minutes.

2. Using an electric mixer on low speed, beat in cake mix, cinnamon, pineapple juice, sour cream alternative and vanilla for 30 seconds or until moistened. Beat on medium speed for 2 minutes. Fold in carrots, raisins and pecans.

3. Spray cake pop wells with baking spray. Fill each well with about 1 tbsp (15 mL) batter.

4. Bake for 7 to 9 minutes or until a tester inserted in the center comes out clean. Transfer cake pops to a wire rack to cool.

5. Repeat steps 3 and 4 with the remaining batter.

If Baking in the Rotating Cake Pop Maker

· ·

In step 4, bake for 2 minutes. Rotate and bake for 3 to 4 minutes. Rotate back before testing for doneness. Continue with step 4.

Gluten-Free, Dairy-Free Maple Pecan Cake Pops

Maple and pecans are a timeless flavor combination, one of Kathy's favorites. You're sure to agree once you sample these cake pops!

Tips

To intensify the maple flavor, substitute maple extract for the vanilla.

Toasting pecans intensifies their flavor. Spread chopped pecans in a single layer on a baking sheet. Bake at 350°F (180°C) for 5 to 7 minutes or until lightly browned. Let cool.

¾ cup	gluten-free all-purpose baking mix (see page 13)	175 mL
¼ cup	granulated sugar	60 mL
¼ cup	packed brown sugar	60 mL
½ tsp	baking soda	2 mL
¼ tsp	salt	1 mL
½ cup	unsweetened plain almond milk	125 mL
2 tsp	cider vinegar	10 mL
1	large egg, at room temperature	1
¼ cup	vegan hard margarine, melted	60 mL
3 tbsp	pure maple syrup	45 mL
¼ tsp	vanilla extract	1 mL
⅓ cup	chopped pecans, toasted (see tip, at left)	75 mL
	Nonstick baking spray	

1. In a small bowl, whisk together baking mix, granulated sugar, brown sugar, baking soda and salt. Set aside.

2. In a large bowl, combine almond milk and vinegar. Let stand for 5 minutes. Using an electric mixer on low speed, beat in egg, margarine, maple syrup and vanilla until moistened. Beat in dry ingredients until moistened. Fold in pecans.

3. Spray cake pop wells with baking spray. Fill each well with about 1 tbsp (15 mL) batter.

4. Bake for 6 to 8 minutes or until a tester inserted in the center comes out clean. Transfer cake pops to a wire rack to cool.

5. Repeat steps 3 and 4 with the remaining batter.

6. If desired, attach sticks to cake pops (see page 27).

If Baking in the Rotating Cake Pop Maker

In step 4, bake for 2 minutes. Rotate and bake for 2 to 3 minutes. Rotate back before testing for doneness. Continue with step 4.

Grasshopper Cake Pops

**Makes 24
to 26 cake pops**

Don't worry — there aren't any insects baked into these cake pops! Rather, they capture the flavor of that alluring green cocktail, first served in New Orleans, that features crème de menthe and chocolate liqueur.

Tips

No buttermilk on hand? See page 15 for substitution suggestions.

Crème de menthe is available in green or clear; either can be used in these cake pops.

Decorating Tip

Coat the cake pops in chocolate candy coating. Or, to accent the mint flavor, choose chocolate mint candy coating.

1⅓ cups	devil's food cake mix	325 mL
1	large egg, at room temperature	1
3 tbsp	buttermilk	45 mL
2 tbsp	crème de menthe	30 mL
2 tbsp	vegetable oil	30 mL
¼ cup	chopped chocolate mint candies	60 mL
	Nonstick baking spray	

1. In a medium bowl, using an electric mixer on low speed, beat cake mix, egg, buttermilk, crème de menthe and oil for 30 seconds or until moistened. Beat on medium speed for 2 minutes. Stir in candies.

2. Spray cake pop wells with baking spray. Fill each well with about 1 tbsp (15 mL) batter.

3. Bake for 4 to 6 minutes or until a tester inserted in the center comes out clean. Transfer cake pops to a wire rack to cool.

4. Repeat steps 2 and 3 with the remaining batter.

5. If desired, attach sticks to cake pops (see page 27).

If Baking in the Rotating Cake Pop Maker

In step 3, bake for 1 minute. Rotate and bake for 2 to 3 minutes. Rotate back before testing for doneness. Continue with step 3.

Chocolate Bourbon Pecan Cake Pops

Makes 34 to 36 cake pops

A front porch surrounded by flowers, glasses filled with sweet tea, and chocolate bourbon pecan cake pops. Sounds like a perfect afternoon in the South.

Tip
Bourbon is a variety of whiskey originally made in Bourbon County, Kentucky, and most of the bourbon sold today still comes from that county. Substitute whiskey for the bourbon in these cake pops, if desired.

Variation
Fold in ¼ cup (60 mL) mini semisweet chocolate chips with the pecans. Bake until cake pops bounce back when gently touched with your finger.

1 oz	unsweetened chocolate, chopped	30 g
2 tbsp	unsalted butter	30 mL
¾ cup	all-purpose flour	175 mL
⅔ cup	granulated sugar	150 mL
¼ cup	unsweetened cocoa powder	60 mL
½ tsp	baking soda	2 mL
½ tsp	baking powder	2 mL
Pinch	salt	Pinch
1	large egg, at room temperature	1
6 tbsp	sour cream	90 mL
2 tbsp	bourbon	30 mL
1 tbsp	water	15 mL
¼ cup	chopped pecans, toasted (see tip, page 72)	60 mL
	Nonstick baking spray	

1. Place chocolate and butter in a small microwave-safe glass bowl. Microwave on High in 30-second intervals, stirring after each, until melted. Let cool to room temperature

2. In a large bowl, whisk together flour, sugar, cocoa powder, baking soda, baking powder and salt. Add egg, sour cream, bourbon and water. Using an electric mixer on medium-high speed, beat for 1 minute or until blended. Fold in pecans.

3. Spray cake pop wells with baking spray. Fill each well with about 1 tbsp (15 mL) batter.

4. Bake for 4 to 6 minutes or until a tester inserted in the center comes out clean. Transfer cake pops to a wire rack to cool.

5. Repeat steps 3 and 4 with the remaining batter.

6. If desired, attach sticks to cake pops (see page 27).

If Baking in the Rotating Cake Pop Maker

In step 4, bake for 1 minute. Rotate and bake for 2 to 3 minutes. Rotate back before testing for doneness. Continue with step 4.

Amaretto Cake Pops

Amaretto, an almond-flavored liqueur, adds a mild yet distinctive flavor to these cake pops. Kathy's daughter Laura loves these and serves them often.

Decorating Tips

Coat the cake pops in white candy coating and sprinkle with toasted chopped almonds. To accent the almond flavor, flavor the candy coating with amaretto or almond-flavored oil-based candy flavoring.

Glaze the cake pops with Almond Glaze (variation, page 106). Remember, if you plan to glaze your cake pops, leave them off the sticks.

1 cup	all-purpose flour	250 mL
1 tsp	baking powder	5 mL
¼ tsp	salt	1 mL
½ cup	granulated sugar	125 mL
½ cup	unsalted butter, softened	125 mL
2	large eggs, at room temperature	2
1 tsp	vanilla extract	5 mL
2 tbsp	amaretto	30 mL
	Nonstick baking spray	

1. In a small bowl, whisk together flour, baking powder and salt. Set aside.

2. In a large bowl, using an electric mixer on medium-high speed, beat sugar and butter for 1 minute or until fluffy. Add eggs, one at a time, beating well after each addition. Beat in vanilla. Add flour mixture alternately with amaretto, making three additions of flour and two of amaretto and beating on low speed until smooth.

3. Spray cake pop wells with baking spray. Fill each well with about 1 tbsp (15 mL) batter.

4. Bake for 4 to 6 minutes or until a tester inserted in the center comes out clean. Transfer cake pops to a wire rack to cool.

5. Repeat steps 3 and 4 with the remaining batter.

6. If desired, attach sticks to cake pops (see page 27).

If Baking in the Rotating Cake Pop Maker

In step 4, bake for 1 minute. Rotate and bake for 2 to 3 minutes. Rotate back before testing for doneness. Continue with step 4.

Gluten-Free, Dairy-Free Almond Amaretto Cake Pops

Makes 20 to 22 cake pops

These tasty cake pops are always a hit. No one will believe they're gluten- and dairy-free!

Decorating Tip

Glaze the cake pops with Almond Glaze (variation, page 106). Remember, if you plan to glaze your cake pops, leave them off the sticks.

1/3 cup	granulated sugar	75 mL
1/4 cup	gluten-free all-purpose baking mix (see page 13)	60 mL
1/4 cup	almond flour	60 mL
1/2 tsp	gluten-free baking powder	2 mL
1/8 tsp	salt	0.5 mL
2	large eggs, at room temperature	2
2 tbsp	amaretto	30 mL
2 tbsp	soy-based dairy-free cream cheese alternative	30 mL
1 tbsp	vegan hard margarine, softened	15 mL
1/2 tsp	almond extract	2 mL
	Nonstick baking spray	

1. In a small bowl, whisk together sugar, baking mix, almond flour, baking powder and salt. Set aside.

2. In a medium bowl, using an electric mixer on medium-high speed, beat eggs, amaretto, cream cheese alternative, margarine and almond extract until blended. Add flour mixture and beat on low speed until smooth.

3. Spray cake pop wells with baking spray. Fill each well with about 1 tbsp (15 mL) batter.

4. Bake for 5 to 7 minutes or until a tester inserted in the center comes out clean. Transfer cake pops to a wire rack to cool.

5. Repeat steps 3 and 4 with the remaining batter.

6. If desired, attach sticks to cake pops (see page 27).

If Baking in the Rotating Cake Pop Maker

In step 4, bake for 2 minutes. Rotate and bake for 2 to 3 minutes. Rotate back before testing for doneness. Continue with step 4.

Apricot Brandy Cake Pops

Makes 42 to 44 cake pops

Apricot brandy was extremely popular in the 1930s and '40s, and trendy bartenders are now rediscovering this golden delight. We've captured its flavor in these cake pops.

Tips

If you prefer, you can substitute regular brandy or another flavored brandy for the apricot brandy.

For a wonderful dessert, serve these with Brandy Cream Sauce (page 109). Arrange the cake pops in pretty martini or cocktail glasses, then drizzle with sauce. If desired, top with whipped cream.

1½ cups	all-purpose flour	375 mL
2 tsp	baking powder	10 mL
¼ tsp	salt	1 mL
¼ cup	milk	60 mL
3 tbsp	apricot brandy	45 mL
¾ cup	granulated sugar	175 mL
6 tbsp	unsalted butter, softened	90 mL
2	large eggs, at room temperature	2
½ tsp	almond extract	2 mL
	Nonstick baking spray	

1. In a small bowl, whisk together flour, baking powder and salt. Set aside.

2. In another small bowl, combine milk and apricot brandy. Set aside.

3. In a large bowl, using an electric mixer on medium-high speed, beat sugar and butter for 1 minute or until fluffy. Add eggs, one at a time, beating well after each addition. Beat in almond extract. Add flour mixture alternately with milk mixture, making three additions of flour and two of milk and beating on low speed until smooth.

4. Spray cake pop wells with baking spray. Fill each well with about 1 tbsp (15 mL) batter.

5. Bake for 4 to 6 minutes or until a tester inserted in the center comes out clean. Transfer cake pops to a wire rack to cool.

6. Repeat steps 4 and 5 with the remaining batter.

7. If desired, attach sticks to cake pops (see page 27).

If Baking in the Rotating Cake Pop Maker

In step 5, bake for 1 minute. Rotate and bake for 2 to 3 minutes. Rotate back before testing for doneness. Continue with step 5.

Trifles and Other Desserts

Chocolate Peanut Butter Trifle

Makes 16 to 20 servings		

Who can resist layers of chocolate cake pops, peanut butter pudding, chocolate pudding and more? This is the perfect dessert for a "bring-a-dish" casual dinner, an office lunch or an old-fashioned potluck.

Tips

Select your favorite chocolate cake pops for this recipe, such as Triple Chocolate Cake Pops (page 54), Chocolate Intensity Cake Pops (page 53) or Chocolate Sour Cream Cake Pops (page 24). Make the cake pops and let them cool completely. Or store leftover cake pops in an airtight container in the freezer and plan to make this trifle when you have collected 20 chocolate cake pops.

You can adjust the number of cake pops you use based on the number you have available and the size of the bowl you are filling.

If you cannot find mini peanut butter cup candies, coarsely chop larger peanut butter cup candies.

- 8-cup (2 L) trifle bowl or straight-sided bowl

1	package (3.4 oz/96 g) vanilla instant pudding mix	1
1	package (3.4 oz/96 g) chocolate instant pudding mix	1
3 cups	milk, divided	750 mL
1/4 cup	creamy peanut butter	60 mL
1	container (8 oz/250 g) frozen whipped topping, thawed	1
20	chocolate cake pops	20
1/2 cup	mini peanut butter cup candies	125 mL
1/4 cup	salted dry-roasted peanuts	60 mL
3 tbsp	chocolate syrup	45 mL

1. Prepare vanilla and chocolate pudding according to package directions, using 1 1/2 cups (375 mL) milk each.

2. Using an electric mixer on low speed, beat peanut butter into vanilla pudding until smooth.

3. Stir 1/4 cup (60 mL) whipped topping into each pudding.

4. Arrange half the cake pops in a single layer in the trifle bowl. Spoon in half the chocolate pudding, spreading until smooth. Spoon in half the peanut butter pudding, spreading until smooth. Sprinkle with 1/4 cup (60 mL) peanut butter candies. Repeat layers of cake pops, chocolate pudding and peanut butter pudding. Spread the remaining whipped topping over top.

5. Cover and refrigerate for at least 30 minutes, until chilled, or overnight. Just before serving, sprinkle with peanuts and the remaining peanut butter candies. Drizzle with chocolate syrup.

> ## Variation
> Slice 1 banana and arrange slices over the first layer of chocolate pudding.

Gingerbread Pumpkin Trifle with Caramelized Pecans

This is the perfect dessert to share when your family and friends gather for the holidays. It is especially convenient since you can make it the day before.

Variations

Substitute toffee bits or crushed toffee candy bars for the caramelized pecans.

Use Brown Sugar Spice Cake Pops (page 32) in place of the Gingerbread Cake Pops.

- 8-cup (2 L) trifle bowl or straight-sided bowl

Gingerbread Cake Pops

1 cup	gingerbread cake or cookie mix	250 mL
1	large egg, at room temperature	1
¼ cup	water	60 mL
2 tbsp	unsalted butter, melted	30 mL
	Nonstick baking spray	

Pumpkin Pudding

1	package (3.4 oz/96 g) butterscotch instant pudding mix	1
1 cup	milk	250 mL
1	can (15 oz/425 mL) pumpkin purée (not pie filling)	1

Whipped Cream

2 cups	heavy or whipping (35%) cream	500 mL
2 tbsp	confectioners' (icing) sugar	30 mL
¼ tsp	ground cinnamon	1 mL
1 tsp	vanilla extract	5 mL

Caramelized Pecans

1 tbsp	unsalted butter	15 mL
2 tbsp	packed brown sugar	30 mL
Pinch	salt	Pinch
⅓ cup	chopped pecans	75 mL

1. *Gingerbread Cake Pops:* In a medium bowl, using an electric mixer on low speed, beat gingerbread mix, egg, water and butter for 30 seconds or until moistened. Beat on medium speed for 2 minutes.

2. Spray cake pop wells with baking spray. Fill each well with about 1 tbsp (15 mL) batter.

3. Bake for 4 to 6 minutes or until a tester inserted in the center comes out clean. Transfer cake pops to a wire rack to cool completely.

4. Repeat steps 2 and 3 with the remaining batter.

5. *Pumpkin Pudding:* Prepare butterscotch pudding according to package directions, using 1 cup (250 mL) milk. Whisk in pumpkin until smooth.

Tips

Gingerbread is a popular flavor, and both cake mixes and cookie mixes are available, as well as mixes that work for both cake and cookies. For this recipe, we recommend using a mix that works for both.

Make the gingerbread cake pops to enjoy on their own. Attach sticks and coat them in vanilla candy coating, or leave them off the sticks and glaze lightly with Lemon Glaze (page 104).

If your can of pumpkin purée is larger than 15 oz (425 mL), measure out 1¾ cups (425 mL) and reserve any extra for another use. Extra pumpkin can be refrigerated in an airtight container for up to 1 week or frozen for up to 6 months.

You could also make individual parfaits, layering the cake pops, pumpkin pudding and whipped cream in parfait glasses or pretty footed goblets.

6. *Whipped Cream:* In a small bowl, using an electric mixer with clean beaters on medium speed, beat cream until frothy. Beat in confectioners' sugar and cinnamon until stiff peaks form. Beat in vanilla.

7. Arrange half the cake pops in a single layer in the trifle bowl. Spoon in half the pudding, spreading until smooth. Spoon in half the whipped cream, spreading until smooth. Repeat layers. Cover and refrigerate for at least 30 minutes, until chilled, or overnight.

8. *Pecans:* In a medium nonstick skillet, melt butter over medium heat. Add brown sugar and salt; cook, stirring constantly, for about 3 minutes or until mixture comes to a boil and sugar is dissolved. Stir in pecans and cook, stirring constantly, for 2 minutes. Pour onto a tray lined with waxed paper and let cool completely. Sprinkle over trifle just before serving.

If Baking in the Rotating Cake Pop Maker

In step 3, bake for 1 minute. Rotate and bake for 2 to 3 minutes. Rotate back before testing for doneness. Continue with step 3.

Individual Brownie Trifle Parfaits

Makes
4 servings

Every time you make a batch of Favorite Brownie Cake Pops, place some in an airtight container in the freezer so you can make these parfaits at a moment's notice.

Tips

Instead of making Hot Fudge Sauce, you can use your favorite brand of hot fudge or chocolate sauce.

Cut the recipe in half to make 2 parfaits, or double it to serve at a party.

• 4 parfait glasses or 12-oz (375 mL) straight-sided glasses

1/3 cup	whipped cream cheese	75 mL
1/3 cup	sour cream	75 mL
3 tbsp	confectioners' (icing) sugar	45 mL
1 tsp	vanilla extract	5 mL
1 cup	frozen whipped topping, thawed	250 mL
16	Favorite Brownie Cake Pops (page 57)	16
1/2 cup	Hot Fudge Sauce (page 110), cooled	125 mL
	Chocolate shavings or chopped milk chocolate candy bar	

1. In a medium bowl, using an electric mixer on medium speed, beat cream cheese, sour cream, sugar and vanilla until smooth. Beat in whipped topping.

2. Place 2 cake pops in each parfait glass. Top with about 2 1/2 tbsp (37 mL) cream cheese mixture. Drizzle with 1 tbsp (15 mL) hot fudge. Repeat layers. Garnish with chocolate shavings. Serve immediately.

Variations

Brownie Trifle Shooters: Make very small trifles in 3- or 5-oz (90 or 150 mL) paper cups. For an adult party, use clear plastic shot glasses and drizzle with crème de cacao or another chocolate liqueur before the hot fudge.

Use this same idea to make any flavor of trifle you like. For example, use Lemon Poppy Seed Cake Pops (page 38) and replace the hot fudge sauce with blueberry or raspberry syrup or lemon curd. Or use white cake pops and caramel sauce.

Marshmallow Puffs

With a can of refrigerated crescent rolls on hand, you can instantly whip up treats and sweets in the cake pop maker.

Tip

If you can only find an 8-oz (227 g) can of refrigerated crescent roll dough, simply double the remaining ingredients and make 24 marshmallow puffs.

Variation

Use 1 marshmallow per square and add a semisweet chocolate chip with the dipped marshmallow.

1	can (4 oz/113 g) refrigerated crescent roll dough	1
3 tbsp	granulated sugar	45 mL
1 tbsp	all-purpose flour	15 mL
½ tsp	ground cinnamon	2 mL
24	miniature marshmallows	24
2 tbsp	unsalted butter, melted	30 mL
	Powdered Sugar Glaze (page 106)	

1. Separate dough into 2 pieces. Using your fingers, pinch perforations together to form 2 rectangles. Cut each rectangle into 3 pieces, then cut each piece in half, making 12 squares total.

2. In a small bowl, combine sugar, flour and cinnamon. Using the fork tool, secure 2 marshmallows on the tines. Dip marshmallows in melted butter, then in sugar mixture. Place marshmallows in the center of a square of dough. Form dough into a ball around the marshmallows and seal well. Repeat with the remaining ingredients.

3. Place a ball in each cake pop well. Bake for 3 to 5 minutes or until golden brown. Transfer puffs to a wire rack to cool slightly.

4. Drizzle generously with Powdered Sugar Glaze. Serve warm.

If Baking in the Rotating Cake Pop Maker

In step 3, bake for 1 minute. Rotate and bake for 2 to 3 minutes. Rotate back before testing for doneness. Continue with step 3.

Macadamia Vanilla Chip Bites

Years ago, Roxanne had two dear neighbors who delivered a version of these cookies to her doorstep. It just goes to show: the gift of friendship, food and caring make an impression that lasts a lifetime.

Tips

If you prefer, you can substitute chopped Brazil nuts, almonds or walnuts for the macadamia nuts.

Note that the amount of dough added to each well is smaller than in most recipes. These are literally bite-size crisp cookies.

¾ cup	all-purpose flour	175 mL
¼ tsp	baking soda	1 mL
¼ tsp	salt	1 mL
¼ cup	packed brown sugar	60 mL
2 tbsp	granulated sugar	30 mL
¼ cup	unsalted butter, softened	60 mL
1	large egg, at room temperature	1
1 tsp	vanilla extract	5 mL
⅓ cup	vanilla baking chips, coarsely chopped	75 mL
½ cup	chopped macadamia nuts	125 mL

1. In a small bowl, whisk together flour, baking soda and salt. Set aside.

2. In a medium bowl, using an electric mixer on medium-high speed, beat brown sugar, granulated sugar and butter for 1 minute or until fluffy. Beat in egg and vanilla. Add flour mixture and beat on low until smooth. Stir in vanilla chips and nuts.

3. Fill each cake pop well with about 1 tsp (5 mL) dough.

4. Bake for 4 to 6 minutes or until golden brown. Transfer cookie bites to a wire rack to cool.

5. Repeat steps 3 and 4 with the remaining dough.

If Baking in the Rotating Cake Pop Maker

In step 4, bake for 1 minute. Rotate and bake for 2 to 3 minutes. Rotate back before testing for doneness. Continue with step 4.

Biscotti Balls

Makes 25 to 27 biscotti balls

Looking for a great teacher gift? Pair these anise-infused biscotti balls with coffee or a gift card from a favorite coffee shop, and shopping is complete.

Tips

Toasting almonds intensifies their flavor. Spread sliced almonds in a single layer on a baking sheet. Bake at 350°F (180°C) for 5 to 7 minutes or until lightly browned. Let cool.

For a different look and taste, substitute white candy coating wafers for the chocolate.

1¼ cups	all-purpose flour	300 mL
¾ tsp	baking soda	3 mL
¼ tsp	salt	1 mL
½ cup	granulated sugar	125 mL
¼ cup	unsalted butter, softened	60 mL
1	large egg, at room temperature	1
1 tsp	anise extract	5 mL
¾ cup	sliced almonds, toasted (see tip at left) and finely chopped	175 mL
½ cup	chocolate candy coating wafers, melted	125 mL

1. In a small bowl, whisk together flour, baking soda and salt. Set aside.

2. In a medium bowl, using an electric mixer on medium-high speed, beat sugar and butter for 1 minute or until fluffy. Beat in egg and anise extract. Add flour and beat on low speed until smooth. Fold in almonds.

3. Fill each cake pop well with about 1 tbsp (15 mL) dough.

4. Bake for 5 minutes. Carefully place the fork tool between each ball and the edge of the well and gently turn the ball over. Bake for 2 to 3 minutes or until golden. Transfer biscotti balls to a wire rack to cool.

5. Repeat steps 3 and 4 with the remaining dough.

6. Using the fork tool, dip half of each biscotti ball in chocolate candy coating and return to the rack to set.

If Baking in the Rotating Cake Pop Maker

In step 4, bake for 3 minutes. Rotate and bake for 3 to 4 minutes. Rotate back before testing for doneness. Continue with step 4.

Baked Sopaipillas with Honey Syrup

Makes 24 sopaipillas

This baked version of sopaipillas, a delightful treat popular in the Southwest, is addictive, so be prepared to make two batches!

Tips

Thaw just the number of puff pastry shells you need. In general, they thaw at room temperature in about 30 minutes or in the refrigerator in about 4 hours.

To coat the hot pastries, place the topping in a brown paper bag, add the pastries and gently shake to coat. Alternatively, place the topping in a shallow bowl, add the pastries and roll to coat evenly. Be sure to coat the pastry immediately after baking.

4	frozen puff pastry shells, thawed	4
2 tbsp	unsalted butter, melted	30 mL
	Cinnamon Sugar Topping (page 112)	
	Honey Syrup (page 111)	

1. Roll out each puff pastry shell to $\frac{1}{8}$ to $\frac{1}{4}$ inch (3 to 5 mm) thick and 5 to $5\frac{1}{2}$ inches (12.5 to 13.5 cm) square. Cut each shell in half, then cut each half into thirds, making 24 pieces total.

2. Brush cake pop wells lightly with melted butter. Place 1 piece of pastry in each well.

3. Bake for 6 minutes or until bottoms are golden brown. Carefully place the fork tool between each pastry and the edge of the well and gently turn the pastry over. Bake for 5 minutes or until golden brown.

4. Immediately coat hot pastry in cinnamon sugar (see tip, at left). Place on a wire rack to cool slightly.

5. Repeat steps 2 to 4 with the remaining pastry pieces.

6. Serve warm, with Honey Syrup.

If Baking in the Rotating Cake Pop Maker

In step 3, bake for 5 minutes or until bottoms are golden brown. Rotate and bake for 3 to 4 minutes. Rotate back before testing for doneness. Continue with step 3.

Apple Dumpling Bites

Makes 14 to 16 dumplings

These bite-size morsels packed with apple are sure to become an all-time classic dessert.

Tips

You can use your favorite single-crust pie crust recipe or use a store-bought prepared crust.

Serve a scoop of vanilla or cinnamon ice cream with 2 or 3 warm apple dumplings, then drizzle generously with warm Cider Sauce.

If Baking in the Rotating Cake Pop Maker

In step 6, bake for 6 minutes. Rotate and bake for 5 to 6 minutes. Rotate back before testing for doneness. Continue with step 6.

- 3-inch (7.5 cm) round cookie cutter

1	Granny Smith apple, peeled and finely chopped	1
2 tbsp	granulated sugar	30 mL
1/2 tsp	ground cinnamon	2 mL
Pinch	salt	Pinch
3 tbsp	water, divided	45 mL
1 tsp	freshly squeezed lemon juice	5 mL
1/2 tsp	cornstarch	2 mL
1	refrigerated pie crust for a 9-inch (23 cm) pie	1
1	large egg, at room temperature	1
	Cider Sauce (page 109)	

1. In a small saucepan, combine apple, sugar, cinnamon, salt, 1 tbsp (15 mL) of the water and lemon juice. Heat over medium heat for 1 minute. Reduce heat to low and simmer gently, stirring often, for 8 to 9 minutes or until apples are tender.

2. Combine cornstarch and 1 tbsp (15 mL) water. Stir into apple mixture and simmer, stirring often, for 1 to 2 minutes or until thickened and bubbly. Remove from heat and let cool for 10 minutes.

3. On a lightly floured board, roll out pie crust to about 1/8 inch (3 mm) thick. Use the cookie cutter to cut out 14 to 16 circles of pie crust, rerolling scraps as needed. Spoon about 1 tsp (5 mL) filling into the center of each circle. Gather all the edges together and pinch to seal tightly.

4. In a small bowl, whisk together egg and the remaining water.

5. Place 1 dumpling in each well. Brush dumplings lightly with egg wash.

6. Bake for 10 minutes. Carefully place the fork tool between each dumpling and the edge of the well and gently turn the dumpling over. Bake for 4 to 5 minutes or until golden brown. Transfer dumplings to a wire rack to cool slightly.

7. Repeat steps 5 and 6 with the remaining dumplings.

8. Serve warm, with Cider Sauce.

Peach Pecan Shortcakes

Capture summer's goodness with warm bite-size peach shortcakes — heavenly!

Tip

Substitute a 16-oz (500 g) package of frozen no-sugar-added sliced peaches for the fresh. Thaw, reserving juice. In step 5, combine peach slices, reserved juice, sugar and ginger.

If Baking in the Rotating Cake Pop Maker

In step 3, bake for 2 minutes. Rotate and bake for 2 to 3 minutes. Rotate back before testing for doneness. Continue with step 3.

Shortcakes

1¼ cups	all-purpose flour	300 mL
2 tbsp	granulated sugar	30 mL
1½ tsp	baking powder	7 mL
¼ tsp	ground ginger	1 mL
Pinch	salt	Pinch
¼ cup	cold butter, cut into small pieces	60 mL
½ cup	milk	125 mL
¼ cup	chopped pecans, toasted (see tip, page 72)	60 mL

Peach Topping

3	ripe peaches, peeled and thinly sliced	3
6 tbsp	granulated sugar (or to taste), divided	90 mL
¼ tsp	ground ginger	1 mL
½ cup	heavy or whipping (35%) cream	125 mL

1. *Shortcakes:* In a medium bowl, whisk together flour, sugar, baking powder, ginger and salt. Using your fingertips or a pastry blender, cut in butter until mixture resembles coarse crumbs. Using a fork, stir in milk just until dough comes together. Stir in pecans.

2. Fill each well with about 1 tbsp (15 mL) batter.

3. Bake for 3 minutes. Carefully place the fork tool between each shortcake and the edge of the well and gently turn the shortcake over. Bake for 3 minutes or until golden brown. Transfer shortcakes to a wire rack to cool slightly.

4. Repeat steps 2 and 3 with the remaining dough.

5. *Topping:* Meanwhile, in a large bowl, toss together peaches, 4 tbsp (60 mL) sugar (or to taste) and ginger. Let stand for 10 minutes. Using the back of a spoon, mash slightly to extract the juice.

6. In a small, deep bowl, using an electric mixer on medium-high speed, beat cream until frothy. Add 2 tbsp (30 mL) sugar and beat until stiff peaks form.

7. Place about 4 shortcakes in each of six dessert dishes. Top with about ⅓ cup (75 mL) peaches and a dollop of whipped cream.

Cherries Jubilee

Makes
8 servings

A classic dessert becomes new again when almond-flavored cake pops are added to the mix.

Tip

If desired, add a small scoop of vanilla ice cream to each serving.

1	can (16 oz/454 mL) pitted dark sweet cherries in heavy syrup	1
3 tbsp	unsalted butter	45 mL
¼ cup	packed brown sugar	60 mL
¼ cup	orange juice	60 mL
¼ cup	brandy	60 mL
1 tbsp	cornstarch	15 mL
2 tbsp	cold water	30 mL
40	Almond Cake Pops (page 44)	40

1. Drain cherries, reserving syrup. Cut cherries in half.

2. In a large skillet, melt butter over medium heat. Add brown sugar and cook, stirring often, until sugar is dissolved. Stir in cherries, reserved syrup and orange juice; bring to a simmer. Stir in brandy.

3. In a small bowl, combine cornstarch and cold water. Stir into cherry mixture and cook, stirring constantly, until thickened and bubbly. Remove from heat.

4. Place 5 cake pops in each of eight dessert dishes. Spoon warm cherry sauce over top.

Caramelized Pineapple Dessert

Makes 6 servings

The flavors in this dessert will remind you of a terrific pineapple upside-down cake.

Tip
There is enough juice in a 20-oz or 540 mL can of crushed pineapple to use in both the cake pops and the topping. Read the label to make sure the fruit is packed in juice and not sweetened syrup.

Variation
Add 1/3 cup (75 mL) chopped pecans with the pineapple.

1	can (20 oz or 540 mL) crushed pineapple in juice	1
2 tbsp	unsalted butter	30 mL
1/2 cup	packed brown sugar	125 mL
24	Pineapple Cake Pops (page 42)	24
	Whipped cream or frozen whipped topping (optional)	

1. Drain pineapple, reserving juice. Measure out 1/2 cup (125 mL) juice.

2. In a large skillet, melt butter over medium heat. Add brown sugar and cook, stirring often, until sugar is dissolved. Stir in pineapple and reserved juice; cook, stirring often, for 10 to 15 minutes or until pineapple is golden and lightly caramelized.

3. Place 4 cake pops in each of six dessert dishes. Spoon warm pineapple sauce over top. If desired, dollop with whipped cream.

Doughnuts

Cinnamon Sour Cream Doughnuts

Makes 25 to 27 doughnuts

This old-fashioned classic, packed with goodness, is just right at any time of the year.

Tip

To coat the hot doughnuts, place the topping in a brown paper bag, add the doughnuts and gently shake to coat. Alternatively, place the topping in a shallow bowl, add the doughnuts and roll to coat evenly. Be sure to coat the doughnuts immediately after baking.

Omit the Cinnamon Sugar Topping and instead drizzle the doughnuts with Powdered Sugar Glaze (page 106).

1 cup	all-purpose flour	250 mL
1½ tsp	baking powder	7 mL
½ tsp	baking soda	2 mL
½ tsp	ground cinnamon	2 mL
¼ tsp	salt	1 mL
¼ cup	granulated sugar	60 mL
¼ cup	packed brown sugar	60 mL
1	large egg, at room temperature	1
½ cup	sour cream	125 mL
¼ cup	vegetable oil	60 mL
½ tsp	vanilla extract	2 mL
	Nonstick baking spray	
	Cinnamon Sugar Topping (page 112)	

1. In a small bowl, whisk together flour, baking powder, baking soda, cinnamon and salt. Set aside.

2. In a medium bowl, using an electric mixer on low speed, beat granulated sugar, brown sugar, egg, sour cream, oil and vanilla for 1 minute or until fluffy. Beat in flour mixture until moistened.

3. Spray cake pop wells with baking spray. Fill each well with about 1 tbsp (15 mL) batter.

4. Bake for 4 to 6 minutes or until a tester inserted in the center comes out clean.

5. Immediately coat hot doughnuts in cinnamon sugar (see tip, at left). Place on a wire rack to cool slightly.

6. Repeat steps 3 to 5 with the remaining batter. Serve warm.

If Baking in the Rotating Cake Pop Maker

In step 4, bake for 1 minute. Rotate and bake for 2 to 3 minutes. Rotate back before testing for doneness as in step 4.

Easy Does It Cinnamon Doughnuts

Makes 20 doughnuts

We had such fun testing these recipes. One day in the test kitchen, Julie Bondank, Amy Dowell, Kathy and Roxanne were remembering fondly the "doughnuts" their moms and grandmothers lovingly prepared for them. We immediately went to the grocery store and purchased the ingredients. The results brought back fond memories in a flash.

Tip

If using a 16.3-oz (462 g) can of 8 larger biscuits, cut each biscuit into quarters, making 32 biscuit balls. Continue as directed. Increase the sugar, cinnamon and butter by about half.

1	can (7.5 oz/213 g) refrigerated biscuit dough (10 biscuits)	1
⅓ cup	granulated sugar	75 mL
¾ tsp	ground cinnamon	3 mL
¼ cup	unsalted butter, melted	60 mL

1. Separate biscuits and cut each in half. Form each half into a ball.

2. In a small bowl, combine sugar and cinnamon. Place melted butter in another small bowl. Set both aside.

3. Place a biscuit ball in each cake pop well.

4. Bake for 3 to 4 minutes or until golden brown.

5. Immediately roll each hot biscuit in butter, then coat in cinnamon sugar. Place on a wire rack to cool slightly.

6. Repeat steps 3 to 5 with the remaining biscuit balls. Serve warm.

If Baking in the Rotating Cake Pop Maker

In step 4, bake for 1 minute. Rotate and bake for 1 to 2 minutes. Rotate back before testing for doneness as in step 4.

Cream-Filled Chocolate Doughnuts

Roxanne's family has a long-standing tradition of visiting a doughnut shop every Saturday morning. But they all love this recipe so much that now they stay home on snowy or rainy days and prepare these delights instead.

Tips

These are also great without the custard filling; simply glaze with the Chocolate Glaze.

Because of the chocolate chips in this recipe, a tester inserted into the cake pops will not come out clean.

If Baking in the Rotating Cake Pop Maker

In step 4, bake for 1 minute. Rotate and bake for 2 to 3 minutes. Rotate back before testing for doneness. Continue with step 4.

• Pastry bag fitted with a medium plain round tip (optional)

1 cup	all-purpose flour	250 mL
3 tbsp	unsweetened cocoa powder	45 mL
1 tsp	baking powder	5 mL
1/4 tsp	baking soda	1 mL
Pinch	salt	Pinch
2/3 cup	granulated sugar	150 mL
2 tbsp	cold unsalted butter, cut into small pieces	30 mL
1	large egg, at room temperature	1
1/2 cup	buttermilk	125 mL
2 tsp	vanilla extract	10 mL
3 tbsp	mini semisweet chocolate chips	45 mL
	Nonstick baking spray	
	Vanilla Custard Filling (page 112)	
	Chocolate Glaze (page 104)	

1. In a large bowl, whisk together flour, cocoa powder, baking powder, baking soda and salt. Stir in sugar. Using a pastry blender or two knives, cut in butter until mixture resembles coarse crumbs. Set aside.

2. In a small bowl, whisk together egg, buttermilk and vanilla. Stir into flour mixture just until moistened. Gently stir in chocolate chips.

3. Spray cake pop wells with baking spray. Fill each well with about 1 tbsp (15 mL) batter.

4. Bake for 4 to 6 minutes or until doughnuts bounce back when gently touched with your finger. Transfer doughnuts to a wire rack set over a sheet of foil or waxed paper to cool.

5. Repeat steps 3 and 4 with the remaining batter.

6. Fill the pastry bag with Vanilla Custard Filling and inject filling into the center of each doughnut (or split doughnuts, fill and stick the halves back together).

7. Using the fork tool, dip the top half of each doughnut in Chocolate Glaze, allowing excess glaze to drip back into the bowl. Return doughnuts to the rack to set.

Strawberry Confetti Doughnuts

Makes 25 to 27 doughnuts

What little girl doesn't like pink confetti doughnuts? They're sure to love our version: the strawberry flavor in these little treats makes them even better.

Tips

These doughnuts are great with the fresh strawberries, but you can leave them out when strawberries aren't in season. The doughnuts will still be delicious!

If you don't have strawberry-flavored milk, use regular milk and increase the strawberry extract to 2 tsp (10 mL). Tint to the desired color with red food coloring.

1¼ cups	all-purpose flour	300 mL
1 tsp	baking powder	5 mL
¼ tsp	salt	1 mL
⅓ cup	granulated sugar	75 mL
¼ cup	unsalted butter, softened	60 mL
1	large egg, at room temperature	1
⅔ cup	strawberry-flavored milk	150 mL
1 tsp	strawberry extract	5 mL
6 to 8	drops red food coloring	6 to 8
¼ cup	finely chopped strawberries	60 mL
2 tbsp	confetti sprinkles	30 mL
	Nonstick baking spray	
	Strawberry Glaze (page 105)	

1. In a medium bowl, whisk together flour, baking powder and salt. Set aside.

2. In a large bowl, using an electric mixer on medium-high speed, beat sugar and butter for 1 minute or until fluffy. Beat in egg. Beat in milk and strawberry extract. Stir in flour mixture just until moistened. Stir in strawberries and enough food coloring to tint to the desired shade of pink. Stir in sprinkles.

3. Spray cake pop wells with baking spray. Fill each well with about 1 tbsp (15 mL) batter.

4. Bake for 4 to 6 minutes or until a tester inserted in the center comes out clean. Transfer doughnuts to a wire rack set over a sheet of foil or waxed paper to cool.

5. Repeat steps 3 and 4 with the remaining batter.

6. Using the fork tool, dip each doughnut in Strawberry Glaze, allowing excess glaze to drip back into the bowl. Return doughnuts to the rack to set.

If Baking in the Rotating Cake Pop Maker

In step 4, bake for 1 minute. Rotate and bake for 2 to 3 minutes. Rotate back before testing for doneness. Continue with step 4.

Apple Cider Doughnuts

Every fall, Roxanne's family heads to a local cider mill to enjoy fresh cider and warm apple cider doughnuts. They always purchase cider to take home so they can make these round replicas and relive the warm memories of the day.

Tip

To coat the hot doughnuts, place the topping in a brown paper bag, add the doughnuts and gently shake to coat. Alternatively, place the topping in a shallow bowl, add the doughnuts and roll to coat evenly. Be sure to coat the doughnuts immediately after baking.

Variation

Stir 3 tbsp (45 mL) toasted finely chopped walnuts or pecans into the batter at the end of step 2.

1 cup	all-purpose flour	250 mL
1/3 cup	packed brown sugar	75 mL
1 tsp	baking soda	5 mL
3/4 tsp	baking powder	3 mL
1/2 tsp	ground cinnamon	2 mL
1/4 tsp	ground nutmeg	1 mL
1/4 tsp	salt	1 mL
1	large egg, at room temperature	1
1/4 cup	unsweetened applesauce	60 mL
3 tbsp	liquid honey	45 mL
3 tbsp	unsweetened apple cider	45 mL
3 tbsp	sour cream	45 mL
1 tbsp	vegetable oil	15 mL
1/2 tsp	vanilla extract	2 mL
	Nonstick baking spray	
	Cinnamon Sugar Topping (page 112)	

1. In a large bowl, whisk together flour, brown sugar, baking soda, baking powder, cinnamon, nutmeg and salt. Set aside.

2. In a medium bowl, whisk together egg, applesauce, honey, apple cider, sour cream, oil and vanilla. Pour into flour mixture and stir to blend. Do not overmix.

3. Spray cake pop wells with baking spray. Fill each well with about 1 tbsp (15 mL) batter.

4. Bake for 4 to 6 minutes or until a tester inserted in the center comes out clean.

5. Immediately coat hot doughnuts in cinnamon sugar (see tip, at left). Place on a wire rack to cool slightly.

6. Repeat steps 3 to 5 with the remaining batter. Serve warm.

If Baking in the Rotating Cake Pop Maker

In step 4, bake for 1 minute. Rotate and bake for 2 to 3 minutes. Rotate back before testing for doneness as in step 4.

Brown Sugar Spice Cake Pops (page 32) and
Gluten-Free, Vegan Oatmeal Raisin Cake Pops (page 46)

Cappuccino Bites (page 61)

Blueberry Cake Pops (page 65) and
Lemon Coconut Cake Pops (page 68)

Grasshopper Cake Pops (page 73)

Pumpkin Donuts (page 98)
and Apple Fritters (page 100)

Gingerbread Ebelskivers (page 121) and Sticky Rolls (page 123)

Bacon Cornbread Muffins (page 133) and Orange Pecan Scones (page 140)

Mini Flowers (from Thinking of You, page 169),
Tie-Dyed Berry Cake Pops (page 63),
and Chocolate Walnut Cake Pops (page 55)

Gluten-Free, Vegan Autumn Apple Doughnuts

Makes 24 to 26 doughnuts

Fall is the perfect time to visit a cider mill and buy apple butter and apple cider. Use some of the cider in these doughnuts. Heat the rest and steep it with cinnamon sticks for a mug of hot apple cider to serve with the doughnuts.

Tip
If desired, serve these doughnuts with warm Gluten-Free Cider Sauce (variation, page 109).

If Baking in the Rotating Cake Pop Maker

In step 5, bake for 1 minute. Rotate and bake for 2 to 3 minutes. Rotate back before testing for doneness as in step 5.

1 tbsp	ground flax seeds (flaxseed meal)	15 mL
3 tbsp	hot water	45 mL
1 cup	gluten-free all-purpose baking mix (see page 13)	250 mL
⅓ cup	packed brown sugar	75 mL
1 tsp	gluten-free baking powder	5 mL
1 tsp	baking soda	5 mL
1 tsp	ground cinnamon	5 mL
¼ tsp	salt	1 mL
¼ cup	apple butter	60 mL
3 tbsp	agave nectar	45 mL
3 tbsp	unsweetened apple cider	45 mL
3 tbsp	soy-based dairy-free sour cream alternative	45 mL
1 tbsp	canola oil	15 mL
1 tsp	vanilla extract	5 mL
	Nonstick baking spray	
	Cinnamon Sugar Topping (page 112)	

1. In a small bowl, combine flax seeds and hot water. Let stand for 10 minutes.

2. In a medium bowl, whisk together baking mix, brown sugar, baking powder, baking soda, cinnamon and salt. Set aside.

3. Whisk apple butter, agave nectar, apple cider, sour cream alternative, oil and vanilla into flaxseed mixture. Stir into flour mixture until smooth.

4. Spray cake pop wells with baking spray. Fill each well with about 1 tbsp (15 mL) batter.

5. Bake for 4 to 6 minutes or until a tester inserted in the center comes out clean.

6. Immediately coat hot doughnuts in cinnamon sugar (see tip, page 96). Place on a wire rack to cool slightly.

7. Repeat steps 4 to 6 with the remaining batter. Serve warm.

Pumpkin Doughnuts

These pumpkin doughnuts are the perfect choice for an autumn event.

Tips

Refrigerate leftover canned pumpkin purée in an airtight container for up to 1 week, or freeze it for up to 3 months. Thaw overnight in the refrigerator, then stir well and use it to bake another batch of doughnuts.

If desired, drizzle the cooled doughnuts with Maple Glaze (variation, page 106).

While they're still hot, coat the doughnuts in Cinnamon Sugar Topping (page 112) or confectioners' (icing) sugar. Then transfer to the rack to cool.

---

1 cup	all-purpose flour	250 mL
1½ tsp	baking powder	7 mL
1 tsp	pumpkin pie spice	5 mL
¼ tsp	salt	1 mL
¼ cup	packed brown sugar	60 mL
½ cup	canned pumpkin purée (not pie filling)	125 mL
2 tbsp	unsalted butter, softened	30 mL
1	large egg, at room temperature	1
1 tbsp	milk	15 mL
½ tsp	vanilla extract	2 mL
	Nonstick baking spray	

1. In a small bowl, whisk together flour, baking powder, pumpkin pie spice and salt. Set aside.

2. In a medium bowl, using an electric mixer on medium-high speed, beat brown sugar, pumpkin and butter for 1 minute or until fluffy. Beat in egg, milk and vanilla until blended. Add flour mixture and beat on low speed until moistened.

3. Spray cake pop wells with baking spray. Fill each well with about 1 tbsp (15 mL) batter.

4. Bake for 4 to 6 minutes or until a tester inserted in the center comes out clean. Transfer doughnuts to a wire rack to cool.

5. Repeat steps 3 and 4 with the remaining batter.

Variation

Stir ⅓ cup (75 mL) toasted finely chopped pecans or walnuts into the batter at the end of step 2.

If Baking in the Rotating Cake Pop Maker

In step 4, bake for 1 minute. Rotate and bake for 2 to 3 minutes. Rotate back before testing for doneness. Continue with step 4.

Baos

Baos, also known as baozi, are pillow-like soft buns that are steamed or baked. Commonly served at dim sum restaurants, they come with a variety of fillings. The buns are usually savory, but of course we like them sweet, for breakfast or a mid-morning snack.

Tip

This dough is fabulous and can be used to make easy appetizers. Omit the candies and confectioners' (icing) sugar. Prepare the dough as directed, then form each portion into a ball around a ½-inch (1 cm) cube of Cheddar or other cheese. Bake as directed.

1 cup	all-purpose flour	250 mL
1 tbsp	granulated sugar	15 mL
½ tsp	baking powder	2 mL
¼ tsp	baking soda	1 mL
Pinch	salt	Pinch
1	large egg, at room temperature	1
1	large egg yolk, at room temperature	1
2 tbsp	unsalted butter, melted	30 mL
2 tbsp	milk	30 mL
12 to 14	milk chocolate drop candies (such as Hershey's Milk Chocolate Drops)	12 to 14
	Nonstick baking spray	
	Confectioners' (icing) sugar	

1. In a medium bowl, whisk together flour, sugar, baking powder, baking soda and salt. Set aside.

2. In a small bowl, whisk together egg, egg yolk, butter and milk.

3. Make a well in the dry ingredients and pour in liquids. Using an electric mixer on medium speed, beat for 1 to 2 minutes or until a dough forms.

4. Place dough on a lightly floured surface and knead for 2 minutes. Wrap dough in plastic wrap and refrigerate for at least 1 hour.

5. Pinch off about 1 tbsp (15 mL) dough and form into a ball around a chocolate drop candy. Repeat with the remaining dough.

6. Spray cake pop wells with baking spray. Place a bun in each well.

7. Bake for 4 to 6 minutes or until golden. Transfer baos to a wire rack set over a sheet of foil or waxed paper. Dust generously with confectioners' sugar.

8. Repeat steps 6 and 7 with the remaining buns.

If Baking in the Rotating Cake Pop Maker

In step 7, bake for 1 minute. Rotate and bake for 2 to 3 minutes. Rotate back before testing for doneness. Continue with step 7.

Apple Fritters

Makes 22
to 24 fritters

We both grew up going to an "apple restaurant" for special occasions. The restaurant is long gone, but we still enjoy reminiscing about its famous fritters. These miniature versions brought us back to our roots.

Variation

Omit the confectioners' (icing) sugar and drizzle the fritters with Powdered Sugar Glaze (page 106).

1½ cups	all-purpose flour	375 mL
¼ cup	granulated sugar	60 mL
1 tsp	baking powder	5 mL
¼ tsp	salt	1 mL
1	large egg, at room temperature	1
½ cup	milk	125 mL
2 tbsp	unsalted butter, melted	30 mL
2 tbsp	orange juice	30 mL
½ tsp	vanilla extract	2 mL
½ cup	finely chopped peeled tart apples (such as Granny Smith)	125 mL
	Nonstick baking spray	
⅓ cup	confectioners' (icing) sugar	75 mL

1. In a medium bowl, whisk together flour, sugar, baking powder and salt. Set aside.

2. In a small bowl, whisk together egg, milk, butter, orange juice and vanilla. Stir into flour mixture until blended. Fold in apples.

3. Spray cake pop wells with baking spray. Fill each well with about 1 tbsp (15 mL) batter.

4. Bake for 4 to 6 minutes or until a tester inserted in the center comes out clean. Transfer fritters to a wire rack to cool slightly.

5. Repeat steps 3 and 4 with the remaining batter.

6. While still warm, roll fritters in confectioners' sugar. Serve warm.

If Baking in the Rotating Cake Pop Maker

In step 4, bake for 1 minute. Rotate and bake for 2 to 3 minutes. Rotate back before testing for doneness. Continue with step 4.

Short John Bites

Makes 32 to 38 bites

What a fun name for these wonderful little bites! Just like traditional Long Johns, these bites are made of pâte à choux.

Tips

It important not to overfill the cake pop wells, as pâte à choux puffs during baking.

Like your Long Johns filled? Slit the baked Short Johns and fill with Vanilla Custard Filling (page 112), then drizzle the tops of the Short Johns with glaze. If desired, use the tip of a knife to gently spread the glaze over the top.

1 cup	water	250 mL
6 tbsp	unsalted butter, cut into pieces	90 mL
¼ tsp	salt	1 mL
1 cup	all-purpose flour	250 mL
3	large eggs, at room temperature	3
	Chocolate Glaze (page 104)	

1. In a medium saucepan, combine water, butter and salt. Bring to a boil over medium-high heat. Reduce heat to medium and, using a wooden spoon, stir in flour; cook, stirring, for 3 minutes.

2. Transfer batter to a medium bowl and stir for 1 minute to cool. Using an electric mixer on medium-high speed, beat in eggs, one at a time, beating well and scraping the sides of the bowl after each addition.

3. Spoon about 2 tsp (10 mL) batter into each cake pop well. *Do not overfill:* it is crucial to allow enough room for the dough to expand.

4. Bake for 10 to 12 minutes or until golden brown and crispy. Do not open before the minimum baking time has elapsed. Transfer bites to a wire rack set over a sheet of foil or waxed paper to cool.

5. Repeat steps 3 and 4 with the remaining batter.

6. Using the fork tool, dip each bite in Chocolate Glaze, allowing excess glaze to drip back into the bowl. Return bites to the rack to set.

If Baking in the Rotating Cake Pop Maker

In step 4, bake for 4 minutes. Rotate and bake for 6 to 7 minutes. Rotate back before testing for doneness. Do not open before the minimum baking time has elapsed. Continue with step 4.

Glazes and Sauces

Cream Cheese Coating

While this coating is not as sweet as melted candy coating wafers, it is firmer than a glaze (though it's still not strong enough to attach a stick securely).

1	container (16 oz/454 g) cream cheese frosting	1
⅓ cup	vanilla baking chips	75 mL

1. Place frosting in a small microwave-safe glass bowl. Microwave on High for 1 minute. Stir well. Stir in baking chips and microwave on High for 1 minute. Stir well. Let stand for 2 to 3 minutes, then stir until chips are completely melted. If necessary, microwave on High for an additional 10 to 15 seconds to melt chips, then stir until smooth.

Variation
This recipe works with any canned frosting flavor. If using chocolate, substitute semisweet chocolate chips for the vanilla baking chips.

Poured Fondant Glaze

This glaze flows on warm and dries to a pretty sheen.

Tips
One cup (250 mL) of this glaze will coat about 24 cake pops.

Keep the glaze warm while coating cake pops. If it cools, it will get too thick.

Tint the glaze any color you like by adding a few drops of food coloring.

2½ cups	confectioners' (icing) sugar	625 mL
¼ cup	water	60 mL
1 tbsp	light (white) corn syrup	15 mL
1 tsp	vanilla extract	5 mL

1. In the top of a double boiler, over simmering water, combine sugar, water and corn syrup. Heat, stirring frequently, for 6 to 7 minutes or until warm and smooth. Stir in vanilla.

Chocolate Glaze

This glaze is a wonderful coating for chocolate doughnuts and cake pops.

Tip

This glaze is gluten-free. Just read the labels on all of the ingredients, especially the confectioners' (icing) sugar, to make sure they were processed in a plant that is gluten-free.

¼ cup	unsalted butter	60 mL
3 tbsp	milk	45 mL
2 tsp	light (white or golden) corn syrup	10 mL
2 oz	semisweet chocolate, finely chopped	60 g
1 tsp	vanilla extract	5 mL
1 cup	confectioners' (icing) sugar	250 mL

1. In a small saucepan, combine butter, milk and corn syrup. Bring to a simmer over medium heat. Remove from heat and stir in chocolate until smooth. Whisk in vanilla. Whisk in sugar.

2. If using glaze as a dip for the top halves of cake pops, let stand for 20 minutes. If fully coating the cake pops, use immediately.

> **Variation**
>
> *Vegan Chocolate Glaze:* Substitute dairy-free chocolate chips and use unsweetened (plain) almond milk. In place of the butter, use ¼ cup (60 mL) hard vegan margarine.

Lemon Glaze

This glaze is perfect for Lemon Poppy Seed Cake Pops (page 38) and numerous other cake pops, doughnuts and desserts.

1 cup	confectioners' (icing) sugar	250 mL
2 tbsp	unsalted butter, melted	30 mL
1½ tbsp	freshly squeezed lemon juice	22 mL

1. In a small bowl, whisk together sugar, butter and lemon juice until smooth.

Orange Glaze

This sweet glaze captures the fresh taste of oranges. We drizzle it on Cranberry Nut Spice Cake Pops (page 67), Vegan Carrot Cake Pops (page 71) and Orange Pecan Scones (page 140).

Tip

This glaze is gluten-free and vegan as long as the confectioners' sugar is gluten-free. Be sure to read the label.

1 cup	confectioners' (icing) sugar	250 mL
2 to 2½ tbsp	orange juice	30 to 37 mL

1. In a small bowl, whisk together sugar and 2 tbsp (30 mL) orange juice. If a thinner glaze is desired, whisk in the remaining orange juice.

Strawberry Glaze

Pink and so inviting, this glaze is great on strawberry doughnuts or cake pops.

Tip

For easy drizzling, fill a sealable food storage bag or disposable pastry bag with glaze, then snip off the corner.

1 cup	confectioners' (icing) sugar	250 mL
2 tbsp	strawberry-flavored milk	30 mL
½ tsp	strawberry extract	2 mL
3 to 5	drops red food coloring	3 to 5

1. In a small bowl, whisk together sugar, 1 tbsp (15 mL) milk and strawberry extract. Stir in enough red food coloring to tint to the desired shade of pink. If a thinner glaze is desired, whisk in the remaining milk.

Tip

If you don't have strawberry-flavored milk, use 1 tbsp (15 mL) regular milk and increase the strawberry extract to 1 tsp (5 mL). Tint pink with food coloring. If a thinner glaze is desired, whisk in more milk, 1 tsp (5 mL) at a time.

Cream Cheese Glaze

Makes about ¾ cup (175 mL)

The tangy, creamy flavor of the classic frosting is captured in a glaze that is perfect for all kinds of treats.

Tip

You can halve this recipe if using it to glaze smaller amounts of cake pops.

2 oz	cream cheese, softened	60 g
2 tsp	unsalted butter, softened	10 mL
1 cup	confectioners' (icing) sugar	250 mL
1 tbsp	milk	15 mL
½ tsp	vanilla extract	2 mL

1. In a small bowl, using an electric mixer on medium speed, beat cream cheese and butter until blended. Reduce mixer speed to low and beat in sugar, milk and vanilla until smooth.

Variation

Vegan Cream Cheese Glaze: Use soy-based dairy-free cream cheese alternative, hard vegan margarine and unsweetened (plain) almond milk.

Powdered Sugar Glaze

Makes about 2 tbsp (30 mL)

This recipe makes just a tiny bit of sweet glaze to drizzle over doughnuts or warm scones. We also love it on Marshmallow Puffs (page 83).

Tip

This recipe can be cut in half if you wish to add just a touch of sweet topping to a smaller recipe. If making a larger batch of doughnuts or cake pops, double the recipe.

½ cup	confectioners' (icing) sugar	125 mL
2 to 4 tsp	milk	10 to 20 mL
½ tsp	vanilla extract	2 mL

1. In a small bowl, whisk together sugar, 2 tsp (10 mL) of the milk and vanilla. Whisk in more milk as needed, 1 tsp (5 mL) at a time, until glaze is the perfect drizzling consistency.

Variations

Almond Glaze: Substitute almond extract for the vanilla.

Amaretto Glaze: Substitute amaretto for the milk.

Maple Glaze: Substitute maple extract for the vanilla.

Vegan Powdered Sugar Glaze: Substitute unsweetened (plain) almond milk for the milk.

Brown Sugar Drizzle

This sweet little drizzle adds the perfect final touch to any scones, muffins or biscuits.

Tips

If a thinner consistency is desired, add more cream or milk, a little bit at a time.

You can halve this recipe if using it to glaze smaller amounts of treats.

2 tbsp	heavy or whipping (35%) cream or milk	30 mL
1 tbsp	unsalted butter	15 mL
¼ cup	packed brown sugar	60 mL
¾ cup	confectioners' (icing) sugar	175 mL

1. In a small saucepan, combine cream and butter. Heat over medium-high heat until butter is melted. Remove from heat and whisk in brown sugar until dissolved. Whisk in confectioners' sugar until smooth.

Brown Sugar Bourbon Dip

This recipe is guaranteed to become a favorite. Try pairing it with Bourbon-Glazed Biscuit and Ham Bites (page 159).

Tips

For a tasty dessert, place a few Brown Sugar Spice Cake Pops (page 32) in a dessert dish and drizzle with this dip.

Brown Sugar Bourbon Dip also makes a great ice cream sauce.

½ cup	unsalted butter	125 mL
1 cup	packed brown sugar	250 mL
¼ cup	water	60 mL
2 tbsp	bourbon	30 mL

1. In a small saucepan, melt butter over medium heat. Stir in brown sugar, water and bourbon; bring to a boil. Reduce heat and simmer, stirring often, for 10 minutes. Remove from heat and let cool for about 15 minutes to thicken slightly. Serve warm.

Variation
Add ¼ cup (60 mL) toasted pecan pieces to make an excellent dip for fruit.

White Chocolate Dip

Makes about 1 cup (250 mL)

This dip pairs perfectly with Kahlúa Fudge Cake Pops (page 56), but is just as tasty with any favorite chocolate cake pops.

Variation

Substitute brewed coffee for the Kahlúa.

½ cup	granulated sugar	125 mL
2 tbsp	cornstarch	30 mL
⅓ cup	water	75 mL
2 tbsp	Kahlúa or other coffee liqueur	30 mL
3 oz	white chocolate, chopped	90 g
1 tbsp	unsalted butter	15 mL

1. In a small saucepan, combine sugar and cornstarch. Stir in water and Kahlúa. Heat over medium heat, stirring constantly, until mixture bubbles and thickens. Remove from heat and stir in white chocolate and butter until melted and smooth. Serve warm.

Mocha Fondue

Makes about 2¾ cups (650 mL)

"F-o-n-d-u-e" spells fun. Serve this mocha-infused chocolate fondue with Favorite White Cake Pops (page 26) or Cappuccino Bites (page 61).

Tip

If you prefer, you can substitute milk chocolate chips for the semisweet.

2 tsp	instant espresso powder	10 mL
2 tbsp	hot water	30 mL
½ cup	confectioners' (icing) sugar	125 mL
2 tbsp	all-purpose flour	30 mL
2 cups	half-and-half (10%) cream	500 mL
1 tsp	vanilla extract	5 mL
1 cup	semisweet chocolate chips	250 mL

1. In a small cup, dissolve espresso powder in hot water. Set aside.

2. In a medium saucepan, whisk together sugar and flour. Whisk in espresso mixture and cream. Bring to a simmer over medium heat, whisking constantly. Reduce heat and simmer, stirring occasionally, for 5 minutes.

3. Place chocolate chips in a medium bowl. Stir in espresso mixture until smooth. Transfer to a fondue pot and keep warm.

Cider Sauce

Makes about 2 cups (500 mL)

Warm apple cider sauce is a perfect match for Apple Cider Donuts (page 96) or Apple Fritters (page 100).

Variation

Gluten-Free Cider Sauce: Substitute 1½ tsp (7 mL) cornstarch for the flour.

⅓ cup	granulated sugar	75 mL
⅓ cup	packed brown sugar	75 mL
1 tbsp	all-purpose flour	15 mL
½ tsp	ground cinnamon	2 mL
1½ cups	unsweetened apple cider	375 mL
1 tbsp	freshly squeezed lemon juice	15 mL
2 tbsp	unsalted butter	30 mL

1. In a medium saucepan, combine granulated sugar, brown sugar, flour and cinnamon. Stir in cider and lemon juice. Bring to a boil over medium-high heat, stirring constantly. Boil, stirring constantly, for 1 minute. Remove from heat and whisk in butter. Let cool for 10 minutes. Serve warm.

Brandy Cream Sauce

Makes about 1 cup (250 mL)

Brown sugar, butter, cream and apricot brandy — this dessert sauce is sure to become an all-time favorite.

3 tbsp	unsalted butter	45 mL
¾ cup	packed brown sugar	175 mL
Pinch	salt	Pinch
6 tbsp	heavy or whipping (35%) cream	90 mL
3 tbsp	apricot brandy or brandy	45 mL
½ tsp	vanilla extract	2 mL

1. In a small saucepan, melt butter over medium heat. Stir in brown sugar and salt; cook, stirring frequently, for 3 minutes or until brown sugar is dissolved. Stir in cream and brandy; cook, stirring, for 1 minute. Remove from heat and stir in vanilla. Serve warm.

Variation

Substitute another flavor of brandy, such as peach, or try a liqueur, such as caramel or coffee liqueur.

Hot Fudge Sauce

Makes about 2 cups (500 mL)

This sauce makes any dessert decadent. Serve it as a dip with just about any flavor of cake pops or doughnuts. For a flavor explosion, layer cake pops, ice cream and hot fudge sauce in a parfait glass.

4 oz	unsweetened chocolate, coarsely chopped	125 g
2 tbsp	unsalted butter	30 mL
1/4 tsp	instant espresso powder (optional)	1 mL
1 cup	granulated sugar	250 mL
1/2 cup	half-and-half (10%) cream	125 mL
1 tsp	vanilla extract	5 mL

1. Place chocolate and butter in a medium microwave-safe glass bowl. Microwave on High in 30-second intervals, stirring after each, until melted and smooth.

2. Stir in espresso powder (if using). Stir in sugar and cream. Microwave on High for 3 minutes, stirring halfway through, until sugar is dissolved and sauce is thickened. Stir in vanilla. Serve hot.

Tip

Store leftover sauce in an airtight container in the refrigerator for up to 1 week. Reheat in the microwave for 1 to 2 minutes on High, stirring halfway through.

Hot Caramel Pecan Sauce

Makes about 1 1/2 cups (375 mL)

This sauce has become a favorite among Kathy's family and friends, and it's sure to be a hit with yours, too!

Variation

Hot Caramel Sauce: Omit the pecans.

1/4 cup	unsalted butter	60 mL
1 cup	packed brown sugar	250 mL
1/2 cup	chopped pecans	125 mL
1/2 cup	whipping or heavy (35%) cream	125 mL
1 tsp	vanilla extract	5 mL

1. In a small saucepan, melt butter over medium heat. Stir in brown sugar and cook, stirring often, for 5 to 7 minutes or until sugar is dissolved. Stir in pecans and cook, stirring constantly, for 1 minute. Stir in cream and cook, stirring constantly, until mixture comes to a full boil. Remove from heat and stir in vanilla. Serve hot.

Honey Syrup

Makes
about ⅔ cup
(150 mL)

We made this warm spiced syrup one day and loved it on Baked Sopaipillas (page 86). We then realized it would also be super on any biscuits, scones, muffins or pancake bites.

½ cup	liquid honey	125 mL
⅓ cup	water	75 mL
1	2-inch (5 cm) cinnamon stick	1

1. In a small saucepan, combine honey, water and cinnamon stick. Bring to a simmer over medium heat. Reduce heat and simmer, stirring occasionally, for 15 minutes. Discard cinnamon stick. Serve warm.

Tip

For this recipe, choose liquid honey, not a whipped or honeycomb variety. Clover and orange blossom honeys are readily available, but if you want to vary the flavor of the sauce slightly, look for local honey at gourmet or natural food stores or farmers' markets.

Blueberry Maple Syrup

Makes
about ¾ cup
(175 mL)

The combination of blueberries and maple syrup creates a fantastic sauce that works with many different desserts.

Tip
The flavor of pure maple syrup is absolutely wonderful with fresh berries. Once opened, store maple syrup in the refrigerator for up to 1 year.

¾ cup	fresh blueberries (or frozen blueberries, thawed and drained)	175 mL
¼ cup	pure maple syrup	60 mL
1 tsp	freshly squeezed lemon juice	5 mL

1. In a small saucepan, combine blueberries and maple syrup. Bring to a simmer over medium heat. Reduce heat and simmer for 2 minutes. Remove from heat and stir in lemon juice. Serve warm.

Vanilla Custard Filling

Makes about 1 ¼ cups (300 mL)

Here it is: the perfect filling for a variety of cake pops.

Tip

Use a pastry bag fitted with a medium plain round tip to inject filling into a cake pop. Or split a cake pop in half and spoon a little filling between the halves.

⅓ cup	granulated sugar	75 mL
1 tbsp	cornstarch	15 mL
1 tbsp	all-purpose flour	15 mL
Pinch	salt	Pinch
2	large egg yolks, at room temperature	2
1 cup	milk	250 mL
1 tbsp	unsalted butter	15 mL
1 tsp	vanilla extract	5 mL

1. In a medium saucepan, whisk together sugar, cornstarch, flour and salt.

2. In a small bowl, whisk together egg yolks and milk. Whisk into flour mixture. Heat over medium heat, stirring frequently, for 5 to 10 minutes or until mixture thickens and begins to boil. Remove from heat and stir in butter and vanilla until smooth. Let cool.

3. If not using custard immediately, transfer to an airtight container and press a piece of plastic wrap on the surface to prevent a skin from forming. Refrigerate until ready to use, for up to 1 day.

Cinnamon Sugar Topping

Makes about ⅓ cup (75 mL)

This old-fashioned, comforting topping is perfect for doughnuts, cake pops, scones and muffins.

⅓ cup	granulated sugar	75 mL
1 tbsp	ground cinnamon	15 mL

1. In a small bowl, whisk together sugar and cinnamon until evenly combined.

Tips

Adjust the amount of cinnamon up or down depending on how much you like it.

Be sure to coat treats with this topping while they're hot.

Treats coated in cinnamon sugar are best served the day they are made.

Part 3

Mealtime Sidekicks

Breakfast Bites

French Toast Bites

Makes about 30 bites

No time to escape to a bed-and-breakfast for a weekend getaway? Prepare these sweet delicacies and enjoy breakfast in bed.

Tips

Roxanne likes to add a pinch of nutmeg along with the cinnamon.

The dimensions of artisan bread vary. We used a loaf about 7½ by 4 inches (19 by 10 cm), but the bread you use may be quite different. Adjust the number of slices as needed to make thirty 1-inch (2.5 cm) bread cubes.

• Preheat oven to 200°F (100°C)

2	slices artisan or country bread (about 1½ inches/4 cm thick)	2
3	large eggs, at room temperature	3
½ tsp	ground cinnamon	2 mL
½ cup	milk	125 mL
1 tsp	vanilla extract	5 mL
	Nonstick baking spray	
1 tbsp	confectioners' (icing) sugar	15 mL
	Pure maple syrup or pancake syrup, warmed	

1. Trim crusts from bread and cut bread into 1-inch (2.5 cm) cubes.

2. In a medium bowl, whisk eggs until blended. Whisk in cinnamon, milk and vanilla until blended.

3. Add 12 of the bread cubes and stir to saturate with egg mixture.

4. Spray cake pop wells with baking spray. Using the fork tool, lift each bread cube from the milk mixture, allowing excess liquid to drain off. Place a bread cube in each cake pop well.

5. Bake for 3 to 4 minutes. Carefully place the fork tool between each bread cube and the edge of the well and gently turn the cube over. Bake for 2 to 3 minutes or until golden. Transfer to an ovenproof plate or pie plate and keep warm in preheated oven.

6. Repeat steps 3 to 5 with the remaining bread cubes and egg mixture.

7. Sprinkle bites with confectioners' sugar. Serve with warm maple or pancake syrup.

If Baking in the Rotating Cake Pop Maker

In step 5, bake for 1 minute. Rotate and bake for 2 to 3 minutes. Rotate back before testing for doneness. Continue with step 5.

Lemon Pancake Bites with Blueberry Maple Syrup

Makes 32 to 34 pancakes

Light and tender, with a delightful, light lemon flavor, these pancakes make breakfast special any time of year. Add the blueberry maple syrup, and they're especially perfect for a spring morning.

Tips

For a more intense lemon flavor, add ¼ tsp (1 mL) lemon extract to the batter along with the lemon juice.

Sometimes, we prefer to turn the pancakes for more even browning. If your cake pop maker doesn't rotate, bake the pancakes for 3 minutes. Carefully place the fork tool between each pancake and the edge of the well and gently turn the pancake over. Bake for 1 to 2 minutes or until golden.

1 cup	all-purpose flour	250 mL
¾ tsp	baking powder	3 mL
¾ tsp	baking soda	3 mL
¼ tsp	salt	1 mL
¾ cup	milk	175 mL
	Grated zest of 1 lemon	
3 tbsp	freshly squeezed lemon juice	45 mL
1	large egg, at room temperature	1
4 tbsp	unsalted butter, melted, divided	60 mL
	Blueberry Maple Syrup (page 111)	

1. In a medium bowl, whisk together flour, baking powder, baking soda and salt. Set aside.

2. In a small bowl, whisk together milk, lemon zest and lemon juice. Whisk in egg and half the butter. Stir into flour mixture until just blended.

3. Brush cake pop wells with the remaining butter. Fill each well with 1 tbsp (15 mL) batter.

4. Bake for 4 to 6 minutes or until a tester inserted in the center comes out clean. Transfer pancakes to a wire rack to cool slightly.

5. Repeat steps 3 and 4 with the remaining batter.

6. Serve warm, with Blueberry Maple Syrup.

If Baking in the Rotating Cake Pop Maker

In step 4, bake for 1 minute. Rotate and bake for 2 to 3 minutes. Rotate back before testing for doneness. Continue with step 4.

Banana Pancake Bites

These flavorful pancake bites will call your family to the table. Serve them with maple syrup or, for a tasty change of pace, try peanut butter syrup (see tip, below).

Tips

No buttermilk on hand? Place 1½ tsp (7 mL) lemon juice or white vinegar in a glass measuring cup, then pour in enough milk to equal ½ cup (125 mL). Let stand for 5 to 10 minutes to thicken. Proceed with the recipe. (See page 15 for other buttermilk substitutions.)

To make peanut butter syrup, in a small microwave-safe glass bowl, combine ¼ cup (60 mL) pure maple syrup and 2 tbsp (30 mL) peanut butter. Microwave on High for 30 seconds. Stir. Microwave on High for 10 to 20 seconds or until peanut butter is melted. Serve drizzled over pancake bites.

1 cup	all-purpose flour	250 mL
2 tsp	baking powder	10 mL
½ tsp	baking soda	2 mL
¼ tsp	salt	1 mL
1	ripe banana	1
1 tbsp	packed brown sugar	15 mL
1	large egg, at room temperature	1
½ cup	buttermilk	125 mL
1 tbsp	unsalted butter, melted	15 mL
½ tsp	vanilla extract	2 mL
¼ cup	chopped walnuts, toasted (see tip, page 136)	60 mL
	Nonstick baking spray	

1. In a medium bowl, whisk together flour, baking powder, baking soda and salt. Set aside.

2. In a small bowl, mash banana with a fork. Whisk in brown sugar, egg, buttermilk, butter and vanilla. Stir into flour mixture until just blended. Stir in walnuts.

3. Spray cake pop wells with baking spray. Fill each well with about 1 tbsp (15 mL) batter.

4. Bake for 4 to 6 minutes or until a tester inserted in the center comes out clean. Transfer pancakes to a wire rack to cool slightly.

5. Repeat steps 3 and 4 with the remaining batter. Serve warm.

If Baking in the Rotating Cake Pop Maker

In step 4, bake for 1 minute. Rotate and bake for 2 to 3 minutes. Rotate back before testing for doneness. Continue with step 4.

Pumpkin Pancake Bites with Cinnamon Honey Butter

Makes 41 to 43 pancakes

These are the perfect breakfast treats for a crisp fall morning.

Tips

Leftover canned pumpkin purée? Refrigerate it in an airtight container for up to 1 week, or freeze it for up to 3 months. To use from frozen, thaw pumpkin overnight in the refrigerator, then stir well and use it to bake another batch of cake pops.

Serve leftover Cinnamon Honey Butter with any pancakes, biscuits or scones

1¼ cups	all-purpose flour	300 mL
2 tsp	baking powder	10 mL
1 tsp	pumpkin pie spice	5 mL
¼ tsp	salt	1 mL
2 tbsp	packed brown sugar	30 mL
1	large egg, at room temperature	1
1 cup	milk	250 mL
⅓ cup	pumpkin purée (not pie filling)	75 mL
2 tbsp	unsalted butter, melted	30 mL
	Nonstick baking spray	

Cinnamon Honey Butter

½ cup	butter, softened	125 mL
¼ cup	liquid honey	60 mL
½ tsp	ground cinnamon	2 mL

1. In a large bowl, whisk together flour, baking powder, pumpkin pie spice and salt. Set aside.

2. In a medium bowl, whisk together brown sugar, egg, milk, pumpkin and butter. Stir into flour mixture until just blended.

3. Spray cake pop wells with baking spray. Fill each well with about 1 tbsp (15 mL) batter.

4. Bake for 4 to 6 minutes or until a tester inserted in the center comes out clean. Transfer pancakes to a wire rack to cool slightly.

5. Repeat steps 3 and 4 with the remaining batter.

6. *Cinnamon Honey Butter:* Meanwhile, in a small bowl, using an electric mixer on medium speed, beat butter, honey and cinnamon until fluffy.

7. Serve pancakes warm, with Cinnamon Honey Butter.

If Baking in the Rotating Cake Pop Maker

In step 4, bake for 1 minute. Rotate and bake for 2 to 3 minutes. Rotate back before testing for doneness. Continue with step 4.

Butter Pecan Pancakes with Caramel Apple Sauce

The caramel apple sauce is a wonderful topping for these yummy pancakes, but they are also great with purchased butter pecan syrup.

Tip

No buttermilk on hand? Place 1 tbsp (15 mL) lemon juice or white vinegar in a glass measuring cup, then pour in enough milk to equal 1 cup (250 mL). Let stand for 5 to 10 minutes to thicken. Proceed with the recipe. (See page 15 for other buttermilk substitutions.)

If Baking in the Rotating Cake Pop Maker

In step 4, bake for 1 minute. Rotate and bake for 2 to 3 minutes. Rotate back before testing for doneness. Continue with step 4.

1 cup	all-purpose flour	250 mL
2 tsp	baking powder	10 mL
1/2 tsp	baking soda	2 mL
1/4 tsp	salt	1 mL
2 tsp	granulated sugar	10 mL
1	large egg, at room temperature	1
1 cup	buttermilk	250 mL
2 tbsp	unsalted butter, melted	30 mL
1/2 cup	chopped pecans, toasted (see tip, page 72)	125 mL
	Nonstick baking spray	

Caramel Apple Sauce

2 tbsp	unsalted butter	30 mL
1	tart apple, peeled and chopped	1
1/2 cup	caramel syrup	125 mL

1. In a medium bowl, whisk together flour, baking powder, baking soda and salt. Set aside.

2. In a small bowl, whisk together sugar, egg, buttermilk and butter. Stir into flour mixture until just moistened. Stir in pecans.

3. Spray cake pop wells with baking spray. Fill each well with about 1 tbsp (15 mL) batter.

4. Bake for 4 to 6 minutes or until a tester inserted in the center comes out clean. Transfer pancakes to a wire rack to cool slightly.

5. Repeat steps 3 and 4 with the remaining batter.

6. *Caramel Apple Sauce:* Meanwhile, in a small saucepan, melt butter over medium heat. Add apples and cook, stirring often, for about 5 minutes or until tender. Stir in caramel syrup and cook, stirring often, for 1 minute or until hot.

7. Serve pancakes warm, topped with warm sauce.

Bacon Pancake Bites

**Makes 28
to 30 pancakes**

Salty bacon and
sweet maple syrup
combine to make this a
winning breakfast dish
any time of year.

Tip

No buttermilk on hand?
Place 1 tbsp (15 mL) lemon
juice or white vinegar in a
glass measuring cup, then
pour in enough milk to
equal 1 cup (250 mL). Let
stand for 5 to 10 minutes
to thicken. Proceed with
the recipe. (See page 15
for other buttermilk
substitutions.)

1 cup	all-purpose flour	250 mL
1/2 tsp	baking powder	2 mL
1/2 tsp	baking soda	2 mL
1/4 tsp	salt	1 mL
2	slices bacon, cooked crisp and crumbled	2
1	large egg, at room temperature	1
1 cup	buttermilk	250 mL
2 tbsp	melted butter	30 mL
1/2 tsp	maple extract	2 mL
	Nonstick baking spray	
	Pure maple syrup or pancake syrup	

1. In a medium bowl, whisk together flour, baking powder, baking soda and salt. Add bacon and toss to coat evenly. Set aside.

2. In a small bowl, whisk together egg, buttermilk, butter and maple extract. Stir into flour mixture until just moistened.

3. Spray cake pop wells with baking spray. Fill each well with about 1 tbsp (15 mL) batter.

4. Bake for 4 to 6 minutes or until a tester inserted in the center comes out clean. Transfer pancakes to a wire rack to cool slightly.

5. Repeat steps 3 and 4 with the remaining batter.

6. Serve pancakes warm, with maple syrup.

If Baking in the Rotating Cake Pop Maker

In step 4, bake for 1 minute. Rotate and bake for 2 to 3 minutes. Rotate back before testing for doneness. Continue with step 4.

Gingerbread Ebelskivers

Makes 22 to 24 ebelskivers

Ebelskivers are light, round Danish pancakes. Kathy is a big fan of all things gingerbread, and these ebelskivers capture that wonderful spicy molasses flavor.

Tips

No paper bag? Place the confectioners' sugar in a small bowl and use a spoon to gently coat the ebelskivers.

Molasses comes from boiling the juice that is extracted from processing sugar beets or cane into sugar. Light (fancy) and dark (cooking) molasses can be used interchangeably in this recipe, but dark molasses gives the ebelskivers a more robust flavor. Unsulfured molasses (no sulfur was used in the processing) is preferred, as the flavor is lighter.

1 cup	all-purpose flour	250 mL
2 tbsp	granulated sugar	30 mL
2 tsp	baking powder	10 mL
1 tsp	ground ginger	5 mL
1 tsp	ground cinnamon	5 mL
1/4 tsp	salt	1 mL
1	large egg, at room temperature	1
1/2 cup	milk	125 mL
2 tbsp	unsulfured dark (cooking) molasses	30 mL
2 tbsp	unsalted butter, melted	30 mL
1 tsp	vanilla extract	5 mL
	Nonstick baking spray	
1 to 1½ cups	confectioners' (icing) sugar	250 to 375 mL

1. In a medium bowl, whisk together flour, sugar, baking powder, ginger, cinnamon and salt. Set aside.

2. In a small bowl, whisk together egg, milk, molasses, butter and vanilla. Stir into flour mixture until blended.

3. Spray cake pop wells with baking spray. Fill each well with about 1 tbsp (15 mL) batter.

4. Bake for 3 to 5 minutes or until golden brown and crisp.

5. Place confectioners' sugar in a paper bag (see tip, at left). Add hot ebelskivers and gently toss to generously coat with sugar. Transfer ebelskivers to a wire rack to cool slightly.

6. Repeat steps 3 to 5 with the remaining batter. Serve warm.

If Baking in the Rotating Cake Pop Maker

In step 4, bake for 1 minute. Rotate and bake for 1 to 2 minutes. Rotate back before testing for doneness as in step 4.

Orange Ebelskivers

This time, we added a light orange flavor to the ebelskivers. They're the perfect way to say good morning to your family.

Tips

No paper bag? Place the confectioners' sugar and orange zest in a small bowl and use a spoon to gently coat the ebelskivers.

Ebelskivers are especially good when served warm. They are puffed and rounded, but very delicate. They are not firm enough to put on cake pop sticks and may actually deflate a bit when cooling. A slightly irregular shape is to be expected.

Omit the confectioners' sugar coating and marmalade and instead drizzle the warm ebelskivers with Orange Glaze (page 105).

1 cup	all-purpose flour	250 mL
2 tbsp	granulated sugar	30 mL
2 tsp	baking powder	10 mL
½ tsp	baking soda	5 mL
¼ tsp	salt	1 mL
1	large egg, at room temperature	1
⅔ cup	milk	150 mL
2 tsp	grated orange zest, divided	10 mL
2 tbsp	freshly squeezed orange juice	30 mL
2 tbsp	unsalted butter, melted	30 mL
½ tsp	vanilla extract	2 mL
	Nonstick baking spray	
½ cup	confectioners' (icing) sugar	125 mL
	Orange marmalade	

1. In a medium bowl, whisk together flour, sugar, baking powder, baking soda and salt. Set aside.

2. In a small bowl, whisk together egg, milk, 1 tsp (5 mL) of the orange zest, orange juice, butter and vanilla. Stir into flour mixture until blended.

3. Spray cake pops wells with baking spray. Fill each well with about 1 tbsp (15 mL) batter.

4. Bake for 3 to 5 minutes or until golden brown and crisp.

5. Place confectioners' sugar in a paper bag (see tip, at left) and add the remaining orange zest. Add hot ebelskivers and gently toss to generously coat with sugar. Transfer ebelskivers to a wire rack to cool slightly.

6. Repeat steps 3 to 5 with the remaining batter.

7. Serve ebelskivers warm, with orange marmalade.

If Baking in the Rotating Cake Pop Maker

In step 4, bake for 1 minute. Rotate and bake for 1 to 2 minutes. Rotate back before testing for doneness as in step 4.

Sticky Rolls

Makes 34
to 36 rolls

Warm sticky rolls, dripping with caramel sauce, make any breakfast or brunch finger-licking good.

Tip

For a quick alternative, thaw nine 38-gram frozen bread rolls according to package directions. Cut each roll into quarters and shape into rounds. Brush cake pop wells with melted butter. Place one roll in each well. Bake for 4 to 5 minutes or until brown (if using the rotating cake pop maker, bake as directed at right). Continue with step 7.

1¾ cups	all-purpose flour	425 mL
2 tbsp	granulated sugar	30 mL
1 tsp	ground cinnamon	5 mL
¾ tsp	salt	3 mL
1	package (¼ oz/7 g) quick-rising (instant) yeast	1
½ cup	milk	125 mL
¼ cup	water	60 mL
3 tbsp	unsalted butter, softened	45 mL
1	large egg, at room temperature	1
2 tbsp	unsalted butter, melted	30 mL
	Hot Caramel Pecan Sauce (page 110)	

1. In a large bowl, whisk together flour, sugar, cinnamon, salt and yeast. Set aside.

2. In a small microwave-safe glass bowl, combine milk, water and softened butter. Microwave on High for 20 to 30 seconds or until warm (butter does not need to be melted).

3. Pour milk mixture into flour mixture and add egg. Using an electric mixer on medium speed, beat for 2 minutes. Cover bowl with a towel and let dough rise in a warm, draft-free place for 30 minutes.

4. Brush cake pop wells with melted butter. Drop about 1½ tsp (7 mL) dough into each well, filling it half to three-quarters full. Quickly and lightly brush the tops of the dough with melted butter.

5. Bake for 5 to 6 minutes or until golden brown and crisp. Transfer rolls to a wire rack to cool slightly.

6. Repeat steps 4 and 5 with the remaining dough.

7. Transfer rolls to a deep serving plate and pour Hot Caramel Pecan Sauce over top. Serve warm.

If Baking in the Rotating Cake Pop Maker

In step 5, bake for 2 minutes. Rotate and bake for 2 to 3 minutes. Rotate back before testing for doneness. Continue with step 5.

Buttermilk Streusel Coffee Cake Bites

Makes 30 to 32 bites

Let's hear it for mini coffee cakes! The next time a friend or neighbor pops by, whip these up and pair them with steaming coffee or cappuccino and a good chat. They're guaranteed to put a smile on your guest's face.

Tip

For optimum enjoyment, serve these mini coffee cakes warm.

If Baking in the Rotating Cake Pop Maker

In step 5, bake for 1 minute. Rotate and bake for 2 to 3 minutes. Rotate back before testing for doneness. Continue with step 5.

1 cup	all-purpose flour	250 mL
1 tsp	baking powder	5 mL
1/2 tsp	baking soda	2 mL
1/4 tsp	salt	1 mL
1/3 cup	granulated sugar	75 mL
2 tbsp	unsalted butter, softened	30 mL
3	large egg whites, at room temperature	3
1/2 cup	buttermilk	125 mL
1 tsp	vanilla extract	5 mL
3 tbsp	packed brown sugar	45 mL
2 tbsp	finely chopped pecans, toasted (see tip, page 72)	30 mL
1/2 tsp	ground cinnamon	2 mL
	Nonstick baking spray	
	Powdered Sugar Glaze (page 106)	

1. In a small bowl, whisk together flour, baking powder, baking soda and salt. Set aside.

2. In a medium bowl, using an electric mixer on medium speed, beat granulated sugar and butter until fluffy. Add egg whites, buttermilk and vanilla and beat for 1 minute. Add flour mixture and beat on low speed just until combined.

3. In a small bowl, stir together brown sugar, pecans and cinnamon. Swirl into batter.

4. Spray cake pop wells with baking spray. Fill each well with about 1 tbsp (15 mL) batter.

5. Bake for 4 to 6 minutes or until a tester inserted in the center comes out clean. Transfer coffee cake bites to a wire rack set over a sheet of foil or waxed paper to cool slightly.

6. Repeat steps 4 and 5 with the remaining batter.

7. Drizzle Powdered Sugar Glaze over warm coffee cake bites.

Muffins and Breads

Chocolate Chip Muffins

Makes 38 to 40 muffins

Roxanne's daughter, Grace, adores chocolate chip muffins. When Roxanne travels out of town on business, Grace can be found in the kitchen preparing these baked bites for her dad to enjoy.

Tip

Because of the chocolate chips in this recipe, a tester inserted into the muffins will not come out clean.

Variation

Instead of the chocolate chips, use ⅔ cup (150 mL) mini semisweet chocolate chips and add ⅓ cup (75 mL) toasted chopped nuts.

1½ cups	all-purpose flour	375 mL
1½ tsp	baking powder	7 mL
¼ tsp	salt	1 mL
¾ cup	granulated sugar	175 mL
6 tbsp	unsalted butter, softened	90 mL
1	large egg, at room temperature	1
1	large egg yolk, at room temperature	1
3 tbsp	milk	45 mL
1 tsp	vanilla extract	5 mL
1 cup	semisweet chocolate chips	250 mL
	Nonstick baking spray	

1. In a medium bowl, whisk together flour, baking powder and salt. Set aside.

2. In a large bowl, using an electric mixer on medium-high speed, beat sugar and butter for 1 minute or until fluffy. Beat in egg and egg yolk, one at a time, beating well after each addition. Beat in vanilla. Add flour mixture alternately with milk, making three additions of flour and two of milk and beating on low speed until smooth. Fold in chocolate chips.

3. Spray cake pop wells with baking spray. Fill each well with about 1 tbsp (15 mL) batter.

4. Bake for 3 to 5 minutes or until golden brown. Transfer muffins to a wire rack to cool.

5. Repeat steps 3 and 4 with the remaining batter.

If Baking in the Rotating Cake Pop Maker

In step 4, bake for 1 minute. Rotate and bake for 2 to 3 minutes. Rotate back before testing for doneness. Continue with step 4.

Chocolate Cherry Muffins

Roxanne's daughter, Grace, makes chocolate chip muffins for the family on the weekends. She perfected this recipe to include maraschino cherries.

Tips

If your package of muffin mix is a different size, use 1⅓ cups (325 mL).

Because of the chocolate chips in the muffin mix, a tester inserted into the muffins will not come out clean.

1	package (6.5 oz/184 g) chocolate chip muffin mix	1
1 tbsp	granulated sugar	15 mL
½ cup	sour cream	125 mL
¼ cup	milk	60 mL
3 tbsp	finely chopped drained maraschino cherries	45 mL
	Nonstick baking spray	

1. In a medium bowl, stir together muffin mix, sugar, sour cream and milk until just combined. Stir in maraschino cherries.

2. Spray cake pop wells with baking spray. Fill each well with about 1 tbsp (15 mL) batter.

3. Bake for 6 to 8 minutes or until golden brown. Transfer muffins to a wire rack to cool.

4. Repeat steps 2 and 3 with the remaining batter.

If Baking in the Rotating Cake Pop Maker

In step 3, bake for 1 minute. Rotate and bake for 3 to 4 minutes. Rotate back before testing for doneness. Continue with step 3.

Dried Cherry Muffins

Makes 37
to 39 muffins

These muffins complete any brunch and can be made ahead for entertaining ease.

Tip

Toasting almonds intensifies their flavor. Spread chopped almonds in a single layer on a baking sheet. Bake at 350°F (180°C) for 5 to 7 minutes or until lightly browned. Let cool.

Variation

Substitute dried blueberries for the cherries.

1½ cups	all-purpose flour	375 mL
1 cup	granulated sugar	250 mL
½ tsp	baking soda	2 mL
½ tsp	ground cinnamon	2 mL
⅔ cup	dried cherries	150 mL
⅓ cup	chopped almonds, toasted (see tip, at left)	75 mL
1	large egg, at room temperature	1
1	large egg yolk, at room temperature	1
⅔ cup	vanilla-flavored yogurt	150 mL
⅓ cup	vegetable oil	75 mL
	Nonstick baking spray	
	Powdered Sugar Glaze (page 106)	

1. In a large bowl, whisk together flour, sugar, baking soda and cinnamon. Stir in cherries and almonds. Set aside.

2. In a medium bowl, whisk together egg, egg yolk, yogurt and oil. Stir into flour mixture until just combined.

3. Spray cake pop wells with baking spray. Fill each well with about 1 tbsp (15 mL) batter.

4. Bake for 4 to 6 minutes or golden brown. Transfer muffins to a wire rack set over a sheet of foil or waxed paper to cool.

5. Repeat steps 3 and 4 with the remaining batter.

6. Drizzle Powdered Sugar Glaze over cooled muffins.

If Baking in the Rotating Cake Pop Maker

In step 4, bake for 1 minute. Rotate and bake for 2 to 3 minutes. Rotate back before testing for doneness. Continue with step 4.

Gluten-Free, Vegan Blueberry Wild Rice Muffins

Makes 16 to 18 muffins

Luscious little blueberry muffins are a universally popular treat. These mini muffins are low in fat, and no one will guess that they are made with wild rice.

Tip

Wild rice is actually a marsh grass, not a rice. It is packed with protein and adds a great nutty flavor to these muffins. Rinse the wild rice well, then cook according to package directions. Let cool to room temperature, then use in these muffins. Any leftover cooked wild rice can be reheated and served as a side dish, added to a soup or stew, or tossed with your favorite vegetables and a vinaigrette dressing and served as a salad.

1 tbsp	ground flax seeds (flaxseed meal)	15 mL
3 tbsp	hot water	45 mL
¾ cup	gluten-free all-purpose baking mix (see page 13)	175 mL
2 tbsp	cornstarch	30 mL
¾ tsp	gluten-free baking powder	3 mL
⅛ tsp	salt	0.5 mL
¼ cup	unsweetened plain almond milk	60 mL
1 tbsp	unsweetened applesauce	15 mL
¾ tsp	vegetable oil	3 mL
¾ tsp	pure maple syrup	3 mL
¼ cup	cooked wild rice, cooled	60 mL
¼ cup	blueberries	60 mL
	Nonstick baking spray	

1. In a small bowl, combine flax seeds and hot water. Let stand for 10 minutes.

2. In a large bowl, whisk together baking mix, cornstarch, baking powder and salt. Set aside.

3. Whisk almond milk, applesauce, oil and maple syrup into flaxseed mixture. Stir into flour mixture until just moistened. Stir in wild rice and blueberries.

4. Spray cake pop wells with baking spray. Fill each well with about 1 tbsp (15 mL) batter.

5. Bake for 8 to 10 minutes or until a tester inserted in the center comes out clean. Transfer muffins to a wire rack to cool slightly.

6. Repeat steps 4 and 5 with the remaining batter. Serve warm.

If Baking in the Rotating Cake Pop Maker

In step 5, bake for 2 minutes. Rotate and bake for 2 to 3 minutes. Rotate back before testing for doneness. Continue with step 5.

Gluten-Free, Vegan Quinoa Cranberry Muffins

These muffins are a powerhouse of nutrition, packed with protein, antioxidants and lots of flavor!

Tips

Ground flax seeds are quite perishable. The exact storage time varies with the brand, but generally, if stored in an airtight container, they will keep in the refrigerator for 1 to 3 months, or in the freezer for about 6 months. Whole flax seeds will keep for up to 1 year in the refrigerator or freezer, and you can grind just the amount you need with a coffee grinder or food mill.

Quinoa is an ancient grain that is especially high in protein. Most quinoa sold today has been washed well to remove the natural bitter residue on the grain, but it is wise to give it a rinse anyway. Follow the package directions for cooking it.

2 tbsp	ground flax seeds (flaxseed meal)	30 mL
1/3 cup	hot water	75 mL
1/2 cup	gluten-free all-purpose baking mix (see page 13)	125 mL
1/2 cup	quinoa flour	125 mL
1/3 cup	granulated sugar	75 mL
1/2 tsp	baking soda	2 mL
1/2 cup	unsweetened plain almond milk	125 mL
1/4 cup	vegetable oil	60 mL
1/2 cup	cooked quinoa, cooled	125 mL
1/4 cup	sweetened dried cranberries	60 mL
	Nonstick baking spray	

1. In a small bowl, combine flax seeds and hot water. Let stand for 10 minutes.

2. In a small bowl, whisk together baking mix, quinoa flour, sugar and baking soda. Set aside.

3. Add almond milk and oil to flaxseed mixture and, using an electric mixer, beat on low speed until blended. Beat in flour mixture until just moistened. Stir in quinoa and cranberries.

4. Spray cake pop wells with baking spray. Fill each well with about 1 tbsp (15 mL) batter.

5. Bake for 5 to 7 minutes or until a tester inserted in the center comes out clean. Transfer muffins to a wire rack to cool.

6. Repeat steps 4 and 5 with the remaining batter.

If Baking in the Rotating Cake Pop Maker

In step 5, bake for 2 minutes. Rotate and bake for 2 to 3 minutes. Rotate back before testing for doneness. Continue with step 5.

Lemon Muffins

When you want to keep it simple, turn to these lemon muffins. The glaze is an added lemon kiss that you won't want to omit.

Tip

Freshly squeezed lemon juice adds so much flavor, and juicing a lemon takes just moments. One lemon will yield about 3 tbsp (45 mL) juice. Leftover lemon juice can be stored in an airtight container in the refrigerator for up to 5 days or in the freezer for up to 6 months.

Variation

Add 1 tbsp (15 mL) poppy seeds to the batter.

Muffins

1½ cups	pound cake mix	375 mL
1	large egg, at room temperature, lightly beaten	1
½ cup	sour cream	125 mL
1 tsp	grated lemon zest	5 mL
2 tbsp	freshly squeezed lemon juice	30 mL
1 tsp	lemon extract	5 mL
½ tsp	vanilla extract	2 mL
	Nonstick baking spray	

Glaze

¾ cup	confectioners' (icing) sugar	175 mL
1 tbsp	freshly squeezed lemon juice	15 mL

1. *Muffins:* In a medium bowl, stir together cake mix, egg, sour cream, lemon zest, lemon juice, lemon extract and vanilla until well blended.

2. Spray cake pop wells with baking spray. Fill each well with about 1 tbsp (15 mL) batter.

3. Bake for 4 minutes. Carefully place the fork tool between each muffin and the edge of the well and gently turn the muffin over. Bake for 2 to 3 minutes or until a tester inserted in the center comes out clean. Transfer muffins to a wire rack set over a sheet of foil or waxed paper to cool slightly.

4. Repeat steps 2 and 3 with the remaining batter.

5. *Glaze:* In a small bowl, whisk together confectioners' sugar and lemon juice until blended. Drizzle over warm muffins. Serve warm.

If Baking in the Rotating Cake Pop Maker

In step 3, bake for 2 minutes. Rotate and bake for 2 to 3 minutes. Rotate back before testing for doneness. Continue with step 3.

Garlic Cheddar Muffins

Roxanne's mother, Colleen Wyss, is known far and wide for her culinary talent. Colleen often served a version of these muffins with family meals.

Variation

Use your favorite cheese, such as pepper Jack or Monterey Jack, in place of the Cheddar.

¾ cup	all-purpose flour	175 mL
3 tbsp	granulated sugar	45 mL
¾ tsp	baking powder	3 mL
¼ tsp	salt	1 mL
3	cloves garlic, minced	3
⅓ cup	buttermilk	75 mL
3 tbsp	unsalted butter, melted	45 mL
½ cup	finely shredded Cheddar cheese	125 mL
	Nonstick baking spray	

1. In a medium bowl, whisk together flour, sugar, baking powder and salt. Set aside.

2. In a small bowl, whisk together garlic, buttermilk and butter. Add to flour mixture, along with cheese, and stir until just combined.

3. Spray cake pop wells with baking spray. Fill each well with about 1 tbsp (15 mL) batter.

4. Bake for 4 to 6 minutes or until a tester inserted in the center comes out clean. Transfer muffins to a wire rack to cool slightly.

5. Repeat steps 3 and 4 with the remaining batter. Serve warm.

If Baking in the Rotating Cake Pop Maker

In step 4, bake for 1 minute. Rotate and bake for 2 to 3 minutes. Rotate back before testing for doneness. Continue with step 4.

Bacon Cornbread Muffins

These savory mini muffins are the perfect accompaniment to so many dinners, but especially ham and beans.

Tip

No buttermilk on hand? Place 2¼ tsp (11 mL) lemon juice or white vinegar in a glass measuring cup, then pour in enough milk to equal ¾ cup (175 mL). Let stand for 5 to 10 minutes to thicken. Proceed with the recipe. (See page 15 for other buttermilk substitutions.)

¾ cup	self-rising cornbread mix	175 mL
¼ cup	all-purpose flour	60 mL
1	large egg, at room temperature	1
¾ cup	buttermilk	175 mL
¼ cup	unsalted butter, melted	60 mL
4	slices bacon, cooked crisp and crumbled	4
	Nonstick baking spray	

1. In a medium bowl, whisk together cornbread mix and flour. Whisk in egg and buttermilk. Stir in butter until blended. Stir in bacon.

2. Spray cake pop wells with baking spray. Fill each well with about 1 tbsp (15 mL) batter.

3. Bake for 4 to 5 minutes or until light brown. Transfer cornbread to a wire rack to cool slightly.

4. Repeat steps 2 and 3 with the remaining batter. Serve warm.

If Baking in the Rotating Cake Pop Maker

In step 3, bake for 1 minute. Rotate and bake for 2 to 3 minutes. Rotate back before testing for doneness. Continue with step 3.

Buttermilk Biscuits

Makes 22 to 24 biscuits

Buttermilk is the "secret" ingredient in these tasty Southern-inspired morsels.

Tips

No buttermilk on hand? Place 2 tsp (10 mL) lemon juice or white vinegar in a glass measuring cup, then pour in enough milk to equal ⅔ cup (150 mL). Let stand for 5 to 10 minutes to thicken. Proceed with the recipe. (See page 15 for other buttermilk substitutions.)

Even though this is a thick dough, it is much easier to use a pastry bag to fill the wells. Use a sharp knife to cut away dough as you fill the wells.

Making a pot of soup or stew? Ladle it into bowls, then, just before serving, top each with a warm biscuit or two. They are just the right size, and the flavor will remind you of an old-fashioned stew topped with dumplings.

1 cup	all-purpose flour	250 mL
1 tsp	baking powder	5 mL
1 tsp	granulated sugar	5 mL
½ tsp	salt	2 mL
¼ tsp	baking soda	1 mL
3 tbsp	shortening	45 mL
⅔ cup	buttermilk	150 mL

1. In a medium bowl, whisk together flour, baking powder, sugar, salt and baking soda. Using your fingertips or a pastry blender, cut in shortening until mixture resembles coarse crumbs. Using a fork, stir in buttermilk just until dough comes together.

2. Fill each cake pop well with about 1 tbsp (15 mL) dough.

3. Bake for 4 to 6 minutes or until golden brown. Transfer biscuits to a wire rack to cool slightly.

4. Repeat steps 2 and 3 with the remaining dough. Serve warm.

If Baking in the Rotating Cake Pop Maker

In step 3, bake for 1 minute. Rotate and bake for 2 to 3 minutes. Rotate back before testing for doneness. Continue with step 3.

Angel Biscuits

Makes 38 to 40 biscuits

This dough can be mixed up and refrigerated overnight. Pull it out in the morning, bake and serve warm, with jam, for breakfast with your family or overnight guests.

. . . .

Tip

No buttermilk on hand? Place 1 tbsp (15 mL) lemon juice or white vinegar in a glass measuring cup, then pour in enough milk to equal 1 cup (250 mL). Let stand for 5 to 10 minutes to thicken. Proceed with the recipe. (See page 15 for other buttermilk substitutions.)

1¼ tsp	active dry yeast	6 mL
¼ cup	warm water	60 mL
2½ cups	all-purpose flour	625 mL
2 tbsp	granulated sugar	30 mL
½ tsp	baking powder	2 mL
½ tsp	baking soda	2 mL
½ tsp	salt	2 mL
⅓ cup	very cold unsalted butter, cut into small pieces	75 mL
1 cup	buttermilk	250 mL

1. In a small cup, stir together yeast and warm water until yeast is dissolved. Set aside.

2. In a large bowl, whisk together flour, sugar, baking powder, baking soda and salt. Using your fingertips or a pastry blender, cut in butter until mixture resembles coarse crumbs.

3. Stir yeast mixture into buttermilk. Pour into flour mixture and stir just until dough comes together. Cover and refrigerate for at least 1½ hours or overnight.

4. Fill each cake pop well with about 1 tbsp (15 mL) dough.

5. Bake for 4 to 6 minutes or until golden brown. Transfer biscuits to wire rack to cool slightly.

6. Repeat steps 4 and 5 with the remaining dough. Serve warm.

If Baking in the Rotating Cake Pop Maker
. . . .

In step 5, bake for 1 minute. Rotate and bake for 2 to 3 minutes. Rotate back before testing for doneness. Continue with step 5.

Sage and Walnut Biscuits

Makes 22 to 24 biscuits

The earthy flavor of sage and the crunch of walnuts combine to make fantastic biscuits. They are great with soup or salad for lunch.

Tip

Toasting walnuts intensifies their flavor. Spread finely chopped walnuts in a single layer on a baking sheet. Bake at 350°F (180°C) for 5 to 7 minutes or until lightly browned. Let cool.

1 cup	all purpose flour	250 mL
2 tsp	baking powder	10 mL
1 tsp	dried rubbed sage	5 mL
½ tsp	salt	1 mL
¼ cup	very cold unsalted butter, cut into small pieces	60 mL
6 tbsp	milk	90 mL
¼ cup	finely chopped walnuts, toasted (see tip, at left)	60 mL

1. In a large bowl, whisk together flour, baking powder, sage and salt. Using your fingertips or a pastry blender, cut in butter until mixture resembles coarse crumbs. Using a fork, stir in milk just until dough comes together. Stir in walnuts.

2. Fill each cake pop well with about 1 tbsp (15 mL) dough.

3. Bake for 4 to 6 minutes or until golden brown. Transfer biscuits to a wire rack to cool slightly.

4. Repeat steps 2 and 3 with the remaining dough. Serve warm.

If Baking in the Rotating Cake Pop Maker

In step 3, bake for 2 minutes. Rotate and bake for 2 to 3 minutes. Rotate back before testing for doneness. Continue with step 3.

Gluten-Free Hush Puppies

Makes 38 to 40 hush puppies

Our friend Johnna Perry is a treasure, and her journey toward healthy gluten-free baking has been an inspiration. Every time we see her, she shares another wonderful gluten-free treat. These low-fat hush puppies, packed with flavor, are a tribute to Johnna.

Tip

Serve these hush puppies with tartar sauce. To keep it healthy, make your own. Start with low-fat or fat-free vegan mayonnaise and season to taste with minced onions, pickle relish and mustard.

1½ cups	cornmeal	375 mL
½ cup	gluten-free all-purpose baking mix (see page 13)	125 mL
½ tsp	baking soda	2 mL
½ tsp	salt	2 mL
¼ tsp	gluten-free baking powder	1 mL
1 cup	unsweetened plain almond milk	250 mL
1 tbsp	cider vinegar	15 mL
1	large egg, at room temperature	1
¾ cup	finely chopped onion	175 mL

1. In a large bowl, whisk together cornmeal, baking mix, baking soda and salt. Set aside.

2. In a small bowl, whisk together almond milk and vinegar. Let stand for 5 minutes. Whisk in egg. Stir in onion. Stir into flour mixture until just moistened.

3. Spray cake pop wells with baking spray. Fill each well with about 1 tbsp (15 mL) batter.

4. Bake for 5 to 7 minutes or until a tester inserted in the center comes out clean. Transfer hush puppies to a wire rack to cool slightly.

5. Repeat steps 3 and 4 with the remaining batter. Serve warm.

If Baking in the Rotating Cake Pop Maker

In step 4, bake for 1 minute. Rotate and bake for 2 to 3 minutes. Rotate back before testing for doneness. Continue with step 4.

Cinnamon Chip Scones

Makes 28 to 30 scones

Savor these cinnamon-infused scones with a cup of tea, and your troubles will float away.

Tip

A half-recipe of Cream Cheese Glaze should be enough for these scones.

Variations

Add ¼ cup (60 mL) toasted chopped pecans with the cinnamon chips.

If cinnamon chips are not available, make chocolate chip scones by substituting semisweet chocolate chips for the cinnamon chips.

2 cups	all-purpose flour	500 mL
⅔ cup	granulated sugar	150 mL
1 tsp	baking powder	5 mL
1 tsp	ground cinnamon	5 mL
½ tsp	salt	2 mL
½ cup	very cold unsalted butter, cut into small pieces	125 mL
½ cup	very cold heavy or whipping (35%) cream	125 mL
1 tsp	vanilla extract	5 mL
½ tsp	baking soda	2 mL
1	large egg, lightly beaten	1
½ cup	cinnamon chips, chopped	125 mL
	Nonstick baking spray	
	Cream Cheese Glaze (page 106)	

1. In a medium bowl, whisk together flour, sugar, baking powder, cinnamon and salt. Using your fingertips or a pastry blender, cut in butter until mixture resembles coarse crumbs. Set aside.

2. In a small bowl, whisk together cream, vanilla and baking soda. Add to flour mixture, along with egg, and, using a fork, stir until just moistened. Stir in cinnamon chips.

3. Spray cake pop wells with baking spray. Fill each well with about 1 tbsp (15 mL) dough.

4. Bake for 6 to 7 minutes or until golden brown. Transfer scones to a wire rack set over a sheet of foil or waxed paper to cool slightly.

5. Repeat steps 3 and 4 with the remaining dough.

6. Drizzle Cream Cheese Glaze over warm scones. Serve warm.

If Baking in the Rotating Cake Pop Maker

In step 4, bake for 1 minute. Rotate and bake for 3 to 4 minutes. Rotate back before testing for doneness. Continue with step 4.

Banana Bread Scones with Brown Sugar Drizzle

Makes 16 to 18 scones

You don't need to be a fan of bananas to fall in love with these scones. Try them once, and you'll be converted.

Variation

Stir 3 tbsp (45 mL) toasted finely chopped pecans into the dough after stirring in the banana mixture.

1¼ cups	all-purpose flour	300 mL
2 tbsp	granulated sugar	30 mL
1 tsp	baking powder	5 mL
½ tsp	ground cinnamon	2 mL
¼ tsp	salt	1 mL
2 tbsp	very cold unsalted butter, cut into small pieces	30 mL
1	ripe banana, mashed	1
¼ cup	sour cream	60 mL
2 tbsp	milk	30 mL
	Nonstick baking spray	
	Brown Sugar Drizzle (page 107)	

1. In a medium bowl, whisk together flour, sugar, baking powder, cinnamon and salt. Using your fingertips or a pastry blender, cut in butter until mixture resembles coarse crumbs. Set aside.

2. In a small bowl, combine banana, sour cream and milk until well blended. Add to flour mixture and, using a fork, stir until just combined. Form dough into 1-inch (2.5 cm) balls.

3. Spray cake pop wells with baking spray. Place a scone in each well.

4. Bake for 4 to 6 minutes or until golden brown. Transfer scones to a wire rack set over a sheet of foil or waxed paper to cool slightly.

5. Repeat steps 3 and 4 with the remaining dough.

6. Drizzle Brown Sugar Drizzle over warm scones. Serve warm.

If Baking in the Rotating Cake Pop Maker

In step 4, bake for 1 minute. Rotate and bake for 2 to 3 minutes. Rotate back before testing for doneness. Continue with step 4.

Orange Pecan Scones

Makes 20 to 22 scones

Orange juice makes these scones wonderful. Serve them warm and watch them disappear quickly.

Tips

For the best flavor from your orange zest, grate only the colored portion of the orange peel, avoiding the bitter white pith underneath.

Toasting pecans intensifies their flavor. Spread chopped pecans in a single layer on a baking sheet. Bake at 350°F (180°C) for 5 to 7 minutes or until lightly browned. Let cool.

1 cup	all-purpose flour	250 mL
¼ cup	granulated sugar	60 mL
1½ tsp	baking powder	7 mL
1 tsp	grated orange zest	5 mL
½ tsp	baking soda	2 mL
¼ tsp	salt	1 mL
3 tbsp	very cold unsalted butter, cut into small pieces	45 mL
¼ cup	very cold buttermilk	60 mL
¼ cup	very cold orange juice	60 mL
¼ cup	chopped pecans, toasted (see tip, at left)	60 mL
	Orange Glaze (page 105)	

1. In a medium bowl, whisk together flour, sugar, baking powder, orange zest, baking soda and salt. Using your fingertips or a pastry blender, cut in butter until mixture resembles coarse crumbs. Using a fork, stir in buttermilk and orange juice just until dough comes together. Stir in pecans.

2. Fill each cake pop well with about 1 tbsp (15 mL) dough.

3. Bake for 4 to 6 minutes or until golden brown. Transfer scones to a wire rack set over a sheet of foil or waxed paper to cool slightly.

4. Repeat steps 2 and 3 with the remaining dough.

5. Drizzle Orange Glaze over warm scones. Serve warm.

If Baking in the Rotating Cake Pop Maker

In step 3, bake for 1 minute. Rotate and bake for 2 to 3 minutes. Rotate back before testing for doneness. Continue with step 3.

Cheddar Herb Scones

**Makes 21
to 23 scones**

Tired of the same
old dinner rolls?
Here's the antidote to
your boredom.

Tips

Use whatever herbs you like
best in these scones — we
like them with rosemary,
basil and/or chives.

For cheese scones, omit the
herbs.

1½ cups	all-purpose flour	375 mL
1½ tsp	baking powder	7 mL
½ tsp	salt	2 mL
¼ tsp	coarsely ground black pepper	1 mL
¼ cup	very cold unsalted butter, cut into small pieces	60 mL
2	cloves garlic, minced	2
¾ cup	shredded sharp (old) Cheddar cheese	175 mL
¼ cup	chopped fresh herbs (see tip, at left)	60 mL
⅓ to ½ cup	very cold heavy or whipping (35%) cream	75 to 125 mL

1. In a medium bowl, whisk together flour, baking powder, salt and pepper. Using your fingertips or a pastry blender, cut in butter until mixture resembles coarse crumbs. Stir in garlic, cheese and herbs until combined.

2. Add ⅓ cup (75 mL) of the cream and, using a fork, stir until blended. If necessary, gradually add more cream, stirring until dough forms a ball. Form dough into 1-inch (2.5 cm) balls.

3. Place a scone in each cake pop well.

4. Bake for 4 minutes. Carefully place the fork tool between each scone and the edge of the well and gently turn the scone over. Bake for 3 to 4 minutes or until golden brown. Transfer scones to a wire rack to cool slightly.

5. Repeat steps 3 and 4 with the remaining dough. Serve warm.

If Baking in the Rotating Cake Pop Maker

In step 4, bake for 2 minutes. Rotate and bake for 2 to 3 minutes. Rotate back before testing for doneness. Continue with step 4.

Butter Rolls

**Makes 22
to 24 rolls**

A basket of warm, bite-size rolls is the perfect accompaniment for a buffet dinner or a soup and salad luncheon.

Tip

Filling the wells half to three-quarters full allows room for the rolls to rise, and brushing the tops of the dough lightly with melted butter improves the browning and adds to the flavor. If the wells are under-filled, the rolls may not rise enough to reach the top of the cake pop maker and they won't brown. If you wonder if the wells are under-filled, bake for 4 minutes, then check on the progress. If desired, use the fork tool to turn each roll over, then continue baking for 2 minutes or until golden brown.

2 tbsp	granulated sugar	30 mL
2 tsp	quick-rising (instant) yeast	10 mL
1/3 cup	warm water	75 mL
1	large egg, at room temperature	1
3 tbsp	unsalted butter, softened	45 mL
1/4 tsp	salt	1 mL
1 1/3 cups	all-purpose flour (approx.)	325 mL
2 tbsp	unsalted butter, melted	30 mL

1. In a large bowl, stir together sugar, yeast and warm water. Let stand for 5 minutes.

2. Using an electric mixer on medium-high speed, beat in egg, softened butter and salt. Add 1 cup (250 mL) of the flour and beat for 1 minute. Stir in enough of the remaining flour to make a soft dough. Cover and let rise in a warm, draft-free place for 30 minutes.

3. Brush cake pop wells with melted butter. Drop about 1 1/2 tsp (7 mL) dough into each well, filling it half to three-quarters full. Quickly and lightly brush the tops of the dough with melted butter.

4. Bake for 6 to 8 minutes or until golden brown and crisp. Transfer rolls to a wire rack to cool slightly.

5. Repeat with the remaining dough. Serve warm.

If Baking in the Rotating Cake Pop Maker

In step 4, bake for 2 minutes. Rotate and bake for 2 to 3 minutes. Rotate back before testing for doneness. Continue with step 4.

Pretzel Rolls

Roxanne's family adores lunching at a Kansas City restaurant, the Webster House, for special occasions before theatrical performances at the Kauffman Center. The high point of the memorable meals is the pretzel rolls that are served warm. This recipe was inspired by those fond memories.

Tip
Serve with mustard.

If Baking in the Rotating Cake Pop Maker

In step 7, bake for 1 minute. Rotate and bake for 2 to 3 minutes. Rotate back before testing for doneness. Continue with step 7.

• Baking sheet, lined with foil

½ cup	warm water	125 mL
1½ tsp	active dry yeast	7 mL
1⅓ cups	all-purpose flour	325 mL
1½ tsp	granulated sugar	7 mL
	Kosher salt	
4 cups	water	1 L
3 tbsp	baking soda	45 mL

1. Pour warm water into a medium bowl and sprinkle with yeast. Let stand for 10 minutes.

2. In a small bowl, whisk together flour, sugar and ½ tsp (2 mL) salt. Add to the yeast mixture and, using an electric mixer on medium speed, beat until a dough forms.

3. Turn dough out onto a floured surface and knead for 5 minutes or until dough is elastic and smooth. Place dough in an oiled bowl, cover and let rise in a warm, draft-free place for about 40 minutes or until doubled in bulk.

4. Punch dough down and turn out onto a floured surface. Knead for about 2 minutes or until dough is smooth and springs back when poked. Form into 1-inch (2.5 cm) balls and place at least 2 inches (5 cm) apart on prepared baking sheet. Cover loosely with plastic wrap and let rise in a warm, draft-free place for about 25 minutes or until doubled in bulk.

5. In a large saucepan, bring 4 cups (1 L) water to a boil over medium-high heat. Stir in baking soda. Add 4 to 6 rolls at a time, reduce heat and simmer for about 1 minute. Using a slotted spoon, transfer rolls to a plate.

6. Place a roll in each cake pop well. Sprinkle lightly with salt.

7. Bake for 5 to 7 minutes or until golden. Transfer rolls to a wire rack to cool slightly.

8. Repeat steps 6 and 7 with the remaining dough. Serve warm or at room temperature.

Sesame Bread Bites

Sesame seeds add a nutty flavor to these bread bites, which would be perfect served with a stir-fry instead of dinner rolls.

Tips

A 1-oz (28 g) bottle of sesame seeds contains about ¼ cup (60 mL).

Once the sesame seeds are golden and fragrant, immediately pour them out of the hot pan to avoid over-toasting.

¼ cup	sesame seeds	60 mL
1	can (8 oz/227 g) refrigerated crescent roll dough	1
3 tbsp	unsalted butter, melted	45 mL

1. In a small skillet, toast sesame seeds over medium heat, stirring frequently, for about 2 minutes or until golden and fragrant. Pour into a small bowl and let cool.

2. Unroll crescent roll dough into triangles. Cut each triangle in half and form into a ball. Roll in melted butter, then in sesame seeds.

3. Place a dough ball in each cake pop well.

4. Bake for 6 to 8 minutes or until golden. Transfer to a wire rack to cool slightly.

5. Repeat steps 3 and 4 with the remaining dough. Serve warm.

If Baking in the Rotating Cake Pop Maker

In step 4, bake for 2 minutes. Rotate and bake for 2 to 3 minutes. Rotate back before testing for doneness. Continue with step 4.

Fig Wonton Bites (page 148) and
Chicken and Mushroom Phyllo Tarts (page 160)

Hoisin-Glazed Turkey Meatballs (page 163)

Gluten-Free Zucchini and Sun-Dried Tomato Fritters (page 154) and
Gluten-Free, Vegan Spicy Tempeh and Rice Balls (page 165)

Birthday Present (page 168)

Bookworm (page 184)

Kitty Cat with Yarn (page 186)

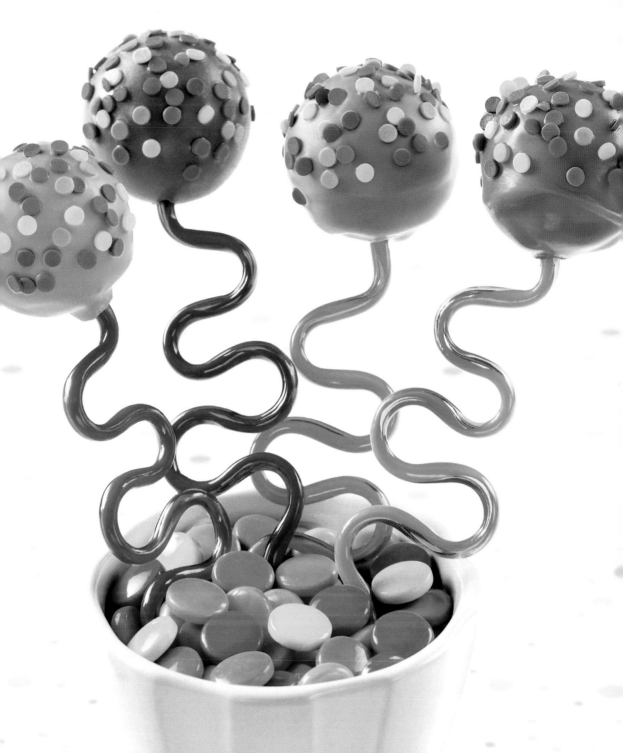

Crazy Straws (page 189)

Movie Night Popcorn (page 200)

Basket of Chicks (page 201)

Summer Fun (page 204)

Gone Fishing (page 205)

Spiders (page 214)

Pumpkin Bread Bites

Makes 34 to 36 bread bites

Old-fashioned pumpkin bread is so inviting and comforting. Fill a basket with these little bites and pour coffee for all. What a treat!

Tip
Refrigerate leftover canned pumpkin purée in an airtight container for up to 1 week, or freeze it for up to 3 months. Thaw overnight in the refrigerator, then stir well and use it to bake another batch of bread bites.

Variation
Stir 1/3 cup (75 mL) toasted chopped pecans or walnuts into the batter at the end of step 2.

1½ cups	all-purpose flour	375 mL
2 tsp	baking powder	10 mL
1 tsp	pumpkin pie spice	5 mL
¼ tsp	salt	1 mL
¾ cup	granulated sugar	175 mL
6 tbsp	unsalted butter, softened	90 mL
1	large egg, at room temperature	1
½ cup	canned pumpkin purée (not pie filling)	125 mL
⅓ cup	milk	75 mL
	Nonstick baking spray	

1. In a small bowl, whisk together flour, baking powder, pumpkin pie spice and salt. Set aside.

2. In a medium bowl, using an electric mixer on medium-high speed, beat sugar and butter for 1 minute or until fluffy. Beat in egg. Beat in pumpkin until blended. Add flour mixture alternately with milk, making three additions of flour and two of milk and beating on low speed until combined.

3. Spray cake pop wells with baking spray. Fill each well with about 1 tbsp (15 mL) batter.

4. Bake for 4 to 6 minutes or until a tester inserted in the center comes out clean. Transfer bread bites to a wire rack to cool.

5. Repeat steps 3 and 4 with the remaining batter.

If Baking in the Rotating Cake Pop Maker

In step 4, bake for 1 minute. Rotate and bake for 2 to 3 minutes. Rotate back before testing for doneness. Continue with step 4.

Tapas and Tidbits

Phyllo Cups

• •

**Makes
20 cups**

Fold, cut, bake and enjoy! It's that easy and oh, so good. Plus, these cups are made without all of the butter typically used when working with phyllo.

• •

Tips

Different brands of phyllo come in different-size sheets. We used sheets that are 14 by 9 inches (35 by 23 cm), which is about half of a 16-oz (454 g) package. If using larger sheets, use 10 and cut them in half crosswise before folding as directed.

Thaw phyllo dough in the refrigerator according to package directions. Wrap any extra sheets tightly in plastic wrap and refrigerate for up to 2 weeks, or refreeze and use within 9 months.

Store baked phyllo cups in an airtight container at room temperature and use within 2 days. Or freeze them for up to 2 months.

• 3-inch (7.5 cm) round cookie cutter

| 20 | sheets frozen phyllo dough (about 8 oz/250 g), thawed (see tips, at left) Nonstick baking spray | 20 |

1. Place 1 phyllo sheet on a cutting board. Immediately cover the remaining phyllo sheets with plastic wrap and then a lightly dampened towel, keeping them covered to prevent them from drying out.

2. Fold the sheet into thirds, making a 9- by $4\frac{1}{2}$-inch (23 by 11 cm) rectangle. Fold the rectangle in half, making a $4\frac{1}{2}$-inch (11 cm) square.

3. Using the cookie cutter, imprint a circle on the phyllo, pressing firmly. Use kitchen shears to cut out the circle, holding the layers together as you cut. Place the circle (there will be 6 layers) over a cake pop well and press down lightly to shape it into a cup. Repeat with 11 more phyllo sheets until all 12 wells are covered. (Keep the remaining phyllo sheets covered.) Spray the inside of each cup with baking spray.

4. Bake for 5 to 7 minutes or until crisp and golden brown. Carefully transfer cups to a wire rack to cool.

5. Repeat steps 1 to 4 with the remaining phyllo sheets.

> ### If Baking in the Rotating Cake Pop Maker
> •
> Bake as directed in step 4, without rotating.

Wonton Cups

The possibilities for these crisp cups are endless — we love them filled with hot cheese dip, pimento cheese or chicken salad. Or fill them with your favorite crab dip for a taste reminiscent of crab Rangoon.

Tip

For a more rustic look, simply cut rough circles from the wonton wrappers with kitchen shears.

- 3-inch (7.5 cm) round cookie cutter

| 24 | wonton wrappers (about 3½ inches/8.5 cm square) | 24 |

1. Using the cookie cutter, cut a circle from each wonton wrapper (see tip, below left).

2. Place a circle over each cake pop well and press down lightly to shape it into a cup.

3. Bake for 2 to 3 minutes or until crisp and golden. Carefully transfer cups to a wire rack to cool.

4. Repeat steps 2 and 3 with the remaining wrappers, using the end of a wooden spoon to press the wrappers into the wells.

> **If Baking in the Rotating Cake Pop Maker**
>
> Bake as directed in step 3, without rotating.

Fig Wonton Bites

These appetizers offer fantastic flavor and are oh so easy.

Variation
Substitute cherry preserves or pepper jelly for the fig preserves.

- 3-inch (7.5 cm) round cookie cutter

12	wonton wrappers (about 3½ inches/8.5 cm square)	12
2 tbsp	fig preserves	30 mL
2 tbsp	crumbled goat cheese	30 mL
2	slices bacon, cooked crisp and finely crumbled	2

1. Using the cookie cutter, cut a circle from each wonton wrapper (see tip, above left).

2. Place a circle over each cake pop well and press down lightly to shape it into a cup. Spoon about ½ tsp (2 mL) preserves into each cup and top with about ½ tsp (2 mL) goat cheese. Sprinkle with bacon.

3. Bake for 2 to 3 minutes or until cups are crisp and golden and filling is hot. Carefully transfer cups to a wire rack to cool slightly. Serve warm.

Roasted Red Pepper Wonton Bites

Makes 34 to 36 cups

Simple pantry ingredients transform into a delightful appetizer, ready in just minutes.

Tips

For a more rustic look, simply cut rough circles from the wonton wrappers with kitchen shears.

Deep-fry or bake the wonton scraps until crisp and add them to soups or salads.

- Food processor
- 3-inch (7.5 cm) round cookie cutter

4	kalamata or other black olives, pitted	4
1	clove garlic	1
½ cup	drained roasted red peppers	125 mL
¼ tsp	dried oregano	1 mL
¼ cup	spreadable cream cheese	60 mL
2 tbsp	freshly grated Parmesan cheese	30 mL
34 to 36	wonton wrappers (about 3½- inches/8.5 cm square)	34 to 36

1. In food processor, combine olives, garlic, roasted peppers and oregano; pulse until finely chopped. Add cream cheese and Parmesan; pulse until combined.

2. Using the cookie cutter, cut a circle from each wonton wrapper (see tip, at left).

3. Place a circle over each cake pop well and, using the end of a wooden spoon, press down lightly to shape it into a cup. Spoon about 1 tsp (5 mL) filling into each cup.

4. Bake for 2 to 3 minutes or until cups are crisp and golden and filling is hot. Carefully transfer cups to a wire rack to cool slightly.

5. Repeat steps 3 and 4 with the remaining wrappers and filling. Serve warm.

If Baking in the Rotating Cake Pop Maker

Bake as directed in step 4, without rotating.

Mushroom Bites

This recipe is a blue ribbon winner. How do we know? At the end of a long day in the test kitchen, there were none left to take home! We had nibbled and snacked on these all day long.

Tips

For the mushrooms, try a mixture of button, cremini and/or shiitake, or use any mushrooms you particularly enjoy.

Try using vegetable-flavored cream cheese instead of regular cream cheese.

- 3-inch (7.5 cm) round cookie cutter

2 tbsp	unsalted butter	30 mL
4 oz	mixed mushrooms, finely chopped (about 2½ cups/625 mL)	125 g
2	green onions, chopped	2
4 oz	cream cheese, softened and cut into small cubes	125 g
⅓ cup	crumbled blue cheese	75 mL
	Salt and freshly ground black pepper	
24	wonton wrappers (about 3½ inches/8.5 cm square)	24

1. In a medium skillet, melt butter over medium-high heat. Add mushrooms and green onions; cook, stirring, for 5 minutes or until most of the liquid has evaporated. Reduce heat to low and stir in cream cheese, blue cheese and salt and pepper to taste; cook, stirring constantly, until cheese is melted and creamy. Remove from heat.

2. Using the cookie cutter, cut a circle from each wonton wrapper (see tip, page 149).

3. Place a circle over each cake pop well and, using the end of a wooden spoon, press down lightly to shape it into a cup. Spoon about 1½ tsp (7 mL) filling into each cup.

4. Bake for 2 to 4 minutes or until cups are crisp and golden and filling is hot. Carefully transfer cups to a wire rack to cool slightly.

5. Repeat steps 3 and 4 with the remaining wrappers and filling. Serve warm.

If Baking in the Rotating Cake Pop Maker

Bake as directed in step 4, without rotating.

Spinach Balls

Remember this old standby from days gone by? It's time for this appetizer to make a comeback, as it is perfect for the cake pop maker.

Tip

The spinach mixture can be made ahead, covered and refrigerated for up to 1 day, and is actually easier to roll into balls when it is chilled.

1	package (10 oz/300 g) frozen chopped spinach, thawed and well drained	1
¾ cup	dry herb stuffing mix	175 mL
½ cup	finely chopped onion	125 mL
¼ tsp	garlic powder	1 mL
	Salt and freshly ground black pepper	
2	large eggs, beaten	2
3 tbsp	freshly grated Parmesan cheese	45 mL
2 tbsp	unsalted butter, melted	30 mL
	Nonstick baking spray	

1. In a large bowl, combine spinach, stuffing mix, onion, garlic powder, salt and pepper to taste, eggs, Parmesan and butter. Form into 1-inch (2.5 cm) balls.

2. Spray cake pop wells with baking spray. Place a ball in each well.

3. Bake for 5 minutes. Carefully place the fork tool between each ball and the edge of the well and gently turn the ball over. Bake for 3 to 4 minutes or until golden brown. Transfer balls to a wire rack to cool slightly.

4. Repeat steps 2 and 3 with the remaining balls. Serve warm.

If Baking in the Rotating Cake Pop Maker

In step 3, bake for 2 minutes. Rotate and bake for 2 to 3 minutes. Rotate back before testing for doneness. Continue with step 3.

Eggplant Balls

Many of our test kitchen tasters were leery of this recipe, but the proof was in the pudding — these meatless morsels won high marks across the board.

Tips

Sprinkle eggplant balls with finely chopped green onions before serving.

Fresh eggplant should be firm, with a smooth skin. The flesh will naturally discolor once cut (like an apple), so eggplants should be peeled and sliced just before cooking.

2	eggplants (each about 1 lb/500 g)	2
1 tbsp	salt	15 mL
2 tbsp	olive oil, divided	30 mL
2	cloves garlic, minced	2
2	large eggs, beaten	2
1 tbsp	reduced-sodium soy sauce	15 mL
1 cup	dry bread crumbs with Italian seasoning	250 mL
	Nonstick baking spray	

1. Peel eggplant and cut crosswise into ½-inch (1 cm) slices. Arrange in a single layer on a tray and sprinkle with salt. Let stand for 10 minutes. Rinse and drain well on paper towels.

2. In a large skillet, heat half the oil over medium-high heat. Add eggplant, in batches as necessary, and cook, turning once, for 6 to 8 minutes or until tender, adding more oil as needed between batches. Using a slotted spoon, transfer eggplant to a cutting board.

3. Cut eggplant into ¼-inch (0.5 cm) pieces and place in a medium bowl. Stir in garlic, eggs and soy sauce. Gently stir in bread crumbs. Form into 1-inch (2.5 cm) balls.

4. Spray cake pop wells with baking spray. Place a ball in each well.

5. Bake for 8 to 10 minutes or until golden brown. Transfer balls to a wire rack to cool slightly.

6. Repeat steps 4 and 5 with the remaining balls. Serve warm.

If Baking in the Rotating Cake Pop Maker

In step 5, bake for 2 minutes. Rotate and bake for 3 to 4 minutes. Rotate back before testing for doneness. Continue with step 5.

Gougères

**Makes 30
to 35 gougères**

These puffs of pâte à choux will forever conjure up fond memories of a trip we took to France. We stayed at cookbook author Anne Willan's chateau in the Burgundy region. Anne and her husband hosted a cocktail party and served icy cold kir royales and warm gougères. It was truly unforgettable.

Tip

It important not to overfill the cake pop wells, as pâte à choux puffs during baking.

Variation

For a truer French experience, substitute shredded Gruyère cheese for the Parmesan.

1 cup	water	250 mL
6 tbsp	unsalted butter, cut into pieces	90 mL
¼ tsp	salt	1 mL
1 cup	all-purpose flour	250 mL
3	large eggs, at room temperature	3
⅔ cup	freshly grated Parmesan cheese	150 mL

1. In a medium saucepan, combine water, butter and salt. Bring to a boil over medium-high heat. Reduce heat to medium and, using a wooden spoon, stir in flour; cook, stirring, for 3 minutes.

2. Transfer batter to a medium bowl and stir for 1 minute to cool. Using an electric mixer on medium-high speed, beat in eggs, one at a time, beating well and scraping the sides of the bowl after each addition. Stir in Parmesan.

3. Spoon about 2 tsp (10 mL) batter into each cake pop well. *Do not overfill*: it is crucial to allow enough room for the dough to expand.

4. Bake for 10 to 12 minutes or until golden brown. Do not open before the minimum baking time has elapsed. Transfer gougères to a wire rack to cool slightly.

5. Repeat steps 3 and 4 with the remaining batter. Serve warm.

If Baking in the Rotating Cake Pop Maker

In step 4, bake for 4 minutes. Rotate and bake for 6 to 7 minutes. Rotate back before testing for doneness. Do not open before the minimum baking time has elapsed. Continue with step 4.

Gluten-Free Zucchini and Sun-Dried Tomato Fritters

Forget deep-fried fritters. These are packed with flavorful vegetables and are low in fat! Serve with a smear of goat cheese.

Tips

You can use yellow summer squash in place of all or some of the zucchini.

Reserve 1 tbsp (15 mL) of the oil you drain from the sun-dried tomatoes and use it in place of the olive oil.

½ cup	gluten-free all-purpose baking mix (see page 13)	125 mL
2 tbsp	granulated sugar	30 mL
½ tsp	gluten-free baking powder	2 mL
¼ tsp	baking soda	1 mL
¼ tsp	salt	1 mL
¼ tsp	freshly ground black pepper	1 mL
¼ tsp	minced garlic	1 mL
1	large egg, at room temperature	1
1 tbsp	olive oil	15 mL
½ cup	shredded zucchini (unpeeled)	125 mL
¼ cup	chopped drained oil-packed sun-dried tomatoes	60 mL
	Nonstick baking spray	

1. In a large bowl, whisk together baking mix, sugar, baking powder, baking soda, salt and pepper.

2. In a small bowl, whisk together garlic, egg and oil. Add to dry ingredients and stir until moistened. Stir in zucchini and tomatoes.

3. Spray cake pop wells with baking spray. Fill each well with about 1 tbsp (15 mL) batter.

4. Bake for 6 to 8 minutes or until golden brown. Transfer fritters to a wire rack to cool slightly.

5. Repeat steps 3 and 4 with the remaining batter. Serve warm.

If Baking in the Rotating Cake Pop Maker

In step 4, bake for 2 minutes. Rotate and bake for 2 to 3 minutes. Rotate back before checking for doneness. Continue with step 4.

Parmesan Garlic Bites

Round out the appetizer buffet with these scrumptious bites. They are perfect to serve with fruit and cheese for a wine tasting.

Tip

If serving these with a variety of cheese and wine, and you want a milder flavor, reduce the garlic powder to a pinch.

1 cup	all-purpose flour	250 mL
2 tsp	baking powder	10 mL
1/4 tsp	salt	1 mL
1/4 tsp	garlic powder	1 mL
1	large egg, at room temperature	1
3/4 cup	milk	175 mL
2 tbsp	unsalted butter, melted	30 mL
1/4 cup	freshly grated Parmesan cheese	60 mL
	Nonstick baking spray	

1. In a medium bowl, whisk together flour, baking powder, salt and garlic powder. Set aside.

2. In a small bowl, whisk together egg, milk and butter. Stir into flour mixture until blended. Stir in Parmesan.

3. Spray cake pop wells with baking spray. Fill each well with about 1 tbsp (15 mL) batter.

4. Bake for 3 to 5 minutes or until golden brown and crispy. Transfer bites to a wire rack to cool slightly.

5. Repeat steps 3 and 4 with the remaining batter. Serve warm.

If Baking in the Rotating Cake Pop Maker

In step 4, bake for 1 minute. Rotate and bake for 2 to 3 minutes. Rotate back before checking for doneness. Continue with step 4.

Bacon Cheese Buttons

Makes 10 to 12 balls

Roxanne loves all foods Southern, and these party pleasers are a great example. They are wonderful with a glass of red wine.

Tip

This recipe can be doubled for a larger crowd.

Variation

After the dough forms a ball, add 3 tbsp (45 mL) toasted finely chopped pecans to the food processor and pulse briefly to combine.

• Food processor

1 cup	shredded sharp (old) Cheddar cheese	250 mL
½ cup	all-purpose flour	125 mL
2 tbsp	crumbled crisply cooked bacon	30 mL
Pinch	salt	Pinch
Pinch	cayenne pepper	Pinch
¼ cup	unsalted butter, softened	60 mL
	Nonstick baking spray	

1. In food processor, combine cheese, flour, bacon, salt, cayenne and butter. Process until mixture forms a ball. Form dough into 1-inch (2.5 cm) balls.

2. Spray cake pop wells with baking spray. Place a ball in each cake pop well.

3. Bake for 10 to 12 minutes or until golden. Carefully transfer to a wire rack to cool slightly. Serve warm.

If Baking in the Rotating Cake Pop Maker

In step 3, bake for 2 minutes. Rotate and bake for 3 to 4 minutes. Rotate back before checking for doneness. Continue with step 3.

Jalapeño Bacon Poppers

These poppers are sure to be a hit at your next football party. Keep plenty of the ingredients on hand and make these appetizers through the first half and well into halftime.

Tips

This recipe is written for a small can of crescent rolls. You can use a larger can (8 oz/227 g) and double the other ingredients to make 32 poppers.

For a vegetarian version, omit the bacon.

1	can (4 oz/113 g) refrigerated crescent roll dough (see tip, at left)	1
4 tsp	spreadable cream cheese	20 mL
2	slices bacon, cooked crisp and cut into 16 pieces	2
8	pickled jalapeño slices, drained and cut in half	8

1. Separate dough into 2 pieces. Using your fingers, pinch perforations together to form 2 rectangles. Cut each rectangle into 4 pieces, then cut each piece in half, making 8 squares.

2. Place $\frac{1}{4}$ tsp (1 mL) cream cheese in the center of each square. Top with a piece of bacon and a jalapeño half. Form dough into a ball around the filling and seal well.

3. Place a ball in each cake pop well.

4. Bake for 2 minutes. Carefully place the fork tool between each ball and the edge of the well and gently turn the ball over. Bake for 2 to 3 minutes or until golden brown. Transfer poppers to a wire rack to cool slightly.

5. Repeat steps 2 and 3 with the remaining balls. Serve warm.

If Baking in the Rotating Cake Pop Maker

In step 4, bake for 2 minutes. Rotate and bake for 2 to 3 minutes. Rotate back before checking for doneness. Continue with step 4.

Bacon and Blue Cheese Potato Cakes

Makes 18 to 20 cakes

These fragrant, flavorful potato morsels are a perfect accompaniment to grilled meats. They're also a fun way to get a dinner party off to a great start.

Tips

Leftover mashed potatoes work well in this recipe, or you can purchase prepared mashed potatoes at the grocery store or deli. Instant mashed potatoes can also be used; prepare according to package directions.

If you don't have blue cheese, a good substitute would be crumbled feta cheese.

1 cup	mashed cooked potatoes (see tip, at left)	250 mL
1/4 cup	crumbled blue cheese	60 mL
2 tbsp	all-purpose flour	30 mL
1/4 tsp	salt	1 mL
Pinch	freshly ground black pepper	Pinch
1	large egg, at room temperature	1
2 tbsp	unsalted butter, melted	30 mL
3	slices bacon, cooked crisp and crumbled	3
	Nonstick baking spray	

1. In a medium bowl, combine mashed potatoes, cheese, flour, salt, pepper, egg and butter. Stir in bacon.

2. Using a small scoop, spoon out 1 tbsp (15 mL) of the potato mixture and form into a 1/2-inch (1 cm) thick disk. Repeat with the remaining potato mixture.

3. Spray cake pop wells with baking spray. Place a disk in each well.

4. Bake for 5 minutes. Carefully place the fork tool between each disk and the edge of the well and gently turn the disk over. Bake for 4 to 6 minutes or until golden. Transfer cakes to a serving plate and keep warm.

5. Repeat steps 3 and 4 with the remaining disks. Serve warm.

If Baking in the Rotating Cake Pop Maker

In step 4, bake for 2 minutes. Rotate and bake for 3 to 4 minutes. Rotate back before checking for doneness. Continue with step 4.

Bourbon-Glazed Biscuit and Ham Bites

Makes 22 to 24 bites

These little bites are packed with flavor, and the stunning arrangement (see tip, below) will be a hit at your next party.

Tips

For the best results, choose a flavorful ham cut into slices about 1/8 to 1/4 inch (3 to 5 mm) thick instead of thinly sliced deli ham.

For a fabulous display, cut a 6- to 8-inch (15 to 20 cm) Styrofoam ball in half. Reserve one half for another use. Place the other half cut side down on a serving plate and cover with leafy lettuce. Use longer cocktail picks or 4-inch (10 cm) skewers to secure the biscuits. Insert the tip of each pick into the Styrofoam, arranging the biscuits decoratively. Place a cup of the dip on the side.

22 to 24	Buttermilk Biscuits (page 134)	22 to 24
44 to 48	1-inch (2.5 cm) squares cooked ham (see tip, at left)	44 to 48
	Brown Sugar Bourbon Dip (page 107)	

1. Using a serrated knife, cut each biscuit in half.

2. Place ham squares between paper towels. Microwave on High for 45 to 60 seconds or until warm.

3. Stack 2 ham squares and sandwich them inside a biscuit. Secure with a toothpick. Repeat with the remaining ham and biscuits.

4. Serve warm, with Brown Sugar Bourbon Dip.

Chicken and Mushroom Phyllo Tarts

Makes 14 to 16 tarts

How can a recipe made with cream cheese and phyllo go wrong?

Tips

Different brands of phyllo come in different-size sheets. For this recipe, we used sheets that are 14 by 9 inches (35 by 23 cm). If using larger sheets, cut them into quarters before folding as directed in step 2.

Thaw phyllo dough in the refrigerator according to package directions. Wrap any extra sheets tightly in plastic wrap and refrigerate for up to 2 weeks, or refreeze and use within 9 months.

Variation

Omit the phyllo dough and substitute 14 to 16 wonton wrappers. Cut and shape wrappers as directed in steps 1 and 2 on page 148. Fill the wonton cups with the chicken filling. Bake for 3 to 4 minutes or until wontons are crisp and filling is hot.

2 tbsp	unsalted butter	30 mL
½ cup	finely chopped mushrooms	125 mL
¼ cup	finely chopped onion	60 mL
1	clove garlic, minced	1
	Salt and freshly ground black pepper	
4 oz	cream cheese, softened	125 g
1	can (4.8 oz/127 g) white chicken, drained	1
7 to 8	sheets frozen phyllo dough, thawed (see tips, at left)	7 to 8

1. In a medium skillet, melt butter over medium-high heat. Add mushrooms and onion; cook, stirring, for 5 to 6 minutes or until lightly browned. Stir in garlic, salt and pepper to taste and cream cheese until cheese is melted. Gently stir in chicken. Remove from heat.

2. Cut each phyllo sheet in half crosswise. As you work with each half-sheet, keep the remaining half-sheets covered with plastic wrap and then a lightly dampened towel, to prevent them from drying out. Fold each half-sheet into fourths. Place about 1 tbsp (15 mL) chicken filling in the center. Gather all the edges up and pinch around filling to make a packet, using water to seal.

3. Place a packet in each cake pop well.

4. Bake for 5 to 7 minutes or until phyllo is crisp. Transfer packets to a wire rack to cool slightly.

5. Repeat steps 3 and 4 with the remaining packets. Serve warm.

If Baking in the Rotating Cake Pop Maker

Bake as directed in step 4, without rotating.

Greek Meatballs with Tzatziki

Makes 30 to 32 meatballs

Serve with Eggplant Balls (page 152), with tzatziki and warm pitas on the side, for a Middle Eastern appetizer buffet.

Tip

Always use very lean ground beef to reduce the amount of fat that collects in the wells. For optimum performance and to minimize fat, turn the unit off between batches, let it cool completely, wipe away any collected fat with a paper towel, then bake the next batch.

1 lb	extra-lean ground beef (see tip, at left)	500 g
1	clove garlic, minced	1
¼ cup	dry bread crumbs	60 mL
1 tsp	paprika	5 mL
1 tsp	dried oregano	5 mL
1	large egg, beaten	1
	Salt and freshly ground black pepper	

1. In a medium bowl, combine beef, garlic, bread crumbs, paprika, oregano and egg. Season with salt and pepper. Form into 1-inch (2.5 cm) meatballs.

2. Place a meatball in each cake pop well.

3. Bake for 5 to 7 minutes or until no longer pink inside. Transfer meatballs to a covered dish and keep warm.

4. Repeat steps 2 and 3 with the remaining meatballs.

If Baking in the Rotating Cake Pop Maker

Bake as directed in step 3, without rotating.

Tzatziki

Makes about 1 cup (250 mL)

Creamy yogurt and cucumber make this sauce a classic.

Tip

Greek yogurt is thicker than regular yogurt and makes a luscious sauce. It commonly comes in 6-oz (175 g) containers, which is the perfect amount for this recipe.

2	cloves garlic, minced	2
½	cucumber, peeled, seeded and shredded	½
⅔ cup	plain Greek yogurt	150 mL
1 tbsp	freshly squeezed lemon juice	15 mL
	Salt and freshly ground black pepper	

1. In a small bowl, combine garlic, cucumber, yogurt and lemon juice. Season to taste with salt and pepper. Cover and refrigerate for up to 1 day.

Ham Meatballs

The tangy sauce the meatballs are tossed with will catapult this recipe to fame.

Tips

When forming meatballs, use a small scoop (one that holds about 1 tbsp/15 mL) to spoon out just the right amount of meat mixture, then lightly shape the mixture into a ball with your hands.

For optimum performance, turn the unit off between batches, let it cool completely, wipe away any collected fat with a paper towel, then bake the next batch.

• Food processor

Meatballs

8 oz	cooked ham, cut into chunks	250 g
8 oz	lean ground pork	250 g
½ cup	dry bread crumbs	125 mL
1 tbsp	packed brown sugar	15 mL
1 tsp	dry mustard	5 mL
½ tsp	salt	2 mL
1	large egg, beaten	1

Sauce

¼ cup	packed brown sugar	60 mL
½ cup	unsweetened pineapple juice	125 mL
¼ cup	cider vinegar	60 mL
2 tsp	ketchup	10 mL
Dash	hot pepper sauce	Dash
1 tbsp	cornstarch	15 mL
2 tbsp	cold water	30 mL

1. *Meatballs:* In food processor, pulse ham to finely chop.

2. In a medium bowl, combine chopped ham, pork, bread crumbs, brown sugar, mustard, salt and egg. Form into 1-inch (2.5 cm) meatballs.

3. Place a meatball in each cake pop well.

4. Bake for 6 to 8 minutes or until no longer pink inside. Transfer meatballs to a covered dish and keep warm.

5. Repeat steps 3 and 4 with the remaining meatballs.

6. *Sauce:* Meanwhile, in a small saucepan, combine brown sugar, pineapple juice, vinegar, ketchup and hot pepper sauce. In a small cup, dissolve cornstarch in cold water; add to pineapple juice mixture. Bring to a simmer over medium heat, stirring often.

7. Pour sauce over cooked meatballs, stirring gently to coat. Serve warm.

If Baking in the Rotating Cake Pop Maker

Bake as directed in step 4, without rotating.

Hoisin-Glazed Turkey Meatballs

Makes 26 to 28 meatballs

Need a fresh, light dinner idea? These Asian-inspired meatballs are sure to please. Pair them with steamed rice and a cup of hot tea.

Tips

Fresh gingerroot can be tightly wrapped and frozen for up to 6 months, and can be grated from frozen.

Toasting sesame seeds intensifies their flavor. Spread them in a small dry skillet and cook over medium heat, stirring often, for 2 to 3 minutes or until golden. Immediately pour the seeds onto a plate to prevent overbrowning. You may also be able to purchase toasted sesame seeds.

For the best results, turn the unit off between batches, let it cool completely, wipe away any collected fat with a paper towel, then bake the next batch.

Variation

Substitute extra-lean ground beef for the turkey.

Meatballs

1 tbsp	grated gingerroot	15 mL
1 tbsp	cornstarch	15 mL
1/4 tsp	hot pepper flakes	1 mL
1/4 tsp	salt	1 mL
2 tbsp	reduced-sodium soy sauce	30 mL
1 tbsp	sesame oil	15 mL
1	green onion, minced	1
1 lb	lean ground turkey	500 g
1/2 cup	finely chopped drained canned water chestnuts	125 mL

Sauce

1/4 cup	hoisin sauce	60 mL
1 tbsp	orange juice	15 mL
1/2 tsp	Asian chili sauce (such as Sriracha)	2 mL
2 tsp	toasted sesame seeds (see tip, at left)	10 mL
	Chopped fresh cilantro	

1. *Meatballs:* In a large bowl, combine ginger, cornstarch, hot pepper flakes, salt, soy sauce and oil, stirring until smooth. Stir in green onion, turkey and water chestnuts until well combined. Form into 1-inch (2.5 cm) meatballs.

2. Place a meatball in each cake pop well.

3. Bake for 5 to 7 minutes or until no longer pink inside. Transfer meatballs to a covered dish and keep warm.

4. Repeat steps 2 and 3 with the remaining meatballs.

5. *Sauce:* In a small bowl, combine hoisin sauce, orange juice and chili sauce. Drizzle over meatballs, stirring gently to coat. Garnish with toasted sesame seeds and cilantro.

If Baking in the Rotating Cake Pop Maker

Bake as directed in step 3, without rotating.

Turkey and Dressing Balls

Makes 16 to 18 meatballs

How could anyone resist turkey and dressing all wrapped up into one delicious bite?

Tips

When forming meatballs, use a small scoop (one that holds about 1 tbsp/15 mL) to spoon out just the right amount of meat mixture, then lightly shape the mixture into a ball with your hands.

Kathy enjoys sweet sauces with her meat, so she would heat a 16-oz (500 mL) can of whole-berry cranberry sauce to serve with these meatballs as a dipping sauce. Roxanne, on the other hand, would heat a 12-oz (375 mL) jar of turkey gravy.

1 cup	finely chopped cooked turkey	250 mL
¼ cup	finely chopped celery	60 mL
2 tbsp	finely chopped onion	30 mL
1½ cups	dry herb stuffing mix	375 mL
¼ cup	all-purpose flour	60 mL
¼ tsp	salt	1 mL
Pinch	freshly ground black pepper	Pinch
½ cup	ready-to-use chicken broth	125 mL
1	large egg, beaten	1

1. In a medium bowl, combine turkey, celery, onion, stuffing mix, flour, salt and pepper. Add broth and combine well. Add egg and combine well. Form into 1-inch (2.5 cm) meatballs.

2. Place a meatball in each cake pop well.

3. Bake for 6 to 8 minutes or until hot in the center. Transfer meatballs to a covered dish and keep warm.

4. Repeat steps 2 and 3 with the remaining meatballs.

If Baking in the Rotating Cake Pop Maker

Bake as directed in step 3, without rotating.

Gluten-Free, Vegan Spicy Tempeh and Rice Balls

Makes 27 to 29 balls

Serve these fantastic morsels in place of other meatballs for a healthy appetizer or main dish.

Tips

Tempeh, a soybean cake, is high in protein but low in fat and cholesterol-free. Many grocery stores now sell this increasingly popular food in vacuum packs, either in the produce section or in a refrigerated case with the health foods or other soy products. To shred it, use a box grater or a food processor fitted with a shredding blade.

If you can't find gluten-free dry bread crumbs, make your own. Arrange slices of gluten-free bread in a single layer on a baking sheet. Bake in a 300°F (150°C) oven for 10 to 20 minutes or until completely dry and light brown. Let cool completely, then tear into pieces. In a food processor, process to fine, even crumbs. Store in an airtight container in the freezer for up to 2 months.

1 tbsp	ground flax seeds (flaxseed meal)	15 mL
3 tbsp	hot water	45 mL
8 oz	gluten-free tempeh, shredded	250 g
¾ cup	cooked brown rice	175 mL
¼ cup	finely chopped celery	60 mL
¼ cup	finely chopped green onion	60 mL
¼ cup	finely chopped red bell pepper	60 mL
1 tsp	minced garlic	5 mL
½ tsp	salt	2 mL
½ tsp	freshly ground black pepper	2 mL
½ tsp	dry mustard	2 mL
½ tsp	ground cumin	2 mL
¼ cup	tomato paste	60 mL
¼ tsp	prepared horseradish	1 mL
1 cup	gluten-free dry bread crumbs, divided	250 mL
	Nonstick baking spray	

1. In a large bowl, combine flax seeds and hot water. Let stand for 10 minutes.

2. Stir in tempeh, brown rice, celery, green onion, red pepper, garlic, salt, pepper, mustard, cumin, tomato paste and horseradish. Stir in ½ cup (125 mL) of the bread crumbs until evenly moistened. Form into 1-inch (2.5 cm) balls.

3. Place the remaining bread crumbs on a plate. Roll balls in bread crumbs until evenly coated.

4. Spray cake pop wells with baking spray. Place a ball in each well.

5. Bake for 8 to 10 minutes or until set, golden brown and hot in the center. Transfer balls to a wire rack to cool slightly.

6. Repeat steps 4 and 5 with the remaining balls. Serve warm.

If Baking in the Rotating Cake Pop Maker

Bake as directed in step 5, without rotating.

Part 4

Gifts and Centerpieces

Creative Gifts

Birthday Present

**Makes
1 gift**

Make this special, colorful gift for anyone celebrating a birthday. It's always in good taste and is easily adaptable: use the recipient's favorite cake pop flavor and colors.

Tips

To make the gift even more decorative and full, tie more ribbon on each cake pop.

To make inserting the cake pops easier, use an ice pick to poke tiny holes in the gift wrap.

Keep cake pops on sticks in an airtight container in the freezer so you can make a great gift in minutes.

Ingredients

	Lavender and yellow candy coating wafers	
7	Lemon Coconut Cake Pops (page 68)	7
	Purple oil-based candy coloring	
	Colorful sprinkles	

Materials

7	cake pop sticks	7
1	Styrofoam block (about 4 inches/ 10 cm cubed)	1
	Colorful gift wrap that coordinates with the candy coating wafers	
	Transparent tape	
6 feet	purple curling ribbon, cut into 12-inch (30 cm) lengths	180 cm
8 feet	yellow curling ribbon, cut into 12-inch (30 cm) lengths	240 cm

1. Melt $1/4$ cup (60 mL) lavender candy coating wafers (see page 19) and use to attach sticks to 4 cake pops (see page 27). Freeze cake pops for at least 15 minutes to set. Reserve the remaining candy coating. Repeat with yellow candy coating wafers, attaching sticks to the remaining cake pops.

2. Add $1/2$ cup (125 mL) lavender candy coating wafers to the reserved lavender coating and melt until smooth. Coat 2 of the cake pops secured with lavender coating (see page 29). Decorate with sprinkles. Set in a cake pop stand to dry.

3. Tint the remaining lavender coating dark purple. Coat the remaining cake pops secured with lavender coating. Decorate with sprinkles. Set in the stand to dry.

4. Add $1/2$ cup (125 mL) yellow candy coating wafers to the reserved yellow coating and melt until smooth. Coat the remaining cake pops. Decorate with sprinkles. Set in the stand to dry.

5. Wrap the Styrofoam block as you would a gift. Tie 2 pieces of ribbon in a knot around each cake pop stick (purple on yellow cake pops, yellow on purple). Slide the knots up to just below the cake pops. Use a scissors blade to curl the ribbons. Push the cake pop sticks into the Styrofoam, arranging the cake pops decoratively.

Thinking of You

· ·

**Makes
3 flowers**

Create your own garden with these special flowers. They're the perfect little gift for a neighbor or friend, just to say "Hello" or "Thinking of You."

· ·

Tips

Choose hard candies in colors that complement the yellow candy coating, such as red, brown or orange.

Babycakes™ cupcakes are the perfect size for these flowers. Of course, if you don't have a Babycakes™ Cupcake Maker, you can substitute regular or mini cupcakes. Adjust the length of the cake pop sticks so they appear balanced with the size of cupcake you are using.

Ingredients

	Yellow candy coating wafers	
3	Lemon Poppy Seed Cake Pops (page 38)	3
27	sweet-tart disk-shaped hard candies (such as Spree)	27
3	Babycakes™ cupcakes (see tip, at left)	3
	Buttercream frosting, tinted green	
	Green sprinkles	

Materials

3	6-inch (15 cm) cake pop sticks	3
12 inches	green tulle (about 6 inches/15 cm wide), cut into 4-inch (10 cm) lengths	30 cm

1. Cut off and discard 1 inch (2.5 cm) from each cake pop stick (6-inch/15 cm sticks are too long, but 4-inch/10 cm sticks are too short).

2. Melt 1 cup (250 mL) yellow candy coating wafers (see page 19) and use to attach sticks to cake pops (see page 27). Freeze cake pops for at least 15 minutes to set. Reserve the remaining candy coating.

3. Reheat yellow coating and coat a cake pop (see page 29). Immediately arrange a ring of 9 hard candies around the cake pop to resemble flower petals. Set in a cake pop stand to dry. Repeat with the remaining cake pops and hard candies.

4. Frost Babycakes™ cupcakes with green buttercream frosting. Sprinkle with green sprinkles.

5. Tie a length of tulle in a knot around each cake pop stick. Insert a cake pop into the center of each cupcake.

Thanks a Latte

Makes
1 gift

This little gift of cake pops in a coffee cup shows your appreciation or thanks, conveying more than words alone can say.

Tips

Blue is a beautiful complement to the coffee colors. However, you can choose any color of mug. Match the piping candy coating and the ribbon to the colors on the mug.

Use flavored coffee beans for added aroma.

Combining equal parts milk chocolate and white candy coating wafers creates a light brown color. Adjust the proportions of candy coating wafers to make the color a little darker or lighter, as you prefer.

Ingredients

	Dark chocolate, milk chocolate, white and blue candy coating wafers	
10	Cappuccino Bites (page 61)	10
	Toffee chips	
8 oz	coffee beans or chocolate-covered espresso beans	250 g

Materials

10	cake pop sticks	10
2	pastry bags or squeeze bottles, each fitted with a fine tip	2
40 inches	blue and ivory print ribbon (about 1 inch/2.5 cm wide), cut into 4-inch (10 cm) lengths	100 cm
1	large coffee cup with matching saucer, in blue and brown color tones	1

1. Melt $1/4$ cup (60 mL) dark chocolate candy coating wafers (see page 19) and use to attach sticks to 6 cake pops (see page 27). Freeze cake pops for at least 15 minutes to set. Reserve the remaining candy coating.

2. Combine 2 tbsp (30 mL) each milk chocolate and white candy coating wafers and melt until smooth. Use to attach sticks to the remaining cake pops. Freeze cake pops for at least 15 minutes. Reserve the remaining candy coating.

3. Add 1 cup (250 mL) dark chocolate candy coating wafers to the reserved dark chocolate coating and melt until smooth. Coat the cake pops secured with dark chocolate coating (see page 29). Immediately sprinkle 3 of the cake pops with toffee chips. Set in a cake pop stand to dry.

4. Add $1/4$ cup (60 mL) each milk chocolate and white candy coating wafers to the reserved light brown coating and melt until smooth. Coat the remaining cake pops. Set in the stand to dry.

5. Melt $\frac{1}{2}$ cup (125 mL) blue candy coating wafers. Use a pastry bag to pipe blue swirls or stripes (see page 33) onto the dark chocolate cake pops not sprinkled with toffee chips. If desired, immediately sprinkle toffee chips over the blue piping. Set in the stand to dry.

6. Reheat dark chocolate coating, adding more wafers as needed. Use another pastry bag to pipe swirls or stripes onto the light brown cake pops. Set in the stand to dry.

7. Tie a length of ribbon in a knot around each cake pop stick. Slide the knots up to just below the cake pops.

8. Place the coffee cup on its saucer. Fill the cup with coffee beans. Arrange the cake pops in the cup, using the beans to steady them. Scatter more beans decoratively in the saucer.

Friends Forever

The black-and-white color theme makes this a gift to remember. Friends from all walks of life will be impressed by its simple sophistication.

Tips

If the box has a cover, turn it upside down and place the box inside it. If necessary, use double-sided tape to hold them together.

Black candy coating wafers may only be available seasonally, for Halloween. Stock up in October, or make your own by stirring a small amount of black oil-based candy coloring into melted dark chocolate candy coating.

Ingredients

	Black and white candy coating wafers	
5	Triple Chocolate Cake Pops (page 54)	5
4	Favorite White Cake Pops (page 26)	4

Materials

9	cake pop sticks	9
2	pastry bags or squeeze bottles, each fitted with a fine tip	2
1	decorative black and white gift box (about 4 inches/10 cm cubed)	1
1	Styrofoam cube (at least 4½ inches/ 11 cm cubed)	1
	Black metallic paper shred	
20 inches	white ribbon (about ½ inch/ 1 cm wide), cut into 4-inch (10 cm) lengths	50 cm
16 inches	black ribbon (about ½ inch/ 1 cm wide), cut into 4-inch (10 cm) lengths	40 cm

1. Melt ¼ cup (60 mL) black candy coating wafers (see page 19) and use to attach sticks to chocolate cake pops (see page 27). Freeze cake pops for at least 15 minutes to set. Reserve the remaining candy coating. Repeat with white candy coating wafers, attaching sticks to white cake pops.

2. Add 1 cup (250 mL) black candy coating wafers to the reserved black coating and melt until smooth. Coat chocolate cake pops (see page 29). Set in a cake pop stand to dry. Repeat with white candy coating wafers and white cake pops.

3. Reheat black coating, adding more wafers as needed. Use a pastry bag to pipe swirls (see page 33), spirals or dots onto white cake pops. Set in the stand to dry. Repeat with white coating and another pastry bag, piping swirls, spirals or dots onto chocolate cake pops.

Tips

Decorate one cake pop for every year of your friendship. For us, that would mean displaying 30 cake pops in a large barrel instead of a cute little gift box!

You can use any cake pop flavor for any of the arrangements in this chapter, though it is wise to use lighter-colored cakes with white or light pastel candy coating wafers. Bright or dark-colored candy coating wafers will coat even the darkest cake pops. So have fun — choose your favorite flavor or mix and match.

4. Measure the dimensions of the box and trim the Styrofoam to fit snugly and be about 1 inch (2.5 cm) shorter than the box. Place Styrofoam in the box and cover it with paper shred.

5. Tie a length of white ribbon in a knot around the stick of each black cake pop, and tie a length of black ribbon in a knot around the stick of each white cake pop. Slide the knots up to just below the cake pops. Push the cake pop sticks into the Styrofoam, arranging the cake pops decoratively.

Girls' Night Out

This creative gift —
a woman's head
popping out of a
decorative box — is the
perfect way to slip a
party invitation or
gift certificate to a
special friend.

Tips

When you're coating cake
pops, the candy coating
needs to be deep enough
that you can dip the cake
pops straight down into it.
If you're only dipping a few
cake pops, there will be
some coating left over, but
it can be melted again and
used another time.

You can also use yellow,
black, orange or white
candy coating wafers for
the hair, and blue or green
candy coating wafers for the
eyes. Customize your gift to
resemble the friend you're
giving it to.

Ingredients

	Pink, yellow, white, milk chocolate and red candy coating wafers	
1	cake pop (any flavor)	1
	Shortening or Paramount Crystals	

Materials

1	cake pop stick	1
1	pastry bag or squeeze bottle, fitted with a fine tip	1
3	fine paintbrushes	3
1	decorative cardboard gift box (about 4 by 2 inches/10 by 5 cm)	1
1	Styrofoam block (at least 5 by 3 by 3 inches/ 12.5 by 7.5 by 7.5 cm)	1
	Pretty stickers	
4 inches	pink ribbon (about $\frac{1}{2}$ inch/ 1 cm wide)	10 cm
4 inches	black ribbon (about $\frac{1}{2}$ inch/ 1 cm wide)	10 cm
2 feet	hot pink tulle (about 6 inches/ 15 cm wide), cut into 6-inch (15 cm) lengths	60 cm

1. Melt 2 tbsp (30 mL) pink candy coating wafers (see page 19) and use to attach stick to cake pop (see page 27). Freeze cake pop for at least 15 minutes to set.

2. To create a mixture the color of a light skin tone, combine equal parts of yellow, pink and white candy coating wafers. For darker skin tones, combine white candy coating wafers with a small amount of chocolate candy coating wafers. Melt $\frac{1}{2}$ cup (125 mL) of the combined wafers. Adjust the tone as desired by adding a little more of one color or another and reheating to melt. Coat the cake pop (see page 29). Set in a cake pop stand to dry.

3. Melt 2 tbsp (30 mL) chocolate candy coating wafers. Use the pastry bag to pipe hair onto the cake pop. Set in the stand to dry.

4. Thin chocolate coating with shortening or Paramount Crystals (see page 20). Use a paintbrush to paint eyes on the cake pop. Set in the stand to dry.

Tips

Be sure to purchase food-safe paintbrushes from a cake decorating shop.

If the gift box has handles, make sure the cake pop sits at a good height above the box. Adjust the length of the cake pop stick before decorating, or fold the box's handles down.

5. Melt 2 tbsp (30 mL) red candy coating wafers and thin with shortening or Paramount Crystals. Use another paintbrush to paint lips on the cake pop. Set in the stand to dry.

6. Reheat red coating, adding more red wafers as needed and adding a few pink candy coating wafers. Thin the coating again, if needed. Use another paintbrush to paint cheeks on the cake pop. Set in the stand to dry.

7. Paint freckles, glasses, hair bows or other details as desired, reheating and thinning coatings as needed. Set in the stand to dry.

8. Measure the dimensions of the gift box and trim the Styrofoam to fit snugly and be 1 inch (2.5 cm) shorter than the box. Place Styrofoam in the box. Embellish the box with stickers.

9. Tie pink ribbon and black ribbon in a knot around the cake pop stick. Slide the knot up to just below the cake pop. Push the cake pop stick into the center of the Styrofoam. If the gift box has handles, use a piece of tulle to partially close them. Stuff the remaining tulle around the Styrofoam, making sure the tulle fluffs out around the top of the box.

Bear Hug

● ●

**Makes
1 gift**

Who can resist
cute, cuddly panda
bears? This yummy
arrangement is an ideal
gift for anyone who
needs a hug.

● ● ● ● ● ● ● ● ● ● ● ● ● ● ● ● ● ● ● ●

Tips

Black candy coating wafers
may only be available
seasonally, for Halloween.
Stock up in October, or
make your own by stirring
a small amount of black
oil-based candy coloring
into melted dark chocolate
candy coating.

Styrofoam blocks can be
purchased at craft stores
and come in a variety of
shapes and sizes. You
may wish to purchase
larger pieces and cut off
the amount you need for
each project.

Ingredients

	White, black and red candy coating wafers	
6	Almond Cake Pops (page 44)	6
	Black and red candy-coated chocolate candies	
	Shortening or Paramount Crystals	

Materials

6	cake pop sticks	6
3	fine paintbrushes	3
12 inches	red ribbon (about ¼ inch/ 0.5 cm wide), cut into 4-inch (10 cm) lengths	30 cm
1	pastry bag or squeeze bottle, fitted with a fine tip	1
12 inches	black ribbon (about ¼ inch/0.5 cm wide), cut into 4-inch (10 cm) lengths	30 cm
1	round wooden bowl (about 4½ inches/11 cm in diameter)	1
1	Styrofoam cube (at least 5 inches/ 12.5 cm cubed)	1

For the Panda Bears

1. Melt ¼ cup (60 mL) white candy coating wafers (see page 19) and use to attach sticks to 3 cake pops (see page 27). Slice a small piece off the front of each cake pop where you'll place the panda's candy eyes. (The flat surface will let the candies sit flat, creating a more realistic-looking panda head.) Freeze cake pops for at least 15 minutes to set. Reserve the remaining candy melts.

2. Add ½ cup (125 mL) white candy coating wafers to the reserved white coating and melt until smooth. Coat a cake pop (see page 29). Immediately position 2 black candy-coated chocolates as eyes and another 2 as ears. Set in a cake pop stand to dry. Repeat with the other 2 cake pops.

3. Reheat white coating and thin with shortening or Paramount Crystals (see page 20). Use a paintbrush to paint the whites of the eyes. Set in the stand to dry.

Tips

Be sure to purchase food-safe paintbrushes from a cake decorating shop.

You can use any cake pop flavor for any of the arrangements in this chapter, though it is wise to use lighter-colored cakes with white or light pastel candy coating wafers. Bright or dark-colored candy coating wafers will coat even the darkest cake pops. So have fun — choose your favorite flavor or mix and match.

4. Melt $\frac{1}{4}$ cup (60 mL) black candy coating wafers and thin with shortening or Paramount Crystals. Use another paintbrush to paint a nose, mouth and pupils in the eyes. Set in the stand to dry. Reserve the remaining candy melts.

5. Melt 2 tbsp (30 mL) red candy coating wafers and thin with shortening or Paramount Crystals. Use another paintbrush to paint a tongue on the panda's mouth. Set in the stand to dry. Reserve the remaining candy melts.

6. Tie a length of red ribbon in a knot around each cake pop stick. Slide the knots up to just below the cake pops.

For the Accent Cake Pops

7. Add $\frac{1}{4}$ cup (60 mL) red candy coating wafers to the reserved red coating and melt until smooth. Use to attach sticks to the remaining cake pops. Freeze cake pops for at least 15 minutes to set. Reserve the remaining candy melts.

8. Add $\frac{1}{2}$ cup (125 mL) red candy coating wafers to the red coating and melt until smooth. Coat cake pops. Set in the stand to dry.

9. Add 2 to 3 tbsp (30 to 45 mL) black candy coating wafers to the reserved black coating and melt until smooth. Use the pastry bag to pipe decorative zigzags on top of each red cake pop. Set in the stand to dry.

10. Tie a length of black ribbon in a knot around each cake pop stick. Slide the knots up to just below the cake pops.

Assembly

11. Measure the dimensions of the bowl and trim the Styrofoam to fit snugly and be about 1 inch (2.5 cm) shorter than the bowl. Place Styrofoam in the bowl and cover it with red and black candy-coated chocolates. Push the cake pop sticks into the Styrofoam, arranging the panda bears and accent cake pops decoratively.

Get Well Cheer

**Makes
1 gift**

A cup of cheer is just what the doctor ordered. Whimsical cake pops — one decorated to look like someone who is sick — in a mug decorated with adhesive bandages will bring a smile and convey best wishes every time.

Tips

Choose the recipient's favorite cake pop flavor. For added fun, decorate the cake pop to resemble your sick friend, melting candy coating wafers that match his or her skin, hair and eye color.

Be sure to purchase food-safe paintbrushes from a cake decorating shop.

Ingredients

	Pink, red, milk chocolate, yellow and white candy coating wafers	
6	Almond Cake Pops (page 44)	6
	Shortening or Paramount Crystals	

Materials

6	cake pop sticks	6
2	pastry bags or squeeze bottles, each fitted with a fine tip	2
2	fine paintbrushes	2
1	large white coffee or latte mug (3 to 4 inches/7.5 to 10 cm in diameter)	1
1	Styrofoam cube (4 inches/10 cm cubed)	1
	White paper shred	
6	adhesive bandages	6
1	sheet thick white printer paper	1
	Red card stock	
	Paper punch	
6 inches	brown, white or red string or cord	15 cm
2 feet	red-checked ribbon (about ½ inch/ 1 cm wide), cut into 4-inch (10 cm) lengths	60 cm
2 feet	brown ribbon (about ½ inch/ 1 cm wide), cut into 4-inch (10 cm) lengths	60 cm

1. Melt 2 tbsp (30 mL) pink candy coating wafers (see page 19) and use to attach a stick to 1 cake pop (see page 27). Freeze cake pop for at least 15 minutes to set. Repeat with ½ cup (125 mL) red candy coating wafers and ½ cup (125 mL) chocolate candy coating wafers, using red to attach sticks to 3 cake pops and chocolate to attach sticks to 2 cake pops. Reserve the remaining red and chocolate candy coating.

2. To create a mixture the color of a light skin tone, combine equal parts of yellow, pink and white candy coating wafers. For darker skin tones, combine white candy coating wafers with a small amount of chocolate candy coating wafers. Melt ½ cup (125 mL) of the combined candy coating wafers. Adjust the tone as desired by adding a little more of one color or another and reheating to melt. Coat the cake pop secured with pink coating (see page 29). Set in a cake pop stand to dry.

Tips

You can use any cake pop flavor for any of the arrangements in this chapter, though it is wise to use lighter-colored cakes with white or light pastel candy coating wafers. Bright or dark-colored candy coating wafers will coat even the darkest cake pops. So have fun — choose your favorite flavor or mix and match.

When you're coating cake pops, the candy coating needs to be deep enough that you can dip the cake pops straight down into it. If you're only dipping a few cake pops, there will be some coating left over, but it can be melted again and used another time.

3. Add 1 cup (250 mL) red candy coating wafers to the reserved red coating and melt until smooth. Coat the cake pops secured with red coating. Set in the stand to dry. Repeat with chocolate candy coating wafers, coating the remaining cake pops.

4. Reheat red coating, adding more wafers as needed. Use a pastry bag to pipe swirls (see page 33), spirals or dots onto the chocolate-coated cake pops. Set in the stand to dry.

5. Thin red coating with shortening or Paramount Crystals (see page 20). Use a paintbrush to paint a sad mouth — perhaps with tongue sticking out — on the face of the "sick person."

6. Reheat chocolate candy coating, adding more wafers as needed. Use another pastry bag to pipe swirls, spirals or dots onto the red cake pops, and to pipe hair onto the "sick person." Set in the stand to dry.

7. Thin chocolate coating with shortening or Paramount Crystals. Use another paintbrush to paint eyes on the "sick person." Set in the stand to dry.

8. Measure the dimensions of the mug and trim the Styrofoam to fit snugly and be 1 inch (2.5 cm) shorter than the mug. Place Styrofoam in the mug and cover it with paper shred. Stick adhesive bandages in a random pattern on the outside of the mug.

9. On printer paper, print "Get Well Soon." Cut out a 3- by 2-inch (7.5 by 5 cm) rectangle, centering the words in the rectangle. Cut a $3\frac{1}{2}$- by $2\frac{1}{2}$-inch (8.5 by 6 cm) rectangle out of red card stock. Glue the white rectangle to the red rectangle, leaving a margin all the way around. Punch a hole in the top left corner of the card and use the string to tie the card to the mug handle.

10. Tie a length of red-checked ribbon and a length of brown ribbon in a knot around each cake pop stick. Slide the knots up to just below the cake pops. Push the cake pop sticks into the Styrofoam, arranging the cake pops decoratively, with the "sick person" set higher than the others.

Welcome Baby

**Makes
1 gift**

Welcoming a bundle of joy is always special — especially when cake pops decorated in pink or blue help announce the arrival. That's just what our friend Sheri Worrel did when her grandson was born, and the cake pops were almost as well received as the sweet arrival himself.

Tip

When selecting the gift box, choose one that has flaps or a top that folds down. If the box has a removable top, remove it and cut a triangle from the center of it.

Ingredients

	Blue and dark chocolate candy coating wafers	
9	Chocolate Sour Cream Cake Pops (page 24)	9

Materials

9	cake pop sticks	9
2	pastry bags or squeeze bottles, each fitted with a fine tip	2
1	white gift box with flaps (about 4 1/2 inches/11 cm cubed)	1
	Double-sided foam tape	
	1/16-inch (2 mm) paper punch	
1	diaper pin	1
1	Styrofoam cube (at least 5 inches/ 12.5 cm cubed)	1
	White paper shred	
63 inches	"It's a Boy" ribbon (about 1/4-inch/ 0.5 cm wide), cut into 7-inch (18 cm) lengths	162 cm

1. Melt 1/4 cup (60 mL) blue candy coating wafers (see page 19) and use to attach sticks to 5 cake pops (see page 27). Freeze cake pops for at least 15 minutes to set. Reserve the remaining candy coating. Repeat with chocolate candy coating wafers, attaching sticks to the remaining cake pops.

2. Add 1 cup (250 mL) blue candy coating wafers to the reserved blue coating and melt until smooth. Coat the cake pops secured with blue coating (see page 29). Set in a cake pop stand to dry. Repeat with chocolate candy coating wafers and the remaining cake pops.

3. Reheat blue coating, adding more wafers as needed. Use a pastry bag to pipe swirls or decorative zigzags (see page 33) over the chocolate cake pops. Set in the stand to dry. Repeat with chocolate coating, using another pastry bag to pipe swirls or zigzags over the blue cake pops.

Tips

For a baby girl, use "It's a Girl" ribbon and decorate 5 of the cake pops with melted pink candy coating wafers. If you don't know the baby's sex, choose any pastel ribbon and candy coating wafers.

When you're coating cake pops, the candy coating needs to be deep enough that you can dip the cake pops straight down into it. If you're only dipping a few cake pops, there will be some coating left over, but it can be melted again and used another time.

4. Cut the flaps off the top of the gift box. Cut the largest flap into a triangle (this will represent the front of the diaper). Fold the bottom of the triangle up $1/2$ inch (1 cm), making a flap. Place the flap under the box and use double-sided tape to stick the triangle to the box. Punch two holes in the top third of the triangle, insert the diaper pin through the holes and close the pin.

5. Measure the dimensions of the box and trim the Styrofoam to fit snugly and be about 1 inch (2.5 cm) shorter than the box. Place Styrofoam in the box and cover it with paper shred.

6. Tie a length of ribbon in a bow around each cake pop stick. Slide the bows up to just below the cake pops. Set aside. Push the cake pop sticks into the Styrofoam, arranging the cake pops decoratively.

Painting a Welcome

This whimsical arrangement of yummy cake pops makes the perfect housewarming gift. Use your friend's favorite color or match a paint color used in the new house. We chose to use blue.

Tip

Make sure to use only new, clean craft paint cans. Avoid used paint cans, which would pose a food safety issue.

Ingredients

	Blue and white candy coating wafers	
8	Favorite Brownie Cake Pops (page 57)	8
	Blue candy-coated chocolate candies	

Materials

8	cake pop sticks	8
1	pastry bag or squeeze bottle, fitted with a fine tip	1
1	clear plastic or metal craft paint can (about 4 inches/10 cm in diameter)	1
1	Styrofoam cube (at least 4 inches/10 cm cubed)	1
	Colorful tissue paper	
	Paint color swatches	
	Glue	
	Black marker	
	Blue ribbon	
	New paintbrush	

1. Melt ¼ cup (60 mL) blue candy coating wafers (see page 19) and use to attach sticks to cake pops (see page 27). Freeze cake pops for at least 15 minutes to set. Reserve the remaining candy coating.

2. Add ½ cup (125 mL) blue candy coating wafers to the reserved blue coating and melt until smooth. Coat 2 or 3 cake pops (see page 29). Set in a cake pop stand to dry.

3. Add a few white candy coating wafers to the blue coating and melt until smooth. Coat 2 or 3 cake pops. Set in the stand to dry. Continue to lighten the coating with white wafers and coat cake pops until all are coated.

4. Melt ¼ cup (60 mL) blue candy coating wafers. Use the pastry bag to pipe swirls (see page 33) and "paint drips" on the cake pops. Set in the stand to dry.

5. Measure the dimensions of the paint can and trim the Styrofoam to fit snugly and be about 1 inch (2.5 cm) shorter than the can. Wrap the Styrofoam in tissue paper and place it in the can.

Tips

This gift is also a great idea for a friend who needs cheering up (write "Paint away the blues" on the swatch) or to say thank you (write "You color my world with happiness").

You can use any cake pop flavor for any of the arrangements in this chapter, though it is wise to use lighter-colored cakes with white or light pastel candy coating wafers. Bright or dark-colored candy coating wafers will coat even the darkest cake pops. So have fun — choose your favorite flavor or mix and match.

6. Reheat blue coating, adding more wafers as needed. Drizzle coating over the Styrofoam, covering it completely, and let coating drip down the sides of the can. Push the cake pop sticks into the Styrofoam, arranging the cake pops decoratively. Let dry, then cover the top of the can with candy-coated chocolates.

7. Arrange several paint color swatches in a fan and glue them together. Place the paint can on top of the fan and secure it with glue.

8. Use the marker to write "Happy Housewarming" on another paint color swatch. Poke a hole in the swatch. Tie blue ribbon in a bow around the paintbrush, tying the swatch into the bow. Present the brush with the can or, if desired, tie a longer blue ribbon around the can and secure the brush to the can.

Bookworm

Who can resist a book when this friendly little bookworm adorns it? Any book lover will love this fun treat. Make several when the book club is gathering at your house.

Tips

For the text pages, you can pull a couple of pages out of a discarded book, use a newspaper or print out a page or two of text designed to resemble a book or textbook.

Attaching sticks to the cake pops makes them much easier to hold when decorating, so we take the time for this extra step even for designs, like this one, where the cake pops are not on sticks in the final presentation.

Ingredients

	Green, yellow, white, dark chocolate and red candy coating wafers	
7	Lemon Poppy Seed Cake Pops (page 38)	7
2	candy-coated chocolate candies (preferably green or yellow)	2
2	green sweet-tart disk-shaped hard candies (such as Spree)	2
	Shortening or Paramount Crystals	

Materials

7	cake pop sticks	7
3	fine food-safe paintbrushes	3
	Decorative square paper punch (2 to 3 inches/5 to 7.5 cm square)	
1 to 2	pages of text (see tip, at left)	1 to 2
	Vellum paper	
1	book	1
1	6-inch (7.5 cm) piece flexible floral wire	1
1	pastry bag or squeeze bottle, fitted with a fine tip	1

1. Melt $1/4$ cup (60 mL) green candy coating wafers (see page 19) and use to attach sticks to cake pops (see page 27). Freeze cake pops for at least 15 minutes to set.

2. Combine one part green, one part yellow and one part white candy coating wafers to make 1 cup (250 mL) total. Melt until smooth. Adjust the tone as desired by adding a little more of one color or another and reheating to melt. Coat cake pops (see page 29). After coating the last cake pop, immediately position the candy-coated chocolates on it as cheeks for the bookworm's head. Set in a cake pop stand to dry.

3. Reheat the combined candy coating and dip the head a second time to coat the candies. Immediately position the disk-shaped hard candies as eyes. Set in the stand to dry. Reserve the remaining candy coating.

4. Melt 1 tbsp (15 mL) white candy coating wafers. Use a paintbrush to paint the whites of the eyes on the hard candies. Set in the stand to dry.

Tips

If you don't have a square paper punch in the right size, use scalloped scissors to cut out 2- to 3-inch (5 to 7.5 cm) squares.

The vellum squares prevent the cake pops from touching the text paper and transferring grease to the book cover or ink to the cake pops.

For a garden party, select a gardening book, then surround the bookworm with flowers.

If you want to add more height to your display, use two books. Stack one on top of the other, with the spines facing you, then rotate the top book slightly counterclockwise for a decorative look.

5. Melt 1 tbsp (15 mL) chocolate candy coating wafers and thin with shortening or Paramount Crystals (see page 20). Use another paintbrush to paint pupils in the eyes. Set in the stand to dry.

6. Melt 1 tbsp (15 mL) red candy coating wafers and thin with shortening or Paramount Crystals. Use another paintbrush to paint a mouth. Set in the stand to dry.

7. Punch out 7 squares from the text pages and 7 squares from the vellum (see tips, at left). Place the book in front of you, with the spine facing you. Arrange the paper squares on top of the book in a loose backwards "S" shape, overlapping squares as needed so that no gaps appear in the curves. Place a matching piece of vellum on top of each piece of paper.

8. Gently twist the stick out of each cake pop. Arrange cake pops, hole side down, along the vellum, with the head closest to the top of the book spine and facing you. Reheat the combined candy coating, then use a drop or two to glue each cake pop to a vellum square and to glue the cake pops to each another. Set aside to dry.

9. Combine eight parts white and one part yellow candy coating wafers to make $1/2$ cup (125 mL) total. Melt until smooth. Use the pastry bag to pipe decorative zigzags onto the bookworm's body.

10. Fashion the floral wire into eyeglasses, using a pencil as a mold so that the frames for each eye are the same size. Set the frames over the worm's eyes (if necessary, use a toothpick to add a tiny drop of candy coating to secure them).

Kitty Cat with Yarn

**Makes
1 gift**

Time to let the cat out of the bag! This cute cat with a ball of yarn makes the perfect gift for any cat lover.

Tips

If desired, decorate several cake pop yarn balls, using a variety of colors, to create a fuller centerpiece. The cat takes some time to create, but the yarn balls are quick and easy.

Be sure to use oil-based coloring specifically designed to tint candy coating. Typical food coloring will cause the coating to solidify.

Ingredients

	White, pink and green candy coating wafers	
3	Hot Chocolate Cake Pops (page 52)	3
4	vanilla baking chips	4
1	gray or black disk-shaped candy wafer (such as Necco)	1
2	brown mini candy-coated chocolate candies	2
	Black oil-based candy coloring	
	Shortening or Paramount Crystals	

Materials

2	cake pop sticks	2
1	toothpick	1
2	fine food-safe paintbrushes	2
1	gray striped pipe cleaner	1
1	pastry bag or squeeze bottle, fitted with a fine tip	1
	Several small balls of yarn (about 2½ inches/6 cm in diameter)	
1	oval basket (about 6 inches/15 cm long)	1

For the Cat

1. Melt 2 tbsp (30 mL) white candy coating wafers (see page 19) and use to attach a stick to a cake pop (see page 27). Push the cake pop down the stick so there is room for another cake pop on top. Immediately add a second cake pop, using a few drops of candy coating to glue the cake pops together. Freeze cake pops for at least 15 minutes to set. Reserve the remaining candy coating.

2. Reheat the reserved white candy coating. For the cat's feet, use coating to glue vanilla baking chips to the front of the bottom cake pop, placing two near the bottom and two near the top and positioning all with the flat side out. Freeze for at least 15 minutes to set.

3. Cut two triangles for the ears out of the candy wafer and set aside.

4. Add ½ cup (125 mL) white candy coating wafers to the white coating and melt until smooth. Tint the coating with black candy coloring to make a light gray. Coat double cake pop (see page 29). Immediately add the candy wafer ears to the top of the cake pop and, at

186   *Creative Gifts*

Tips

You can use any cake pop flavor for any of the arrangements in this chapter, though it is wise to use lighter-colored cakes with white or light pastel candy coating wafers. Bright or dark-colored candy coating wafers will coat even the darkest cake pops. So have fun — choose your favorite flavor or mix and match.

When you're coating cake pops, the candy coating needs to be deep enough that you can dip the cake pops straight down into it. If you're only dipping a few cake pops, there will be some coating left over, but it can be melted again and used another time.

the front of the top cake pop, position 2 candy-coated chocolates as the muzzle. Drag the toothpick out from the muzzle through the wet coating, drawing whiskers. Set in a cake pop stand to dry.

5. Reheat gray coating and tint darker by stirring in more black candy coloring. Use a paintbrush to paint stripes on the head and back of the cat. Set in the stand to dry.

6. Melt 1 tbsp (15 mL) pink candy coating wafers and thin with shortening or Paramount Crystals (see page 20). Use another paintbrush to paint a tongue and a nose. Set in the stand to dry.

7. Reheat gray coating and tint darker by stirring in more black candy coloring. Using the end of the first paintbrush (opposite the bristles), make two dots of coating for the eyes. Use the brush to paint freckles on the muzzle and tiny claws on the feet. Set in the stand to dry.

8. Wind one end of the pipe cleaner around the cake pop stick, then slide it up to the base of the bottom cake pop to make the tail. Curl the tail as desired.

For the Cake Pop Yarn Ball

9. Combine 2 tbsp (30 mL) each white and green candy coating wafers and melt until smooth, making a light green color. Use to attach a stick to the remaining cake pop. Freeze cake pop for at least 15 minutes to set. Reserve the remaining candy coating.

10. Reheat the reserved light green coating. Coat cake pop. Set in the stand to dry.

11. Reheat light green coating. Use the pastry bag to pipe lines that resemble strands of yarn over the cake pop. Set in the stand to dry.

Assembly

12. Fit the balls of yarn snugly into the basket. Pull a few strings out to hang over the edge of the basket. Arrange the cat and yarn cake pops in the basket by pushing the sticks into the yarn.

Theme Party and Special Occasion Centerpieces

Crazy Straws

· ·

Any celebration is a good time for a fun cake pop display on crazy straws! The cake pops bounce on the straws, adding whimsical movement to the arrangement.

· ·

Tips

Crazy straws are festive straws that can be purchased at discount or party stores. Because the straws add height and movement to the arrangement, make sure the glass you use is heavy; otherwise, fill the bottom with marbles or glue the glass to a board before adding the cake pops.

Be sure the crazy straws fit in your cake pop stand and are held upright securely before you begin. If not, use a Styrofoam block instead.

Ingredients

	Blue, red, yellow, lavender, orange and green candy coating wafers	
6	Chocolate Sour Cream Cake Pops (page 24)	6
	Brightly colored decorative sprinkles	
	Sweet-tart disk-shaped hard candies (such as Spree)	

Materials

6	crazy straws	6
1	parfait or decorative glass (about 3 inches/7.5 cm in diameter)	1
1	Styrofoam cube (at least 3 inches/ 7.5 cm cubed)	1
7½ feet	colorful ribbons (about ½ inch/ 1 cm wide), 3 pieces cut into 16-inch (40 cm) lengths and 6 pieces cut into 7-inch (18 cm) lengths	228 cm

1. Melt 2 tbsp (30 mL) blue candy coating wafers (see page 19) and use to attach a crazy straw to 1 cake pop (see page 27). Freeze cake pop for at least 15 minutes to set. Reserve the remaining candy coating. Repeat with red, yellow, lavender, orange and green candy coating wafers, using each color to attach a straw to 1 cake pop.

2. Add ½ cup (125 mL) blue candy coating wafers to the reserved blue coating and melt until smooth. Coat the cake pop secured with blue coating (see page 29). Decorate with sprinkles. Set in a cake pop stand to dry. Repeat with red, yellow, lavender, orange and green candy coating wafers.

3. Tie three 16-inch (40 cm) ribbons around the center of the parfait glass. Measure the dimensions of the glass and trim the Styrofoam to fit snugly and be about 1 inch (2.5 cm) shorter than the glass. Place some candies in the bottom of the glass. Place Styrofoam in the glass and surround and cover it with candies.

4. Tie a 7-inch (18 cm) ribbon around each straw. Push the straws into the Styrofoam, arranging the cake pops decoratively.

Goldilocks and the Three Bears

Makes 1 centerpiece

Set the stage for a child's birthday party with this centerpiece based on a beloved fairy tale. For a fun presentation, insert the finished cake pops into a thick, heavy hardcover book that will stand upright on the table.

Tip

You can use any cake pop flavor for any of the arrangements in this chapter, though it is wise to use lighter-colored cakes with white or light pastel candy coating wafers. Bright or dark-colored candy coating wafers will coat even the darkest cake pops. So have fun — choose your favorite flavor or mix and match.

Ingredients

	White, yellow, pink, dark chocolate and red candy coating wafers	
3	Favorite White Cake Pops (page 26)	3
2	red jumbo heart sprinkles	2
	Shortening or Paramount Crystals	
2	white candy-coated drop candies (such as Hershey's Cookies 'n' Creme Drops)	2
4	brown candy-coated chocolate candies	4
2	pink jumbo heart sprinkles	2
1	milk chocolate drop candy (such as Hershey's Milk Chocolate Drops)	1
2	mini brown candy-coated chocolate candies	2
	Black edible ink food marker	

Materials

4	cake pop sticks	4
3	pastry bags or squeeze bottles, each fitted with a fine tip	3
3	food-safe fine paintbrushes	3
	2-inch (5 cm) scalloped paper punch (see tip, at right)	
3	2½-inch (6 cm) squares of decorative card stock in coordinating colors	3
	Glue stick	
6 inches	black ribbon (about ¼ inch/ 0.5 cm wide)	15 cm
1	old hardcover book (about 8½ by 6 by 1½ inches/21 by 15 by 4 cm)	1
2	8½- by 11-inch (21 by 28 cm) sheets of card stock (any color)	2
1	8½- by 3½-inch (21 by 8.5 cm) strip of decorative card stock	1
	Black marker	
3 feet	ribbon (about 1 inch/2.5 cm wide)	90 cm

For Goldilocks

1. Melt 1 tbsp (15 mL) white candy coating wafers (see page 19) and use to attach a stick to 1 cake pop (see page 27). Freeze cake pop for at least 15 minutes to set. Reserve the remaining candy coating.

Tips

When you're coating cake pops, the candy coating needs to be deep enough that you can dip the cake pops straight down into it. If you're only dipping a few cake pops, there will be some coating left over, but it can be melted again and used another time.

Be sure to purchase food-safe paintbrushes from a cake decorating shop.

If you don't have a paper punch, trace circles on the card stock with a 2-inch (5 cm) scalloped circle cookie cutter, then use scissors to cut out the shapes.

2. To create a mixture the color of a light skin tone, combine equal parts of yellow, pink and white candy coating wafers. Melt $\frac{1}{2}$ cup (125 mL) of the combined wafers. Adjust the tone as desired by adding a little more of one color or another and reheating to melt. Coat the cake pop (see page 29). Set in a cake pop stand to dry.

3. Melt 2 to 3 tbsp (30 to 45 mL) yellow candy coating wafers. Use a pastry bag to pipe hair in tight curls on the cake pop. Immediately place 2 red heart sprinkles, with points touching, in the hair to create a bow. Set in the stand to dry.

4. Melt 2 to 3 tbsp (30 to 45 mL) chocolate candy coating wafers and thin with shortening or Paramount Crystals (see page 20). Use a paintbrush to paint eyes and eyelashes. Set in the stand to dry.

5. Melt 2 to 3 tbsp (30 to 45 mL) red candy coating wafers. Use another pastry bag to pipe a dot in the center of the bow. Thin the remaining red coating with shortening or Paramount Crystals. Use another paintbrush to paint a mouth. Set in the stand to dry.

6. Add a little red coating to the reserved white coating, stirring to make a light pink color, and reheat as needed. Use another paintbrush to paint cheeks. Set in the stand to dry.

7. For her collar, use the scalloped paper punch to cut a circle from a square of card stock. Poke a small hole in the center of the circle, fold the circle in half and slide it up the cake pop stick to the base of the cake pop.

For Mama and Papa Bear

8. Melt 2 tbsp (30 mL) chocolate candy coating wafers and use to attach sticks to the remaining cake pops. Slice a small piece off the front of each cake pop where you'll place the drop candy muzzle. (The flat surface will let the candy sit flat, creating a more realistic-looking muzzle.) Freeze cake pops for at least 15 minutes to set. Reserve the remaining candy coating.

Tip

When you're melting just 1 to 2 tbsp (15 to 30 mL) of candy coating wafers to paint fine details, be careful not to overheat them; heat in 10- or 15-second intervals rather than 30-second intervals.

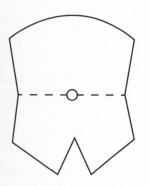

Papa Bear's collar

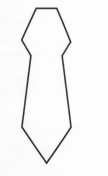

Papa Bear's tie

9. Add ½ cup (125 mL) chocolate candy coating wafers to the reserved chocolate coating and melt until smooth. Coat 1 cake pop. Immediately position 1 white drop candy on the flat spot as the muzzle, and 2 brown candy-coated chocolates as the ears. Set in the stand to dry. Repeat with the remaining cake pop, placing 2 pink heart sprinkles, with points touching, in front of one of the ears to be a bow on Mama Bear. Set in the stand to dry.

10. Melt 1 tbsp (15 mL) pink candy coating wafers. Use another pastry bag to pipe a dot in the center of the bow. Set in the stand to dry.

11. Melt 1 tbsp (15 mL) white candy coating wafers and thin with shortening or Paramount Crystals. Use the end of a paintbrush (opposite the bristles) to make two dots of coating for the eyes on each cake pop. Set in the stand to dry.

12. Reheat chocolate coating, adding more wafers as needed, and thin with shortening or Paramount Crystals. On each cake pop, paint a nose and a mouth on the muzzle and pupils in the eyes. Set in the stand to dry.

13. Melt 1 tbsp (15 mL) red candy coating wafers and thin with shortening or Paramount Crystals. Paint a tongue on each bear's mouth. Reserve the remaining coating.

14. For Papa Bear's collar, use the paper punch to cut a circle from a square of card stock. Using scissors, trim the circle to look like the pattern at left. Poke a small hole in the center of the collar, fold it according to the dotted line in the pattern, and slide it up the cake pop stick to the base of the cake pop. For his tie, trim a scrap of coordinating card stock to look like the pattern at left. Glue the tie in place on the collar.

15. For Mamma Bear's collar, use the paper punch to cut a circle from the remaining square of card stock. Poke a small hole in the center of the circle, fold the circle in half and slide it up the cake pop stick to the base of the cake pop.

Tips

If desired, use a sewing machine to zigzag-stitch the pieces of card stock for the book jacket together, making it look like old-fashioned binding.

For the book title, you could also use a computer to print the title in an old-fashioned font on printer paper the same color as the sheets of card stock, then cut out the title and glue it to the book jacket.

Be sure to place the cake pops in different parts of the book, as this will help them stay securely in place.

For Baby Bear

16. Melt 1 tbsp (15 mL) chocolate candy coating wafers. Dip about $\frac{1}{2}$ inch (1 cm) of a cake pop stick in the coating and press it to the back of the chocolate drop candy. Let dry.

17. Reheat chocolate coating as needed and use to glue the mini candy-coated chocolates onto the chocolate drop for the ears.

18. Melt 1 tbsp (15 mL) white candy coating wafers and thin with shortening or Paramount Crystals. Use the end of a paintbrush (opposite the bristles) to make two dots of coating for the eyes and to paint a small muzzle.

19. Use the black food marker to draw pupils in the eyes, a nose and a mouth.

20. Reheat the reserved red coating and paint a small tongue on the mouth.

21. Tie the black ribbon in a bow around the cake pop stick. Slide the bow up to just below the chocolate drop.

Assembly

22. Measure the book. Trim the 2 sheets of card stock to be the same height as the book and 3 inches (7.5 cm) wider. Trim the strip of card stock to be the same height as the book. Glue the three pieces of card stock together, with the strip in the center and overlapping both sheets, to make a book jacket. Let dry.

23. Use the marker to write "Goldilocks and the Three Bears" on the front of the jacket. Wrap the book jacket around the book, folding the edges inside the covers.

24. Insert the cake pop sticks into the book, placing each stick between different pages, so that the cake pops peek out over the top. Tie the book very firmly shut with ribbon, then tie the ribbon into a bow at the front of the book, underneath the title.

Jack-in-the-Box

· ·

This fun, colorful centerpiece is a show-stopper for a baby shower or a child's birthday party.

....

Tips

Crazy straws are festive straws that can be purchased at discount or party stores. Be sure the crazy straw fits in your cake pop stand and is held upright securely before you begin. If not, use a Styrofoam block instead.

If desired, you can add a crank to the jack-in-the-box. Bend a wire to resemble a crank. Drill a hole the diameter of the wire in the side of the box. Insert one end of the wire through the hole and bend it to secure the wire. Finish the outer end of the wire with a decorative bead, securing it with glue.

Ingredients

	White, red, blue and orange candy coating wafers	
1	White Spice Cake Pop (page 28)	1
1	marshmallow	1
	Green sprinkles	
2	round, flat jumbo pink sprinkles	2
1	mini red candy-coated chocolate candy	1
1	striped candy kiss	1
	Purple sprinkles	

Materials

1	wooden box with a hinged lid (about 4 inches/10 cm cubed)	1
1	Styrofoam cube (at least 4 inches/ 10 cm cubed)	1
	Variety of brightly colored paints and a paintbrush	
1	crazy straw	1
2	food-safe fine paintbrushes	2
1	pastry bag or squeeze bottle, fitted with a fine tip	1
	Colorful tissue paper, cut into 3-inch (7.5 cm) squares	

1. Measure the dimensions of the box and trim the Styrofoam to fit snugly and be about 1 inch (2.5 cm) shorter than the box. Set Styrofoam aside.

2. Paint the box and lid as desired, using brightly colored paints. Let dry.

3. Melt $1/4$ cup (60 mL) white candy coating wafers (see page 19) and use to attach the crazy straw to the cake pop (see page 27). Freeze cake pop for at least 15 minutes to set. Reserve the remaining candy coating.

4. Cut a $1/4$-inch (0.5 cm) thick round from the marshmallow (eat the rest of the marshmallow). Reheat the reserved white coating. Use a food-safe paintbrush to paint the outer edge of the marshmallow slice with coating. Roll the edge in green sprinkles. Poke a hole in the center of the marshmallow slice and slide it about halfway up the crazy straw.

Tips

When you're melting just 1 to 2 tbsp (15 to 30 mL) of candy coating wafers to paint fine details, be careful not to overheat them; heat in 10- or 15-second intervals rather than 30-second intervals.

Be sure to purchase food-safe fine paintbrushes from a cake decorating shop.

Use the jack-in-the-box model to make cake pop clowns for another occasion.

5. Coat the cake pop in white coating (see page 29). Slide the marshmallow slice up to just below the cake pop. Immediately position the pink sprinkles on the cake pop as cheeks and the mini red candy-coated chocolate as the nose. Set in a cake pop stand to dry.

6. Melt 1 tbsp (15 mL) red candy coating wafers and thin with shortening or Paramount Crystals (see page 20). Use another paintbrush to paint a mouth. Set in the stand to dry.

7. Melt 1 tbsp (15 mL) blue candy coating wafers and thin with shortening or Paramount Crystals. Use the end of a paintbrush (opposite the bristles) to make two dots of coating for the eyes. Set in the stand to dry.

8. Melt 2 to 3 tbsp (30 to 45 mL) orange candy coating wafers. Use a pastry bag to pipe hair in tight curls on the cake pop. Immediately place the candy kiss on top as a hat. Set in the stand to dry.

9. Reheat white coating, adding more wafers as needed. Dip the tip of the candy kiss hat in coating, then dip in purple sprinkles. Let dry.

10. Place the Styrofoam in the box and push the crazy straw into the Styrofoam. Arrange tissue paper squares over the Styrofoam, using a toothpick or pencil to poke them down into the Styrofoam and fluffing them up around the crazy straw.

Hedgehog Crossing

● ●

**Makes
1 centerpiece**

These adorable
hedgehogs signal fun
times ahead — perfect
for any occasion!

· ·

Tip

To make the crossing sign
on a computer, create a
diamond shape that is
2½ inches (6 cm) on each
side. Search the Internet
for a small drawing of a
hedgehog, and copy and
paste it into the middle of
the diamond. If desired,
add the word "Hedgehog"
above the drawing and
"Crossing" below it. Fill
the diamond with yellow
shading. Print and cut out
the sign. If using thin paper,
paste the sign to a slightly
larger diamond of brown
card stock to give it more
weight. (If you prefer to
hand-make the sign, simply
cut a diamond shape out
of yellow card stock and
write "Caution: Hedgehog
Crossing" on it.)

Ingredients

	Dark chocolate and white candy coating wafers	
3	Triple Chocolate Cake Pops (page 54)	3
3	candy kisses	3
18	vanilla baking chips	18
	Chocolate jimmies	
	Shortening or Paramount Crystals	

Materials

3	4-inch (10 cm) cake pop sticks	3
3	toothpicks	3
1	food-safe fine paintbrush	1
1	open tin container (about 8 by 4 by 3 inches/ 20 by 10 by 7.5 cm)	1
1	Styrofoam block (at least 8 by 4 by 3 inches/ 20 by 10 by 7.5 cm)	1
	Green paper shred	
1	diamond-shaped crossing sign (see tip, at left)	1
1	7- to 8-inch (18 to 20 cm) wooden skewer	1
	Transparent tape	

1. Melt ¼ cup (60 mL) chocolate candy coating wafers (see page 19) and use to attach sticks to cake pops (see page 27). Freeze cake pops for at least 15 minutes to set. Reserve the remaining candy coating.

2. Poke a toothpick into the flat bottom of each candy kiss, allowing the toothpick to protrude. Melt ¼ cup (60 mL) white candy coating wafers. Using the toothpick to hold the candy kisses, coat the kisses in white coating. Push toothpicks into a piece of Styrofoam and set aside to dry.

Tips

We used shorter cake pop sticks than usual so the hedgehogs would appear close to the ground.

Be sure to purchase a food-safe paintbrush from a cake decorating shop.

You can use any cake pop flavor for any of the arrangements in this chapter, though it is wise to use lighter-colored cakes with white or light pastel candy coating wafers. Bright or dark-colored candy coating wafers will coat even the darkest cake pops. So have fun — choose your favorite flavor or mix and match.

3. Add ½ cup (125 mL) chocolate candy coating wafers to the reserved chocolate coating and melt until smooth. Coat 1 cake pop (see page 29). Immediately push the toothpick of a candy kiss into the side of the cake pop, to be the hedgehog's face. Position 2 vanilla chips as ears, placing them on the cake pop above the face, with the flat side toward the face. Holding the cake pop upside down, position 4 vanilla chips as feet, with the flat side out. Set in a cake pop stand to dry. Repeat with the remaining cake pops.

4. Reheat chocolate coating. Working in small sections at a time, use the paintbrush to paint the hedgehogs' bodies with chocolate coating, then sprinkle with jimmies to resemble prickly fur. Set in the stand to dry.

5. Reheat chocolate coating and thin with shortening or Paramount Crystals (see page 20). Use the end of the paintbrush (opposite the bristles) to make two dots of coating for the eyes on each candy kiss. Add one dot of coating for a nose on the tip of each kiss. Set in the stand to dry.

6. Measure the dimensions of the container and trim the Styrofoam to fit snugly and be about 1 inch (2.5 cm) shorter than the container. Place Styrofoam in the container and cover it with paper shred. Push the cake pop sticks into the Styrofoam, arranging the hedgehogs in a line.

7. Tape the crossing sign to the skewer and push the skewer into the Styrofoam.

Barrel of Monkeys

Serve up a barrel of
fun with this barrel of
monkeys.

Tips

Twelve inches (30 cm) of
ribbon allows for nice curls
on each cake pop, but you
may want to adjust the
length depending on the
width and stiffness of the
ribbon you choose.

If desired, add a green
leaf-shaped sprinkle to any
strawberry-shaped candies
you decorate the accent
cake pops with.

Ingredients

	Milk chocolate, white and dark chocolate candy coating wafers	
8	Chocolate Sour Cream Cake Pops (page 24)	8
3	white candy-coated drop candies (such as Hershey's Cookies 'n' Creme Drops)	3
6	whole cashews	6
	Shortening or Paramount Crystals	
	Small fruit-shaped candies (such as Runts)	

Materials

8	cake pop sticks	8
2	food-safe fine paintbrushes	2
1	empty soup can (about 3 inches/ 7.5 cm in diameter)	1
	Duct tape	
	Craft or Popsicle sticks	
2	1/8-inch (3 mm) gold brads	2
2	10- by 3/8-inch (25 cm by 9 mm) strips brown card stock	2
	Glue dots	
1	Styrofoam block (about 4 by 2½ by 2½ inches/ 10 by 6 x 6 cm)	1
8 feet	yellow curling ribbon, cut into 12-inch (30 cm) lengths	240 cm

1. Melt ¼ cup (60 mL) milk chocolate candy coating wafers (see page 19) and use to attach sticks to cake pops (see page 27). For each of the 3 cake pops that will be monkeys, slice a small piece off the front where you'll place the drop candy muzzle. (The flat surface will let the candy sit flat, creating a more realistic-looking muzzle.) Freeze cake pops for at least 15 minutes to set. Reserve the remaining candy coating.

For the Monkeys

2. Add ½ cup (125 mL) milk chocolate candy coating wafers to the reserved chocolate coating and melt until smooth. Coat 1 of the cake pops with a flat surface (see page 29). Immediately position 1 white drop candy on the flat spot as the muzzle, and 2 cashews as the ears. Set in a cake pop stand to dry. Repeat with the other 2 cake pops with a flat surface.

Tips

Be sure to purchase food-safe paintbrushes from a cake decorating shop.

When you're coating cake pops, the candy coating needs to be deep enough that you can dip the cake pops straight down into it. If you're only dipping a few cake pops, there will be some coating left over, but it can be melted again and used another time.

3. Melt 2 to 3 tbsp (30 to 45 mL) white candy coating wafers and thin with shortening or Paramount Crystals (see page 20). Use a paintbrush to paint eyes on the monkeys. Set in the stand to dry.

4. Melt 2 to 3 tbsp (30 to 45 mL) dark chocolate candy coating wafers and thin with shortening or Paramount Crystals. Use the end of a paintbrush (opposite the bristles) to make dots of coating for pupils in the eyes and nostrils on the muzzles. Turn the paintbrush around and paint a mouth on each monkey. Set in the stand to dry.

For the Accent Cake Pops

5. Reheat milk chocolate coating and coat the remaining cake pops. Immediately decorate the top of each cake pop with a fruit-shaped candy. Set in the stand to dry.

For the Barrel

6. Wrap the can tightly with duct tape, sticky side out. Place craft sticks vertically around the can, touching each other, with the bottom of the sticks even with the bottom of the can. Surround the can completely, making it look like a wooden barrel.

7. Push a gold brad onto the end of each strip of card stock. Wrap the strips around the barrel, one near the top and one near the bottom, and adhere with a small glue dot underneath each brad.

Assembly

8. Measure the dimensions of the can and trim the Styrofoam to fit snugly and be about 1 inch (2.5 cm) shorter than the can. Place Styrofoam in the can and cover it with fruit-shaped candies.

9. Tie a length of ribbon in a knot around each cake pop stick. Slide the knots up to just below the cake pops. Use a scissors blade to curl the ribbons. Push the cake pop sticks into the Styrofoam, arranging the monkeys and accent cake pops decoratively.

Movie Night Popcorn

**Makes
1 centerpiece**

When you're hosting a movie night, chances are you'll be serving popcorn. Continue the theme with this fun centerpiece.

Tip

When cutting the marshmallows into two pieces, cut pieces of various sizes. The cake pops will look more like popcorn if the marshmallows are not in perfect halves.

Ingredients

	White candy coating wafers	
8	Favorite White Cake Pops (page 26)	8
40 to 45	mini marshmallows, each cut into two pieces (see tip, at left)	40 to 45
1	bag unpopped yellow popcorn	1

Materials

8	cake pop sticks	8
8 feet	red metallic curling ribbon, cut into 12-inch (30 cm) lengths	240 cm
1	popcorn container (about 8 inches/ 20 cm tall)	1
1	Styrofoam block (about 8 by 2 by 2 inches/ 20 by 5 by 5 cm)	1

1. Melt $1/4$ cup (60 mL) white candy coating wafers (see page 19) and use to attach sticks to cake pops (see page 27). Freeze cake pops for at least 15 minutes to set. Reserve the remaining candy coating.

2. Add 1 cup (250 mL) white candy coating wafers to the reserved white coating and melt until smooth. Coat cake pops (see page 29). Immediately arrange marshmallow halves, cut side down, over cake pops, making them look like popcorn. Set in a cake pop stand to dry.

3. Tie a length of ribbon in a knot around each cake pop stick. Slide the knots up to just below the cake pops. Use a scissors blade to curl the ribbons.

4. Measure the dimensions of the popcorn container and trim the Styrofoam to fit snugly and be about 1 inch (2.5 cm) shorter than the container. Place Styrofoam in the container and cover it with unpopped popcorn. Push the cake pop sticks into the Styrofoam, arranging the cake pops decoratively.

Basket of Chicks

· ·

**Makes
1 centerpiece**

Announce spring with
this basket of chicks,
or display it as a
whimsical centerpiece
for a "hen party" or
anytime you're hanging
out with your "peeps."

· ·

Tips

Use tweezers to grasp and
arrange small candies, such
as the sunflower seeds in
this recipe.

Be sure to purchase a
food safe paintbrush from
a cake decorating shop.

If necessary, thin the dark
chocolate coating with
shortening or Paramount
Crystals in step 4 before
making the eyes.

Ingredients

	Yellow and dark chocolate candy coating wafers	
7	Lemon Coconut Cake Pops (page 68)	7
7	vanilla baking chips	7
21	orange-candy-and-chocolate-covered sunflower seeds	21
	Yellow sanding sugar	

Materials

7	cake pop sticks	7
1	food-safe fine paintbrush	1
28 inches	ribbon (about $\frac{1}{4}$ inch/0.5 cm wide), cut into 4-inch (10 cm) lengths	70 cm
1	basket (about 6 inches/15 cm)	1
1	Styrofoam cube (at least $6\frac{1}{2}$ inches/16 cm cubed)	1
	Green paper shred	

1. Melt $\frac{1}{4}$ cup (60 mL) yellow candy coating wafers (see page 19) and use to attach sticks to cake pops (see page 27). Freeze cake pops for at least 15 minutes to set. Reserve the remaining candy coating.

2. Add $\frac{3}{4}$ cup (175 mL) yellow candy coating wafers to the reserved yellow coating and melt until smooth. Use to glue a white baking chip to one side of each cake pop, for a tail. Set in a cake pop stand to dry.

3. Reheat yellow coating as needed. Coat 1 cake pop (see page 29). Immediately position 1 sunflower seed as a beak and 2 as feet. Sprinkle the cake pop with sanding sugar. Set in the stand to dry. Repeat with the remaining cake pops.

4. Melt 2 to 3 tbsp (30 to 45 mL) dark chocolate candy coating wafers. Use the end of the paintbrush to make eyes. Set in the stand to dry.

5. Tie a length of ribbon in a knot around each cake pop stick. Slide the knots up to just below the cake pop.

6. Measure the basket and trim the Styrofoam to fit snugly and be about 1 inch (2.5 cm) shorter than the basket. Place Styrofoam in the basket and cover it with paper shred. Push the cake pop sticks into the Styrofoam, arranging the cake pops decoratively.

Tea Party

• •

Nothing could be more glamorous than sipping tea and sampling miniature treats, both sweet and savory. Set an elegant table with this centerpiece in the middle, then let guests helps themselves to the cake pops. Round out the menu with Chicken and Mushroom Phyllo Tarts (page 160) and Lemon Muffins (page 131).

• •

Tip
Keep your eyes open for distinctive, colorful teacups at antique stores and flea markets.

Ingredients

	Lavender and white candy coating wafers	
6	Apricot Brandy Cake Pops (page 77) or Strawberry Cake Pops (page 40)	6
	White sugar pearls	
	White sparkling sugar	

Materials

6	cake pop sticks	6
1	pastry bag or squeeze bottle, fitted with a fine tip	1
1	teacup (about 3 inches/ 7.5 cm in diameter) and saucer	1
	Styrofoam cube (at least 3 inches/ 7.5 cm cubed)	
2 feet	white tulle (about 6 inches/ 15 cm wide)	60 cm
	Straight pins	
6 feet	lavender ribbon (about ½ inch/ 1 cm wide), cut into 12-inch (30 cm) lengths	180 cm

1. Melt ¼ cup (60 mL) lavender candy coating wafers (see page 19) and use to attach sticks to cake pops (see page 27). Freeze cake pops for at least 15 minutes to set. Reserve the remaining candy coating.

2. Add 1 cup (250 mL) lavender candy coating wafers to the reserved lavender coating and melt until smooth. Coat cake pops (see page 29). Immediately sprinkle 1 cake pop with sugar pearls and 1 cake pop with sparkling sugar (leave the rest plain). Set in a cake pop stand to dry.

3. Melt ½ cup (125 mL) white candy coating wafers. Use the pastry bag to pipe spirals, dots or filigree over the 4 cake pops without pearls or sugar. Immediately sprinkle sparkling sugar over the moist decorations on 1 cake pop (do not sprinkle the others). Set in the stand to dry.

Tips

Trim the Styrofoam to fit snugly so that it doesn't slip once the cake pops are inserted. If necessary, pile polished clear floral stones, gems or pebbles (available from a craft shop) over the Styrofoam for stability.

For a marbleized effect, pipe white spirals over a freshly coated lavender cake pop, then use a toothpick to swirl the white coating through the lavender coating.

Coordinate the color of the cake pops with the colors on the teacup. Lavender works well with a teacup decorated with spring violets, for example.

4. Measure the dimensions of the teacup and trim the Styrofoam to fit snugly and be 1 inch (2.5 cm) shorter than the cup. Place Styrofoam in the cup. Loosely gather the tulle, then, using straight pins, pin the tulle to the Styrofoam. (Keep the tulle loosely gathered so that it looks full and generously covers the Styrofoam.)

5. Tie a length of ribbon in a bow around each cake pop stick. Slide the bows up to just below the cake pops. Push the cake pop sticks into the Styrofoam, arranging the cake pops decoratively.

Summer Fun

• •

Summer fun means watermelon time. Set the table with this fun centerpiece, then serve the little watermelon cake pops for dessert, alongside the real thing!

• •

Tips

The mini chocolate chips baked into the cake pops will resemble watermelon seeds when you take a bite.

Ideally, the yellow-green color you make in step 2 will contrast brightly with the green coating on the cake pops.

Ingredients

	Green and yellow candy coating wafers	
7	Strawberry Chocolate Chip Cake Pops (variation, page 40)	7
	Green oil-based candy coloring	

Materials

7	cake pop sticks	7
1	pastry bag or squeeze bottle, fitted with a fine tip	1
28 inches	pink ribbon (about ¼ inch/ 0.5 cm wide), cut into 4-inch (10 cm) lengths	70 cm
1	pink polka dot can or flower pot (about 5 inches/12.5 cm in diameter)	1
1	Styrofoam cube (at least 5½ inches/ 13.5 cm cubed)	1
	Green paper shred	

1. Melt ¼ cup (60 mL) green candy coating wafers (see page 19) and use to attach sticks to cake pops (see page 27). Freeze cake pops for at least 15 minutes to set. Reserve the remaining candy coating.

2. Melt ¼ cup (60 mL) yellow candy coating wafers. Tint with green candy coloring to make a bright yellow-green (see tip, at left). Fill the pastry bag with yellow-green coating.

3. Add 1 cup (250 mL) green candy coating wafers to the reserved green coating and melt until smooth. Coat cake pops (see page 29). Immediately pipe yellow-green squiggly stripes, similar to those found on a watermelon, on the cake pops. Set in a cake pop stand to dry.

4. Tie a length of ribbon in a knot around each cake pop stick. Slide the knot up so it is just below the cake pop.

5. Measure the dimensions of the can and trim the Styrofoam to fit snugly and be about 1 inch (2.5 cm) shorter than the can. Place Styrofoam in the can and cover it with paper shred. Push the cake pop sticks into the Styrofoam, arranging the cake pops decoratively.

Gone Fishing

· ·

**Makes
1 centerpiece**

Celebrate Father's Day with a trip to the nearest fishing hole — or create your own tasty fishing hole with cake pops.

....

Tips

You can use any cake pop flavor for any of the arrangements in this chapter, though it is wise to use lighter-colored cakes with white or light pastel candy coating wafers. Bright or dark-colored candy coating wafers will coat even the darkest cake pops. So have fun — choose your favorite flavor or mix and match.

When you're coating cake pops, the candy coating needs to be deep enough that you can dip the cake pops straight down into it. If you're only dipping a few cake pops, there will be some coating left over, but it can be melted again and used another time.

Ingredients

4	flat sugared gummy candies, ribbons or gum drops	4
	Yellow, dark chocolate, white and red candy coating wafers	
4	Favorite White Cake Pops (page 26)	4
	Green oil-based candy coloring	
2	jumbo pink heart sprinkles	2
2	round white candy beads or small candy balls	2
	Shortening or Paramount Crystals	
3	red ring-shaped candies	3
3	gummy worms	3

Materials

4	cake pop sticks	4
1	food-safe fine paintbrush	1
1	2-inch (5 cm) long upholstery needle with a large eye	1
3	28-inch (70 cm) lengths cotton string	3
1	pastry bag or squeeze bottle, fitted with a fine tip	1
3	10- to 12-inch (25 to 30 cm) wooden skewers	3
3	1-inch (2.5 cm) square pieces of foil	3
1	small glass fish bowl (about 4 inches/ 10 cm in diameter)	1
1	Styrofoam block (about 4 by 3 by 3 inches/ 10 by 7.5 by 7.5 cm)	1
	Blue flat polished glass marbles or pebbles	
1	sheet thick white printer paper	1
1	3- by 2¼-inch (7.5 by 5.5 cm) piece blue card stock	1
	Double-sided tape	
3 feet	blue feathered yarn	90 cm

For the Fish

1. Cut the flat gummy candies into a tail, 2 side fins and 1 back fin for the fish (if using gum drops, roll flat before cutting). Set aside.

Gone Fishing (continued)

Tips

Be sure to purchase a food-safe paintbrush from a cake decorating shop.

When you're melting just 1 to 2 tbsp (15 to 30 mL) of candy coating wafers to paint fine details, be careful not to overheat them; heat in 10- or 15-second intervals rather than 30-second intervals.

You will be making the bobbers upside down on the stick so they can be right side up when you remove the stick.

Avoid handling the bobbers much and work gently, as the heat of your hands can melt the candy coating. If the coating softens while you're working with the bobbers, place it in the refrigerator for a few minutes to chill.

2. Melt ¼ cup (60 mL) yellow candy coating wafers (see page 19). Tint with green candy coloring to the desired fish color. Use the tinted coating to attach a stick to 1 cake pop (see page 27). Freeze cake pop for at least 15 minutes to set. Reserve the remaining candy coating.

3. Reheat green-tinted coating and coat the cake pop (see page 29). Immediately position the tail, side fins, back fin, 2 heart sprinkles, positioned point to point, for the mouth and white candy beads for the eyes. Set in a cake pop stand to dry.

4. Melt 2 tbsp (30 mL) chocolate candy coating wafers and thin with shortening or Paramount Crystals (see page 20). Use the end of the paintbrush (opposite the bristles) to make a dot of coating for a pupil in each eye. Set in the stand to dry.

For the Bobbers

5. Melt ¼ cup (60 mL) white candy coating wafers and use to attach sticks to the remaining cake pops. Freeze cake pops for at least 15 minutes to set. Reserve the remaining candy coating.

6. Add ½ cup (125 mL) white candy coating wafers to the reserved white coating and melt until smooth. Coat cake pops. Slide a ring-shaped candy up the stick to the base of each cake pop. Set in the stand to dry.

7. Melt ½ cup (125 mL) red candy coating wafers and coat the top half of each cake pop. Set in the stand to dry. Reserve the remaining candy coating.

8. Gently twist the stick out of a cake pop. Thread the needle with a length of cotton string. Insert the needle through the ring-shaped candy into the hole in the candy coating and gently work it straight through the cake pop to emerge directly opposite the hole. Draw the thread through the cake pop until at least 8 inches (20 cm) of string emerges on the red side, leaving about 18 inches (45 cm) of string dangling from the ring-shaped candy.

9. Tie a knot in the string close to the red side of the cake pop to hold it in place on the string. Trim the remaining string on that side to about 4 inches (10 cm).

Tips

When you're adjusting the length of the string in step 10, keep in mind that the bobber should hang at least 5 inches (12.5 cm) above the tabletop so that the hook and worm dangle freely. Also consider that the arrangement will look nicest if the bobbers hang at slightly different heights. If necessary, when you're assembling the centerpiece, you can readjust the string lengths.

For the sign, you might say, "Gone Fishing" or "Find me and my dad at the fishing hole" or "For my best fishing buddy, my dad."

10. Reheat red coating. Use the pastry bag to fill the ring-shaped candy with coating, to secure the string. Tie that end of the string tightly to a skewer, adjusting the length of the string so that the bobber will hang an appropriate length from the fishing pole and above the table once the skewer is inserted into the Styrofoam in the fish bowl (see tip, at left).

11. Roll a square of foil tightly around the bottom of the 4-inch (10 cm) tail of string. Bend it into a hook shape by wrapping it around a thick pencil. Trim, if necessary.

12. Repeat steps 8 to 11 with the remaining cake pops.

Assembly

13. Measure the dimensions of the fish bowl and trim the Styrofoam to fit snugly and be about 1 inch (2.5 cm) shorter than the bowl. Place Styrofoam in the bowl and surround and cover it with marbles. Push the cake pop stick and the skewers into the Styrofoam, arranging the fish and bobbers decoratively.

14. On the printer paper, write or print an appropriate message (see tip, at left). Centering the message, trim the paper to fit onto the card stock, leaving a $\frac{1}{8}$-inch (3 mm) border. Use double-sided tape to mount the paper on the card stock. Poke a tiny hole in the corner of the sign.

15. Tie the yarn around the top of the fish bowl and tie a bow, threading the sign onto the bow.

16. Drape a gummy worm over the hook on each bobber.

Soccer Team Party

With this centerpiece, your favorite team will have a ball celebrating their winning season. Make one soccer ball for each player on the team.

Variation

Basketballs: Substitute orange candy coating wafers for the white. Pipe black lines onto the cake pops to resemble the lines on basketballs.

Ingredients

	White and black candy coating wafers	
12	Favorite White Cake Pops (page 26)	12

Materials

13	cake pop sticks	13
1	pastry bag or squeeze bottle, fitted with a fine tip	1
1	decorative bucket or bowl, in team colors (6 to 7 inches/ 15 to 18 cm in diameter)	1
	Styrofoam cube (at least 7 inches/ 18 cm cubed)	
	Paper shred in team colors	
	White and another color of card stock	
	Glue	
	Marker	

1. Melt $1/2$ cup (125 mL) white candy coating wafers (see page 19) and use to attach sticks to cake pops (see page 27). (You will have 1 stick left over.) Freeze cake pops for at least 15 minutes to set. Reserve the remaining candy coating.

2. Add 1 cup (250 mL) white candy coating wafers to the reserved white coating and melt until smooth. Coat cake pops (see page 29). Set in a cake pop stand to dry.

3. Melt $1/2$ cup (125 mL) black candy coating wafers. Use the pastry bag to pipe black pentagons and lines onto the cake pops to resemble soccer balls.

4. Measure the dimensions of the bucket and trim the Styrofoam to fit snugly and be about 1 inch (2.5 cm) shorter than the bucket. Place Styrofoam in the bucket and cover with paper shred. Push the cake pop sticks into the Styrofoam, arranging the cake pops decoratively.

Tips

Want each player to have a favor to take home as a gift? Be sure to make enough cake pops for everyone on the team. Once they are dry and set, cover each cake pop with a 7-inch (18 cm) square of clear cellophane and secure it with ribbon.

This centerpiece is also great for a child's birthday party or a gathering to watch the game on television.

Instead of piping the lines, you can use a black edible ink food marker to draw the lines.

Black candy coating wafers may only be available seasonally, for Halloween. Stock up in October, or make your own by stirring a small amount of black oil-based candy coloring into melted dark chocolate candy coating.

5. Cut a triangle out of white card stock to resemble a pennant about $1\frac{1}{2}$ by $2\frac{1}{2}$ inches (4 by 6 cm). Cut a second triangle, about $\frac{1}{4}$ inch (0.5 cm) larger than the first, out of colored card stock. Glue the white pennant onto the colored pennant, leaving a margin all the way around. Use the marker to write the name of the team or "Go Team!" on the pennant. Glue the pennant to the remaining cake pop stick and push it into the Styrofoam.

Take Me Out to the Ball Game

● ●

**Makes
1 centerpiece**

Cake pops decorated as baseballs and a ball player make a show-stopping centerpiece for the team party or a special gift for a favorite coach. Match the cap, paper shred and ribbon to the team colors.

● ●

Tips

When you're coating cake pops, the candy coating needs to be deep enough that you can dip the cake pops straight down into it. If you're only dipping a few cake pops, there will be some coating left over, but it can be melted again and used another time.

If desired, you could melt red candy coating wafers and use a pastry bag or squeeze bottle fitted with a fine tip to pipe the stitching on the baseballs.

Ingredients

	White, yellow, pink, milk chocolate, red and dark chocolate candy coating wafers	
7	White Spice Cake Pops (page 28)	7
	Red and black edible ink food markers	
1	disk-shaped candy wafer (such as Necco)	1
1	round jumbo sprinkle	1
	Shortening or Paramount Crystals	

Materials

7	cake pop sticks	7
1	pastry bag or squeeze bottle, fitted with a fine tip	1
1	food-safe fine paintbrush	1
1	Styrofoam cube (at least 4 inches/ 10 cm cubed)	1
	New baseball cap	
	Paper shred	
28 inches	ribbon (about ¼ inch/ 0.5 cm wide), cut into 4-inch (10 cm) lengths	70 cm

1. Melt ½ cup (125 mL) white candy coating wafers (see page 19) and use to attach sticks to cake pops (see page 27). Freeze cake pops for at least 15 minutes to set. Reserve the remaining candy coating.

For the Baseballs

2. Add 1 cup (250 mL) white candy coating wafers to the reserved white coating and melt until smooth. Coat 6 cake pops (see page 29). Set in a cake pop stand to dry.

3. Use the red food marker to draw stitching on the cake pops to resemble baseballs. Set in the stand to dry.

For the Baseball Player

4. To make the bill on the ball player's cap, break off a small piece of the candy wafer to flatten one side of the circle. Set aside.

Tips

Match the hair and eye color of your favorite ball player, substituting yellow, orange or milk chocolate candy coating wafers for the hair, and blue or green candy coating wafers for the eyes. Make the hair short or long, straight or curly.

Be sure to purchase a food-safe paintbrush from a cake decorating shop.

When you're melting just 1 to 2 tbsp (15 to 30 mL) of candy coating wafers to paint fine details, be careful not to overheat them; heat in 10- or 15-second intervals rather than 30-second intervals.

5. To create a mixture the color of a light skin tone, combine equal parts of yellow, pink and white candy coating wafers. For darker skin tones, combine white candy coating wafers with a small amount of milk chocolate candy coating wafers. Melt $\frac{1}{2}$ cup (125 mL) of the combined wafers. Adjust the tone as desired by adding a little more of one color or another and reheating to melt. Coat the remaining cake pop. Set in the stand to dry.

6. Melt 2 tbsp (30 mL) red candy coating wafers. Dip the top third of the cake pop in red coating to make a cap. Immediately position the sprinkle at the top of the cap as a button. Place the candy wafer on one side to form the bill, with the flat side against the cake pop, and gently hold in place until set. Set in the stand to dry.

7. Use the black food marker to draw stitching lines from the button down to the edge of the cap.

8. Melt 2 to 3 tbsp (30 to 45 mL) dark chocolate candy coating wafers. Use a pastry bag to pipe hair on the cake pop. Set in the stand to dry.

9. Press 1 tbsp (15 mL) of the dark chocolate coating out of the pastry bag and back into the bowl. Reheat as needed and thin with shortening or Paramount Crystals (see page 20). Use the end of the paintbrush (opposite the bristles) to make two dots of coating for the eyes. Set in the stand to dry.

10. Reheat red coating and thin with shortening or Paramount Crystals. Use the paintbrush to paint a mouth. Set in the stand to dry.

Assembly

11. Tie a length of ribbon in a knot around each cake pop stick. Slide the knots up to just below the cake pops.

12. Place the Styrofoam in the baseball cap. Pull the strap on the cap as tight as possible without disrupting the shape of the cap too much. Fill the cap with paper shred, covering the Styrofoam. Push the cake pop sticks into the Styrofoam, arranging the cake pops decoratively.

Tailgate Party

Football season means tailgate parties and gatherings to watch the game on TV. This centerpiece will score winning points with your guests.

Tip

Adjust the color and look of the helmets and the jerseys to represent the team you are cheering for. Instead of a stripe on each helmet, for example, you could write the team's initials with edible ink food markers.

Ingredients

	Pink, yellow, white, milk chocolate, dark chocolate and red candy coating wafers	
5	Peanut Butter Cake Pops (page 36)	5
	Blue and yellow fondant	
	Shortening or Paramount Crystals	
	Black edible ink food marker	

Materials

7	cake pop sticks	7
	Rolling pin	
	3-inch (7.5 cm) round cookie cutter	1
	Straw	
1	pastry bag or squeeze bottle, fitted with a fine tip	1
1	food-safe fine paintbrush	1
	⅛-inch (3 mm) paper punch	
5	2-inch (5 cm) circles of yellow card stock	5
	Blue colored pencil or marker	
	Foam football	
	Green paper shred	

1. Melt ¼ cup (60 mL) pink candy coating wafers (see page 19) and use to attach sticks to cake pops (see page 27). (You will have 2 extra sticks.) Freeze cake pops for at least 15 minutes to set.

2. To create a mixture the color of a light skin tone, combine equal parts of yellow, pink and white candy coating wafers. For darker skin tones, combine white candy coating wafers with a small amount of milk chocolate candy coating wafers. Melt ½ cup (125 mL) of the combined wafers. Adjust the tone as desired by adding a little more of one color or another and reheating to melt. Coat cake pops (see page 29). Set in a cake pop stand to dry.

3. For the helmets, roll out blue fondant to about ⅛ inch (3 mm) thick and cut into 5 circles with the cookie cutter. Using a sharp knife, trim the circles to look like the pattern at left. Use the straw to cut out holes on either side of each helmet where the chin guard will attach. Wrap each piece of fondant around a cake pop, gently forming it into a helmet by molding the fondant

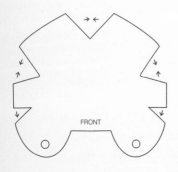

Football helmet

Tips

Be sure to purchase a food-safe paintbrush from a cake decorating shop.

Match the skin tone and hair and eye colors of your favorite football players, substituting yellow, orange or milk chocolate candy coating wafers for the hair, and blue or green candy coating wafers for the eyes.

If desired, use a black edible ink food marker to draw lines under each of player's eyes.

with your fingers. Trim the fondant as needed, taking care not to cut or dent the candy coating.

4. Melt $\frac{1}{4}$ cup (60 mL) dark chocolate candy coating wafers. Use a pastry bag to pipe hair in short lines around the helmet on each cake pop. Set in the stand to dry.

5. Press 1 tbsp (15 mL) of the dark chocolate coating out of the pastry bag and back into the bowl. Reheat as needed and thin with shortening or Paramount Crystals (see page 20). Use the end of the paintbrush (opposite the bristles) to make two dots of coating for the eyes on each cake pop. Set in the stand to dry.

6. Melt 2 to 3 tbsp (30 to 45 mL) red candy coating wafers and thin with shortening or Paramount Crystals. Use the paintbrush to paint a mouth on each cake pop. Set in the stand to dry.

7. Roll a small pinch of yellow fondant into a narrow strip to create a chin guard. Press the chin guard into position on a helmet. Repeat to create chin guards on each helmet.

8. Roll out a piece of yellow fondant to about $\frac{1}{8}$ inch (3 mm) thick and cut into 5 narrow strips. Place a strip across the top of each helmet, running front to back, as a stripe. Carefully trim the ends as needed.

9. Use the paper punch to punch a hole in the center of each card stock circle. Fold the circles in half and write a number on the front of each. Slide each "jersey" up the cake pop stick to the base of the cake pop.

10. Cut the remaining 2 cake pop sticks in half to use as support legs for the bottom of the football. To make it easier to push each stick into the foam, first cut a tiny hole with the tip of a sharp knife. Slide the sticks in deep enough and distribute them evenly enough that they will hold the football level. Once the football is stable, push the cake pops into the foam, distributing them evenly so that the football is still stable. Arrange paper shred around the bottom of the football to hide the support sticks.

Spiders

● ●

**Makes
1 centerpiece**

Kathy hates spiders,
but she'll make an
exception for these
cute edible arachnids.
They're perfect for a
Halloween gathering.

....

Tips

When you're combining or
tinting candy coating wafers
to make a custom color, be
sure to melt as much as you
need for the entire project.
If you have to melt more, it
will be difficult to match the
color perfectly.

If you can't find black
candy melts, substitute
dark chocolate candy melts
and tint them black with
oil-based candy coloring.

Ingredients

	Yellow, green, orange, lavender and black candy coating wafers	
7	Pistachio Marble Cake Pops (page 34)	7
	Orange and purple oil-based candy coloring	
7	black candy-coated chocolate candies	7
14	white, yellow and/or orange confetti sprinkles	14

Materials

7	cake pop sticks	7
1	pastry bag or squeeze bottle, fitted with a fine tip	1
1	food-safe fine paintbrush	1
49 inches	ribbon (about ¼ inch/0.5 cm wide), cut into 7-inch (18 cm) lengths	123 cm
1	decorative Halloween motif pail or vase (about 2½ inches/6 cm in diameter)	1
1	Styrofoam block (about 4 by 2½ by 2½ inches/ 10 by 6 by 6 cm)	1
	Black paper shred	

1. Combine ¼ cup (60 mL) each yellow and green candy coating wafers. Melt until smooth (see page 19). Adjust the tone to make a bright green by adding a little more of one color or the other and reheating to melt. Use to attach sticks to 3 cake pops (see page 27). Freeze cake pops for at least 15 minutes to set. Reserve the remaining candy coating.

2. Melt ½ cup (125 mL) orange candy coating wafers. Tint with orange candy coloring to make a bright, deep orange. Use to attach sticks to 2 cake pops. Freeze cake pops for at least 15 minutes to set. Reserve the remaining candy coating.

3. Melt ½ cup (125 mL) lavender candy coating wafers. Tint with purple candy coloring to make a bright, deep purple. Use to attach sticks to the remaining cake pops. Freeze cake pops for at least 15 minutes to set. Reserve the remaining candy coating.

Tips

Vary the spot on the cake pops where the spiders rest. For some, place the spider on top; for others, place it on the side. The bouquet will look like it is crawling with spiders.

Be sure to purchase a food-safe paintbrush from a cake decorating shop.

4. Reheat each of the candy coatings and coat the corresponding cake pops (see page 29). Set in a cake pop stand to dry.

5. Melt 2 to 3 tbsp (30 to 45 mL) black candy coating wafers. Use the pastry bag to pipe a dot of black coating near the top or on the side of each cake pop (see tip, at left). Place a candy-coated chocolate on each dot. Carefully pipe 8 legs around each candy-coated chocolate to make a spider. Use tiny drops of coating to glue 2 confetti sprinkles to each spider as eyes. Set in the stand to dry.

6. Press 1 tbsp (15 mL) of the black coating out of the pastry bag and back into the bowl. Reheat as needed and thin with shortening or Paramount Crystals. Use the end of the paintbrush (opposite the bristles) to make dots of coating for pupils in the eyes. Set in the stand to dry.

7. Tie a length of ribbon in a small bow around each cake pop stick. Slide the bow up so it is just below the cake pop.

8. Measure the dimensions of the pail and trim the Styrofoam to fit snugly and be about 1 inch (2.5 cm) shorter than the pail. Place Styrofoam in the pail and cover it with paper shred. Push the cake pop sticks into the Styrofoam, arranging the cake pops decoratively.

Ghosts

These cute little ghosts add spooky fun to your Halloween celebration.

Tips

When you're coating cake pops, the candy coating needs to be deep enough that you can dip the cake pops straight down into it. If you're only dipping a few cake pops, there will be some coating left over, but it can be melted again and used another time.

If you can't find black candy melts, substitute dark chocolate candy melts and tint them black with oil-based candy coloring.

Ingredients

	White and black candy coating wafers	
3	Favorite White Cake Pops (page 26)	3
15	pieces candy corn	15
	Shortening or Paramount Crystals	

Materials

3	cake pop sticks	3
1	food-safe fine paintbrush	1
	Double-sided tape	
1	computer-generated Halloween scene (about 6½ inches/16 cm square)	1
1	6¾-inch (17 cm) square of black card stock	1
1	10- to 12-inch (25 to 30 cm) wooden skewer	1
1	black mug (about 2 inches/ 5 cm in diameter)	1
1	Styrofoam block (at least 3 by 2 by 2 inches/ 7.5 by 5 by 5 cm)	1
	Black paper shred	
1 foot	orange ribbon (about ½ inch/ 1 cm wide)	30 cm
1 foot	black ribbon (about ½ inch/ 1 cm wide)	30 cm

1. Melt ¼ cup (60 mL) white candy coating wafers (see page 19) and use to attach sticks to cake pops (see page 27). Dip the larger end of 5 pieces of candy corn in white coating and arrange the pieces around the bottom of a cake pop, holding each piece for a moment so it adheres. Repeat with the remaining cake pops and candy corn. Freeze cake pops for at least 15 minutes to set. Reserve the remaining candy coating.

2. Add 1 cup (250 mL) white candy coating wafers to the reserved white coating and melt until smooth. Coat cake pops and candy corn down to and including the tips (see page 29). Set in a cake pop stand to dry. (It is fine if the coating drips off the candy corn unevenly.)

Tips

Be sure to purchase a food-safe paintbrush from a cake decorating shop.

You can use any cake pop flavor for any of the arrangements in this chapter, though it is wise to use lighter-colored cakes with white or light pastel candy coating wafers. Bright or dark-colored candy coating wafers will coat even the darkest cake pops. So have fun — choose your favorite flavor or mix and match.

3. Melt 2 tbsp (30 mL) black candy coating wafers and thin with shortening or Paramount Crystals (see page 20). Use the end of the paintbrush (opposite the bristles) to make two dots of coating for the eyes on each cake pop. Set in the stand to dry.

4. Use double-sided tape to mount the Halloween scene onto the black card stock, leaving a $\frac{1}{8}$-inch (3 mm) border around the scene. Tape the skewer to the back of the card stock.

5. Measure the dimensions of the mug and trim the Styrofoam to fit snugly and be about 1 inch (2.5 cm) shorter than the mug. Place Styrofoam in the mug and cover with paper shred. Place the Halloween scene at the back of the mug, pushing the skewer into the Styrofoam. Push the cake pop sticks into the Styrofoam, arranging the cake pops decoratively in front of the Halloween scene. Tie the orange and black ribbons to the handle of the mug.

Bewitched

Makes 1 centerpiece

Plan for a wicked awesome time with this centerpiece of witches.

Tip

To make the festive sign on a computer, create a 3- by 2-inch (7.5 by 5 cm) rectangle. Search the Internet for a silhouette of a witch, and copy and paste it into the middle of the rectangle. Add a message such as "Have a Bewitching Time" or "Best Witches." Print and cut out the sign. (If you prefer to hand-make the sign, cut the silhouette of a witch out of black paper, paste it to a rectangle of white paper and write your message.)

Ingredients

	Green, dark chocolate, yellow and red candy coating wafers	
3	Pistachio Marble Cake Pops (page 34)	3
3	milk chocolate candy coins	3
3	milk chocolate kisses	3
3	green-candy-and-chocolate-covered sunflower seeds	3
	Green and black oil-based candy coloring	
	Shortening or Paramount Crystals	
	Foil-covered Halloween candies	

Materials

3	cake pop sticks	3
1	pastry bag or squeeze bottle, fitted with a fine tip	1
1	food-safe fine paintbrush	1
1	orange mug (about 3 inches/ 7.5 cm in diameter)	1
1	Styrofoam block (at least 4 by 3 by 3 inches/ 10 by 7.5 by 7.5 cm)	1
	Double-sided tape	
1	festive sign (see tip, at left)	1
1	3¼- by 2¼-inch (8 by 5.5 cm) rectangle of black card stock	1
2 feet	black tulle (about 6 inches/ 15 cm wide), 3 pieces cut into 4-inch (10 cm) lengths and 2 pieces cut into 6-inch (15 cm) lengths	60 cm

1. Melt 2 tbsp (30 mL) green candy coating wafers (see page 19) and use to attach sticks to cake pops (see page 27). Freeze cake pops for at least 15 minutes to set.

2. Melt 2 to 3 tbsp (30 to 45 mL) chocolate candy coating wafers. Unwrap chocolate coins. Using the coating as glue, attach a chocolate kiss to the top of each coin, making a witch hat. Set aside to dry. Reserve the remaining candy coating.

Tips

Use tweezers to grasp and arrange small candies, such as the sunflower seeds in this recipe.

If you would like to add warts to the witches, use a pastry bag to pipe a dot or two of the bright green candy coating onto each face.

Be sure to purchase a food-safe paintbrush from a cake decorating shop.

You can use any cake pop flavor for any of the arrangements in this chapter, though it is wise to use lighter-colored cakes with white or light pastel candy coating wafers. Bright or dark-colored candy coating wafers will coat even the darkest cake pops. So have fun — choose your favorite flavor or mix and match.

3. Combine ¼ cup (60 mL) each yellow and green candy coating wafers. Melt until smooth. Tint with green candy coloring to make a bright green. Coat cake pops (see page 29). Immediately position 1 sunflower seed on each cake pop as a nose. Set in a cake pop stand to dry.

4. Add 2 to 3 tbsp (30 to 45 mL) chocolate candy coating wafers to the reserved chocolate coating and melt until smooth. Tint black with black candy coloring. Use a pastry bag to pipe hair on the cake pops. Immediately place a hat on each witch. Set in the stand to dry.

5. Press 1 tbsp (15 mL) of the black-tinted chocolate coating out of the pastry bag and back into the bowl. Reheat as needed and thin with shortening or Paramount Crystals (see page 20). Use the end of the paintbrush (opposite the bristles) to make two dots of coating for the eyes on each cake pop.

6. Melt 2 to 3 tbsp (30 to 45 mL) red candy coating wafers and thin with shortening or Paramount Crystals. Use the paintbrush to paint a mouth on each cake pop. Set in the stand to dry.

7. Tie a 4-inch (10 cm) length of tulle in a knot around each cake pop stick. Slide the knots up to just below the cake pops.

8. Use double-sided tape to mount the festive sign onto the black card stock, leaving a ⅛-inch (3 mm) border around the sign. Poke a small hole in the corner of the note.

9. Measure the dimensions of the mug and trim the Styrofoam to fit snugly and be about 1 inch (2.5 cm) shorter than the mug. Place Styrofoam in the mug. Tie the remaining pieces of tulle around the handle of the mug. Thread a little bit of tulle through the hole in the sign. Push the cake pop sticks into the Styrofoam, arranging the cake pops decoratively. Fill the mug with Halloween candies.

Pumpkin Patch

Create a tasty
pumpkin patch with
a collection of cake
pops decorated to look
like pumpkins — a
perfect centerpiece
for Halloween,
Thanksgiving or any
harvest-time gathering.

Tips

If you can't find jumbo
green leaf sprinkles,
substitute jumbo green star
sprinkles and place each
one on its edge to resemble
a leaf.

Using the same color of
candy coating wafers to
attach the sticks and to coat
the cake pops ensures that
any drips will be disguised.

When you're coating cake
pops, the candy coating
needs to be deep enough
that you can dip the cake
pops straight down into it.
If you're only dipping a few
cake pops, there will be
some coating left over, but
it can be melted again and
used another time.

Ingredients

	Orange, milk chocolate and green candy coating wafers	
9	Brown Sugar Spice Cake Pops (page 32)	9
	Orange oil-based candy coloring	
9	green-candy-and-chocolate-covered sunflower seeds	9
9	jumbo green leaf sprinkles	9
	Shortening or Paramount Crystals	

Materials

9	cake pop sticks	9
1	food-safe fine paintbrush	1
3 feet	green ribbon (about 1/4 inch/ 0.5 cm wide), cut into 4-inch (10 cm) lengths	90 cm
	Brown paper lunch bag	
1	Styrofoam block (about 5 by 3 by 3 inches/ 12.5 by 7.5 by 7.5 cm)	1
	Brown paper shred	
3 feet	jute	90 cm

1. Melt 1/4 cup (60 mL) orange candy coating wafers (see page 19) and use to attach sticks to cake pops (see page 27). Freeze cake pops for at least 15 minutes to set. Reserve the remaining candy coating.

2. Add 1 cup (250 mL) orange candy coating wafers to the reserved orange coating and melt until smooth. Tint with orange candy coloring to make a bright orange. Coat cake pops (see page 29). Immediately position a sunflower seed on the top of each cake pop as a stem. Place a leaf sprinkle near each stem. Set in a cake pop stand to dry.

3. Melt 2 to 3 tbsp (30 to 45 mL) chocolate candy coating wafers. Dip a butter knife into the coating, then scrape off both sides of the knife, leaving only a small ridge of coating along the top of the knife. Place the top of the knife near the top of a pumpkin and gently "roll" it down the side, making a straight line. Make several lines on each pumpkin.

Tips

Use tweezers to grasp and arrange small candies, such as the sunflower seeds and sprinkles in this recipe.

Be sure to purchase a food-safe paintbrush from a cake decorating shop.

You can use any cake pop flavor for any of the arrangements in this chapter, though it is wise to use lighter-colored cakes with white or light pastel candy coating wafers. Bright or dark-colored candy coating wafers will coat even the darkest cake pops. So have fun — choose your favorite flavor or mix and match.

4. Melt 2 to 3 tbsp (30 to 45 mL) green candy coating wafers and thin with shortening or Paramount Crystals (see page 20). Use the paintbrush to paint a curly vine on some of the pumpkins. Set in the stand to dry.

5. Tie a length of ribbon in a knot around each cake pop stick. Slide the knots up to just below the cake pops.

6. Roll down the top of the lunch bag so that the bag stands 5 to 6 inches (12.5 to 15 cm) tall. Place the Styrofoam cube in the bag and surround and cover it with paper shred. Tie jute around the bag, about 1 inch (2.5 cm) from the top. Push the cake pop sticks into the Styrofoam, arranging the cake pops decoratively.

Angels

Makes
1 centerpiece
or 3 gifts

Make a heavenly host
of angels as a divine
centerpiece for your
holiday table, or
make individual
angels as gifts.

Tip

Instead of using white
doilies, try dressing your
angels in silver or gold
metallic doilies. Use a
contrasting color for the
paper shred.

Ingredients

	Pink, yellow, white, milk chocolate and dark chocolate candy coating wafers	
3	Strawberry Cake Pops (page 40)	3
	Gold sparkling sanding sugar	
	Shortening or Paramount Crystals	

Materials

3	cake pop sticks	3
3	pastry bags or squeeze bottles, each fitted with a fine writing tip	3
1	food-safe fine paintbrush	1
2	5-inch (12.5 cm) white paper doilies	2
	Double-sided tape	
3 feet	white ribbon (1/8 to 1/4 inch/ 3 to 5 mm wide), 3 pieces cut into 7-inch (18 cm) lengths and 3 pieces cut into 5-inch (12.5 cm) lengths	90 cm
	Permanent glue dots	
18 inches	stiff gold, silver or white ribbon (about 2 inches/5 cm wide), cut into three 6-inch (15 cm) lengths	45 cm
3	stemmed clear glass wine goblets (about 3 inches/7.5 cm in diameter)	3
3	Styrofoam cubes (each about 3 inches/7.5 cm cubed)	3
	Gold metallic paper shred	

1. Melt 1/4 cup (60 mL) pink candy coating wafers (see page 19) and use to attach sticks to cake pops (see page 27). Freeze cake pops for at least 15 minutes to set.

2. To create a mixture the color of a light skin tone, combine equal parts of yellow, pink and white candy coating wafers. For darker skin tones, combine white candy coating wafers with a small amount of milk chocolate candy coating wafers. Melt 1/2 cup (125 mL) of the combined wafers. Adjust the tone as desired by adding a little more of one color or another and reheating to melt. Coat cake pops (see page 29). Set in a cake pop stand to dry.

3. Melt 2 to 3 tbsp (30 to 45 mL) dark chocolate candy coating wafers. Use a pastry bag to pipe curly hair on 1 cake pop. Set in the stand to dry.

Tips

Be sure to purchase a food-safe paintbrush from a cake decorating shop

You can use any cake pop flavor for any of the arrangements in this chapter, though it is wise to use lighter-colored cakes with white or light pastel candy coating wafers. Bright or dark-colored candy coating wafers will coat even the darkest cake pops. So have fun — choose your favorite flavor or mix and match.

4. Melt 2 to 3 tbsp (30 to 45 mL) yellow candy coating wafers. Use another pastry bag to pipe curly hair on the remaining cake pops. Set in the stand to dry.

5. Melt 2 to 3 tbsp (30 to 45 mL) white candy coating wafers. Use another pastry bag to pipe a circle on top of each cake pop, as a halo. Immediately sprinkle the halos with gold sanding sugar. Set in the stand to dry.

6. Press 1 tbsp (15 mL) of the dark chocolate coating out of the pastry bag and back into the bowl. Reheat as needed and thin with shortening or Paramount Crystals (see page 20). Use the end of the paintbrush (opposite the bristles) to make two dots of coating for the eyes on each cake pop.

7. Melt 2 to 3 tbsp (30 to 45 mL) red candy coating wafers and thin with shortening or Paramount Crystals. Use the paintbrush to paint a mouth on each cake pop. Set in the stand to dry.

8. Cut doilies in half. Shape each half into a cone and use double-sided tape to hold it together and to attach the cake pop stick to the inside back of the cone.

9. Tie each 7-inch (18 cm) length of white ribbon into a tiny bow, trimming it as needed. Use a glue dot to glue a bow to the front neckline of each doily.

10. Pinch each length of stiff ribbon in the middle and tie it with a 5-inch (12.5 cm) length of white ribbon, making wings. Use a glue dot to glue wings to the back of each angel.

11. Measure the dimensions of a goblet and trim each Styrofoam cube to fit snugly and be about 1 inch (2.5 cm) shorter than the goblet. Place some paper shred in the bottom of each goblet. Place Styrofoam in the goblet and, using the tip of a butter knife, push shred down around the Styrofoam to hide it. Pile more shred on top of the Styrofoam, allowing some of it to spill over the edge of the goblet. Push a cake pop stick into the Styrofoam in each goblet so that the angel floats above the goblet.

Santa Claus

**Makes
1 centerpiece**

No Christmas celebration is complete without this jolly old elf! You might want to make several of these centerpieces as holiday gifts for neighbors and friends.

....

Tips

If you cannot find tiny marshmallows, use scissors to cut mini marshmallows into small pieces, wiping scissors with a warm cloth when they get sticky.

When you're coating cake pops, the candy coating needs to be deep enough that you can dip the cake pops straight down into it. If you're only dipping a few cake pops, there will be some coating left over, but it can be melted again and used another time.

Ingredients

	Red, pink, yellow, white, milk chocolate, blue and green candy coating wafers	
1	candy kiss	1
7	Minted Brownie Cake Pops (page 59)	7
	Tiny marshmallows (such as Kraft Mallow Bits)	
	Shortening or Paramount Crystals	

Materials

1	toothpick	1
7	cake pop sticks	7
2	pastry bags or squeeze bottles, each fitted with a fine tip	2
1	food-safe fine paintbrush	1
28 inches	red Christmas ribbon (about ¼ inch/0.5 cm wide), cut into 4-inch/10 cm lengths	70 cm
1	round red ceramic pot (about 4 inches/10 cm in diameter)	1
1	Styrofoam cube (at least 4 inches/10 cm cubed)	1
2 feet	white feather boa	90 cm

For Santa

1. For Santa's hat, poke a toothpick into the flat bottom of the candy kiss, allowing the toothpick to protrude. Melt 2 to 3 tbsp (30 to 45 mL) red candy coating wafers. Using the toothpick to hold the candy kiss, coat the kiss in red coating. Immediately place 1 tiny marshmallow on the point. Poke into Styrofoam to dry.

2. Melt 1 tbsp (15 mL) pink candy coating wafers (see page 19) and use to attach a stick to 1 cake pop (see page 27). Freeze cake pop for at least 15 minutes to set.

3. To create a mixture the color of a light skin tone, combine equal parts of yellow, pink and white candy coating wafers. For darker skin tones, combine white candy coating wafers with a small amount of chocolate candy coating wafers. Melt ½ cup (125 mL) of the combined wafers. Adjust the tone as desired by adding a little more of one color or another and reheating to melt. Coat the cake pop (see page 29). Immediately arrange tiny marshmallows as a beard. Set in a cake pop stand to dry.

Tips

Use tweezers to grasp and arrange small candies, such as the marshmallows for the beard.

Be sure to purchase food-safe paintbrushes from a cake decorating shop.

When you're melting just 1 to 2 tbsp (15 to 30 mL) of candy coating wafers to paint fine details, be careful not to overheat them; heat in 10- or 15-second intervals rather than 30-second intervals.

4. Melt 2 to 3 tbsp (30 to 45 mL) white candy coating wafers. Push the hat's toothpick into the top of the cake pop and glue the hat in place with white coating. Set in the stand to dry.

5. Reheat white coating. Use a pastry bag to pipe curly hair and a mustache on the cake pop. Pipe a hat band beneath the hat. Set in the stand to dry.

6. Melt 2 tbsp (30 mL) pink candy coating wafers and thin with shortening or Paramount Crystals (see page 20). Use the paintbrush to paint a nose. Stir a drop of two of white coating into the pink coating and paint cheeks. Set in the stand to dry.

7. Melt 1 tbsp (15 mL) blue candy coating wafers and thin with shortening or Paramount Crystals. Use the end of the paintbrush (opposite the bristles) to make two dots of coating for the eyes. Set in the stand to dry.

For the Accent Cake Pops

8. Melt $\frac{1}{4}$ cup (60 mL) green candy coating wafers and use to attach sticks to the remaining cake pops. Freeze cake pops for at least 15 minutes to set. Reserve the remaining candy coating.

9. Add 1 cup (250 mL) green candy coating wafers to the reserved green coating and melt until smooth. Coat cake pops. Set in the stand to dry.

10. Melt $\frac{1}{4}$ cup (60 mL) red candy coating wafers. Use another pastry bag to pipe decorative swirls (see page 33) on cake pops. Set in the stand to dry.

Assembly

11. Tie a length of ribbon in a knot around each cake pop stick. Slide the knots up to just below the cake pops.

12. Measure the dimensions of the pot and trim the Styrofoam to fit snugly and be about 1 inch (2.5 cm) shorter than the pot. Place Styrofoam in the pot and cover it with the feather boa. Push the cake pop sticks into the Styrofoam, arranging the cake pops decoratively.

Black Tie Affair

● ●

**Makes
1 centerpiece**

This centerpiece is breathtaking — yet it's incredibly easy to create.

● ●

Tips

Before beginning, check that the cake pops will be a good height in the candelabra. You may want to check local craft stores for lollipop sticks of different lengths to balance the look. If needed, you can always shorten the sticks, but there's no way to lengthen short ones.

Where can you find an elegant yet inexpensive candelabra for this centerpiece? Check antique stores and estate sales for old, tarnished silver candelabras. Wedding and party supply stores may also rent silver pieces.

Ingredients

	Milk or dark chocolate and white candy coating wafers	
8	Chocolate Intensity Cake Pops (page 53)	8
7	Favorite White Cake Pops (page 26)	7
	White sugar pearls	
	White sparkling sugar (optional)	

Materials

15	cake pop sticks	15
2	pastry bags or squeeze bottles, each fitted with a fine tip	2
1	elegant candelabra that holds 5 candles	1
6½ feet	white tulle (about 12 inches/ 30 cm wide), cut into 6-inch (15 cm) squares	195 cm
	Styrofoam block	
	Pearl strings	

1. Melt ¼ cup (60 mL) chocolate candy coating wafers (see page 19) and use to attach sticks to the chocolate cake pops (see page 27). Freeze cake pops for at least 15 minutes to set. Reserve the remaining candy coating. Repeat with white candy coating wafers, attaching sticks to the white cake pops.

2. Add 1 cup (250 mL) chocolate candy coating wafers to the reserved chocolate coating and melt until smooth. Coat the cake pops secured with chocolate coating (see page 29). Immediately sprinkle 2 or 3 cake pops with sugar pearls. Set in a cake pop stand to dry. Repeat with white candy coating wafers, coating the remaining cake pops and sprinkling 2 or 3 of them with sugar pearls.

3. Reheat white coating, adding more wafers as needed. Use a pastry bag to pipe swirls (see page 33), dots or filigree on a few of the chocolate-coated cake pops without pearls. If desired, sprinkle the moist decorations with sparkling sugar. Repeat with a few of the white cake pops without pearls. Set in the stand to dry.

Tips

Using the same color of candy coating wafers to attach the sticks and to coat the cake pops ensures that any drips will be disguised.

You can use any cake pop flavor for any of the arrangements in this chapter, though it is wise to use lighter-colored cakes with white or light pastel candy coating wafers. Bright or dark-colored candy coating wafers will coat even the darkest cake pops. So have fun — choose your favorite flavor or mix and match.

4. Reheat chocolate coating, adding more wafers as needed. Use another pastry bag to pipe swirls, dots or filigree on the remaining cake pops without pearls. If desired, sprinkle the moist decorations with sparkling sugar. Set in the stand to dry.

5. Measure the diameter and height of an opening for a candle. Cut 5 small cubes from the Styrofoam and trim cubes to fit snugly in candle openings. Make a stack of 5 squares of tulle and place the stack over a candle opening. Place a Styrofoam cube on top of the tulle and press it gently into the opening (this will make the edges of the tulle stand up). Repeat with the remaining tulle and Styrofoam cubes.

6. Push 3 cake pop sticks into each Styrofoam cube, arranging the cake pops so that the colors and patterns alternate. Drape the pearl strings over and around the candelabra.

New Year's Centerpiece

. . . .

**Makes
1 centerpiece**

Celebrate the new year in good taste with this festive, glittery centerpiece that is also a supply of party favors!

. . . .

Tip

Make several of these centerpieces and set them around the party room so that you have at least one favor for each of your guests.

Ingredients

	Milk or dark chocolate and white candy coating wafers	
4	Chocolate Bourbon Pecan Cake Pops (page 74)	4
	Gold edible glitter or sprinkles	

Materials

4	cake pop sticks	4
1	pastry bag or squeeze bottle, fitted with a fine tip	1
1	stemmed clear glass wine goblet (about 3 inches/7.5 cm in diameter)	1
1	Styrofoam cube (about 3 inches/ 7.5 cm cubed)	1
	Gold metallic paper shred	
1	sheet thick white printer paper	1
	Black and gold card stock	
	Glue	
1	12-inch (30 cm) wooden skewer	1
4 feet	gold curling ribbon, cut into 12-inch (30 cm) lengths	120 cm

1. Melt $1/4$ cup (60 mL) chocolate candy coating wafers (see page 19) and use to attach sticks to cake pops (see page 27). Freeze cake pops for at least 15 minutes to set. Reserve the remaining candy coating.

2. Add $1/2$ cup (125 mL) chocolate candy coating wafers to the reserved chocolate coating and melt until smooth. Coat cake pops (see page 29). Immediately sprinkle cake pops with glitter. Set in a cake pop stand to dry.

3. Melt $1/4$ cup (60 mL) white candy coating wafers. Use the pastry bag to pipe one numeral onto each cake pop so that, when displayed together, the cake pops give the date of the coming year. (For example, 2, 0, 1 and 3 for the year 2013.) Set in the stand to dry.

Tips

This would also be a great centerpiece for a graduation party. Use school colors for the cake pops, paper shred and card stock. Pipe the graduation year onto the cake pops. Print "Congratulations!" on the sign and insert the cake pops into a colorful vase.

When you're coating cake pops, the candy coating needs to be deep enough that you can dip the cake pops straight down into it. If you're only dipping a few cake pops, there will be some coating left over, but it can be melted again and used another time.

4. Measure the dimensions of the goblet and trim the Styrofoam to fit snugly and be 1 inch (2.5 cm) shorter than the goblet. Place some paper shred in the bottom of the goblet. Place Styrofoam in the goblet and, using the tip of a butter knife, push shred down around the Styrofoam to hide it. Pile more shred on top of the Styrofoam, allowing some of it to spill festively over the edge of the goblet.

5. On printer paper, print "Happy New Year!" Cut out a starburst shape, centering the words in the starburst. Cut another starburst, $\frac{1}{8}$ inch (3 mm) larger than the first, out of black stock. Glue the white starburst to the black starburst, leaving a margin all the way around. Cut another starburst, $\frac{1}{8}$ inch (3 mm) larger than the black one, out of gold stock. Glue the black and white starburst to the gold starburst, leaving a margin all the way around. Glue the starburst to one end of the skewer.

6. Tie a length of ribbon in a knot around each cake pop stick. Slide the knots up to just below the cake pops. Use a scissors blade to curl the ribbons. Push the cake pop sticks into the Styrofoam, arranging the cake pops in the correct order. Push the skewer into the Styrofoam, positioning the sign slightly behind the cake pops.

Cake Pops
Problem Solver

EVERYONE OCCASIONALLY has questions. Let us help you by sharing some of the answers we learned in the test kitchen.

Problem	Cause	Prevention/Solution
The cake pops don't brown evenly.	The bottoms of the cake pops began baking slightly before the tops.	A little of this is to be expected, since as you fill the wells of the hot cake pop maker the bottoms of the cake pops will begin baking right away. This will be minimized if you use the rotating cake pop maker. It will be most evident when you're baking white or light-colored cakes and less obvious with chocolate treats. In general, don't worry about this: the coating will conceal the problem.
The cake pops are not round.	The wells were not full enough.	Fill each well until the batter is level with the top edge of the well. This should take about 1 tbsp (15 mL) of batter.
	The cake mix brand you chose doesn't make firm, rounded cake pops.	Some cake mixes bake into firmer, more rounded cake pops than others. Experiment to see if you prefer the results of another brand. Cake mixes labeled "extra moist" or "pudding in the mix," such as those by Betty Crocker or Pillsbury, bake into more rounded cake pops. If you are having trouble making nice rounds when using other brands, try adding 2 tbsp (30 mL) non-dairy whipped topping mix to the batter.
	You underbaked the cake pops.	Be sure to bake the cake pops until a tester inserted in the center comes out clean.
	You weren't gentle enough when removing the cake pops.	Lift each cake pop out by slipping the fork tool gently between the cake pop and the edge of the well, then lifting gently from underneath. Gently place the cake pop on a wire rack to cool completely.
The cake pops have ridges.	You overfilled the wells or batter dripped around the wells.	Fill each well only until level full. If you use too much batter, it may seep around the edges of the cake pop as it bakes and form a ridge. Once the cake pops are completely cool, you can gently rub off the ridges.

Problem	Cause	Prevention/Solution
The cake pops stick to the cake pop maker.	The appliance was not clean.	After each use, let the appliance cool completely, then thoroughly wipe the plates clean.
	You forgot to use nonstick baking spray.	Spray the wells with nonstick baking spray before each batch, or as needed.
The melted candy coating is too thick or stiff.	You overheated the candy coating wafers.	Microwave in 30-second intervals, stirring after each, just until the candy coating wafers are melted.
	The candy coating has cooled.	Candy coating thickens as it cools, so dip quickly. Reheat in 30-second intervals as needed.
	The candy coating needs to be thinned.	Add a little shortening, vegetable oil or Paramount Crystals to the coating (see page 20).
	You have chosen a thicker brand.	Candy coating wafers vary by brand, and each brand melts a little differently. Experiment to see which brand you prefer.
	Your bowl, cup or spoon is wet.	Water causes candy coating to stiffen, or "freeze." Be sure the spoons, cups or bowls you use are dry.
	You added food coloring or flavoring made with water or alcohol.	Food colorings and flavorings that have water or alcohol in them cause candy coating to stiffen. Use only those specifically designed for candy coating.
The cake pops are not evenly coated.	The candy coating was too thick.	Make sure to reheat the candy coating in 30-second intervals as needed. See above for other solutions for thinner candy coating.
	You did not dip evenly.	Be sure to dip the cake pop straight down into the candy coating and coat it completely. Lift it straight up, hold the coated cake pop over the cup and let the excess drip off, gently tapping the stick against your fingers. Place the coated cake pop in the stand to dry.
The cake shows through the coating.	You used a glaze to coat the cake pops.	Glazes are generally thinner than candy coating, so the cake may well show through. This is to be expected, especially with thinner glazes.
	The color of the candy coating is lighter than the color of the cake.	Make sure the candy coating wafers you choose are a darker color than your baked cake pops.

Problem	Cause	Prevention/Solution
The cake pops fall off their sticks.	You didn't let the cake balls cool completely.	Be sure the freshly baked cake pops are completely cool before attaching the sticks.
	You didn't secure the sticks with candy coating.	See the step-by-step instructions for attaching the sticks on page 27. Once the cake pops are on the sticks, make sure to chill them in the freezer for about 15 minutes to firmly secure the sticks.
	The coating is too thick.	Dip cake pops in freshly melted candy coating, and dip just once, coating thoroughly. A thick coating may cause the cake pops to break apart.

Library and Archives Canada Cataloguing in Publication

Moore, Kathy, 1954-
   The big book of babycakes cake pop maker recipes : homemade bite-sized fun! /
Kathy Moore & Roxanne Wyss.

Includes index.
ISBN 978-0-7788-0418-5

   1. Cake. 2. Cookbooks. I. Wyss, Roxanne II. Title.

TX771.M648 2012   641.86'53   C2012-902829-0

Internet Support and Mail Order Sources

The Electrified Cooks, LLC:
  www.electrifiedcooks.com

Our blog, filled with recipes, tips, classes
  and more: www.pluggedintocooking.com

Select Brands: www.selectbrands.com

Babycakes®: www.thebabycakesshop.com

Cake Decorating Supplies

Beryl's: www.beryls.com

Candy Warehouse:
  www.candywarehouse.com

Fancy Flours: www.fancyflours.com

Golda's Kitchen: www.goldaskitchen.com

N.Y. Cake: www.nycake.com

Sweet! Baking & Candy Making Supply:
  www.sweetbakingsupply.com

Wilton: www.wilton.com

Kitchen Utensils, Kitchen Equipment, Spices, Serving Platters and Packaging

Bridge Kitchenware:
  www.bridgekitchenware.com

Crate & Barrel: www.crateandbarrel.com

Sur la Table: www.surlatable.com

Williams-Sonoma:
  www.williamssonoma.com

Flours, Sugars, Spices, Extracts and Premium Ingredients

C&H Pure Cane Sugar:
  www.chsugar.com

The Stafford County Flour Mills Co.:
  www.hudsoncream.com

King Arthur Flour:
  www.kingarthurflour.com

Land O'Lakes: www.landolakes.com

Penzeys Spices: www.penzeys.com

Sarabeth's Kitchen (we adore her
  preserves): www.sarabeth.com

Index

Be sure to visit our website

for product reviews, community tips, great recipes, decorating ideas and more!

thebabycakesshop.com is your online home for all things Babycakes®. Peruse the full line of Babycakes baking appliances, order accessories and utensils, view photos and recipes from the Babycakes experts and share tips with fellow Babycakes enthusiasts.

Fun and delicious treats are always just a click away!

connect with others in the Babycakes online community.

discover tips and tricks to make your baking experience even more fun.

create your own recipes and baking tips and upload your photos to share.

www.thebabycakesshop.com

THE ORIGINAL
babycakes™

Donut Maker

Pie Pop Maker

Flip-Over Cake Pop Maker

 mini donuts

 pie pops

 cake pops

enjoy the *Sweetness* of life...

Chocolatier

Pie Maker

Flip-Over Donut Maker

coated treats

mini pies

mini donuts

babycakes™
accessories

Baking Mixes

Cake/Pie
Pop Stand

Mini Cupcake
Paper Liners

Wooden
Treat Sticks

Paper
Treat Sticks

Every Babycakes™ baking appliance comes with valuable accessories that make the baking experience both fun and easy. To view our full offering of baking accessories or to purchase our baking mixes created specifically for Babycakes products, visit us online at
www.thebabycakesshop.com